MARVEL

SPIDER-MAN

THE BLACK CAT STRIKES

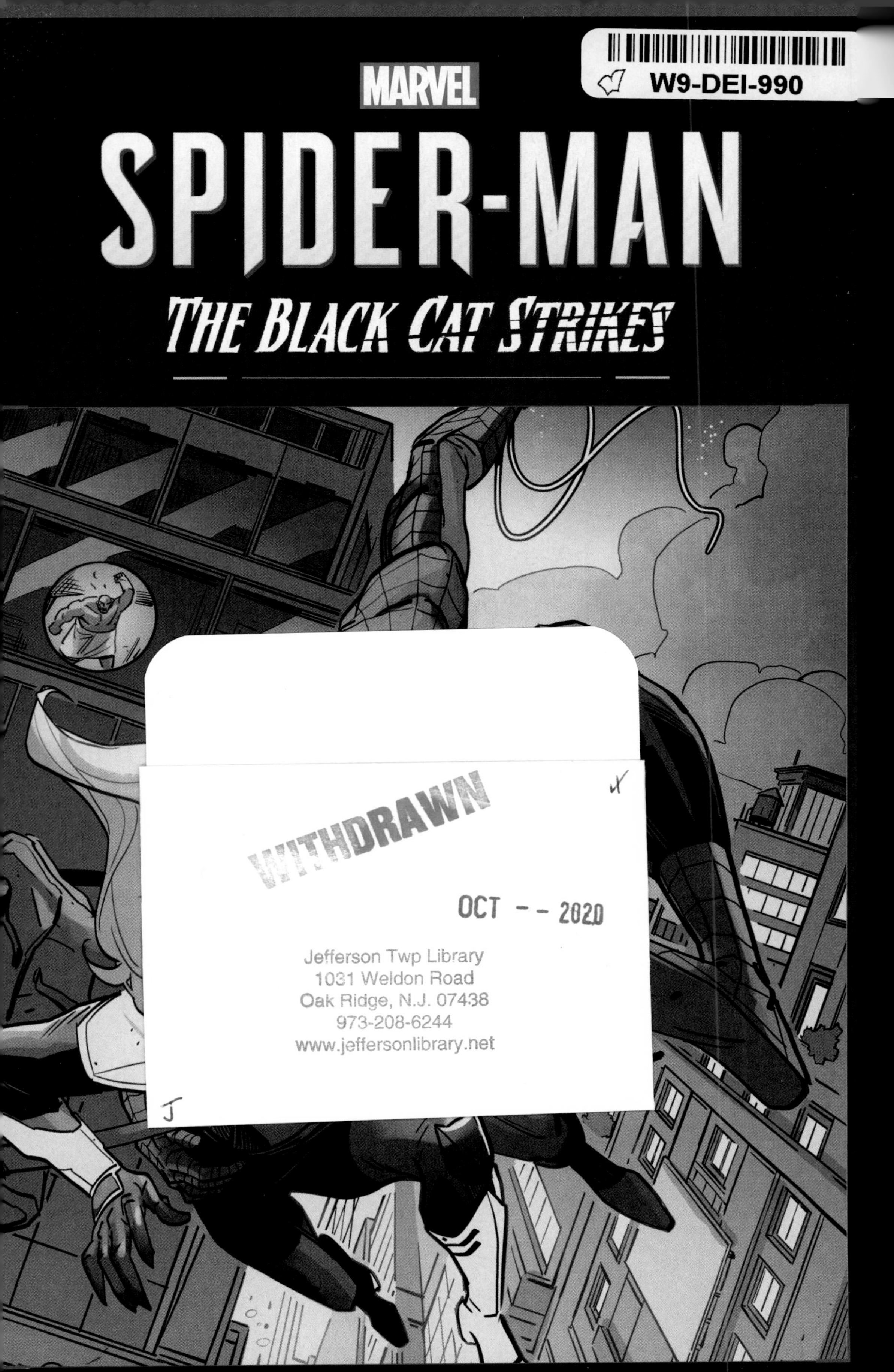

MARVEL

SPIDER-MAN

THE BLACK CAT STRIKES

PETER PARKER HAS FACED A SERIES OF CHALLENGES AND TRAGEDIES AS SPIDER-MAN AND IN HIS PERSONAL LIFE — MOST NOTABLY THE DEATHS OF HIS BELOVED UNCLE BEN AND AUNT MAY. HOWEVER, HE'S MANAGED TO TRIUMPH OVER ADVERSITY AND REKINDLE HIS RELATIONSHIP WITH *DAILY BUGLE* REPORTER MARY JANE WATSON. BUT LIFE AS SPIDER-MAN IS NEVER THAT EASY...

WRITER
DENNIS HOPELESS

ARTIST
LUCA MARESCA

COLORIST
RACHELLE ROSENBERG

LETTERER
VC's TRAVIS LANHAM

COVER ART
SANA TAKEDA

ASSISTANT EDITORS
MARTIN BIRO & SHANNON ANDREWS BALLESTEROS

EDITOR
MARK BASSO

FOR INSOMNIAC GAMES & MARVEL GAMES

STUDIO ART DIRECTOR, INSOMNIAC GAMES
JACINDA CHEW

LEAD WRITER, INSOMNIAC GAMES
JON PAQUETTE

CREATIVE ASSISTANT, MARVEL GAMES
DAKOTA MAYSONET

DIRECTOR OF GAME PRODUCTION, MARVEL GAMES
ERIC MONACELLI

VP & CREATIVE DIRECTOR, MARVEL GAMES
BILL ROSEMANN

SPIDER-MAN
CREATED BY
STAN LEE & STEVE DITKO

COLLECTION EDITOR **JENNIFER GRÜNWALD**
ASSISTANT MANAGING EDITOR **MAIA LOY**
ASSISTANT MANAGING EDITOR **LISA MONTALBANO**
EDITOR, SPECIAL PROJECTS **MARK D. BEAZLEY**

VP PRODUCTION & SPECIAL PROJECTS **JEFF YOUNGQUIST**
BOOK DESIGNER **ADAM DEL RE** WITH **NICK RUSSELL**
SVP PRINT, SALES & MARKETING **DAVID GABRIEL**
EDITOR IN CHIEF **C.B. CEBULSKI**

MARVEL'S SPIDER-MAN: THE BLACK CAT STRIKES. Contains material originally published in magazine form as MARVEL'S SPIDER-MAN: THE BLACK CAT STRIKES (2020) #1-5. First printing 2020. ISBN 978-1-302-91925-2. Published by MARVEL WORLDWIDE, INC., a subsidiary of MARVEL ENTERTAINMENT, LLC. OFFICE OF PUBLICATION: 1290 Avenue of the Americas, New York, NY 10104. © 2020 MARVEL No similarity between any of the names, characters, persons, and/or institutions in this magazine with those of any living or dead person or institution is intended, and any such similarity which may exist is purely coincidental. **Printed in Canada.** KEVIN FEIGE, Chief Creative Officer; DAN BUCKLEY, President, Marvel Entertainment; JOHN NEE, Publisher; JOE QUESADA, EVP & Creative Director; TOM BREVOORT, SVP of Publishing; DAVID BOGART, Associate Publisher & SVP of Talent Affairs; Publishing & Partnership; DAVID GABRIEL, VP of Print & Digital Publishing; JEFF YOUNGQUIST, VP of Production & Special Projects; DAN CARR, Executive Director of Publishing Technology; ALEX MORALES, Director of Publishing Operations; DAN EDINGTON, Managing Editor; SUSAN CRESPI, Production Manager; STAN LEE, Chairman Emeritus. For information regarding advertising in Marvel Comics or on Marvel.com, please contact Vit DeBellis, Custom Solutions & Integrated Advertising Manager, at vdebellis@marvel.com. For Marvel subscription inquiries, please call 888-511-5480. **Manufactured between 7/24/2020 and 8/25/2020 by SOLISCO PRINTERS, SCOTT, QC, CANADA.**

10 9 8 7 6 5 4 3 2 1

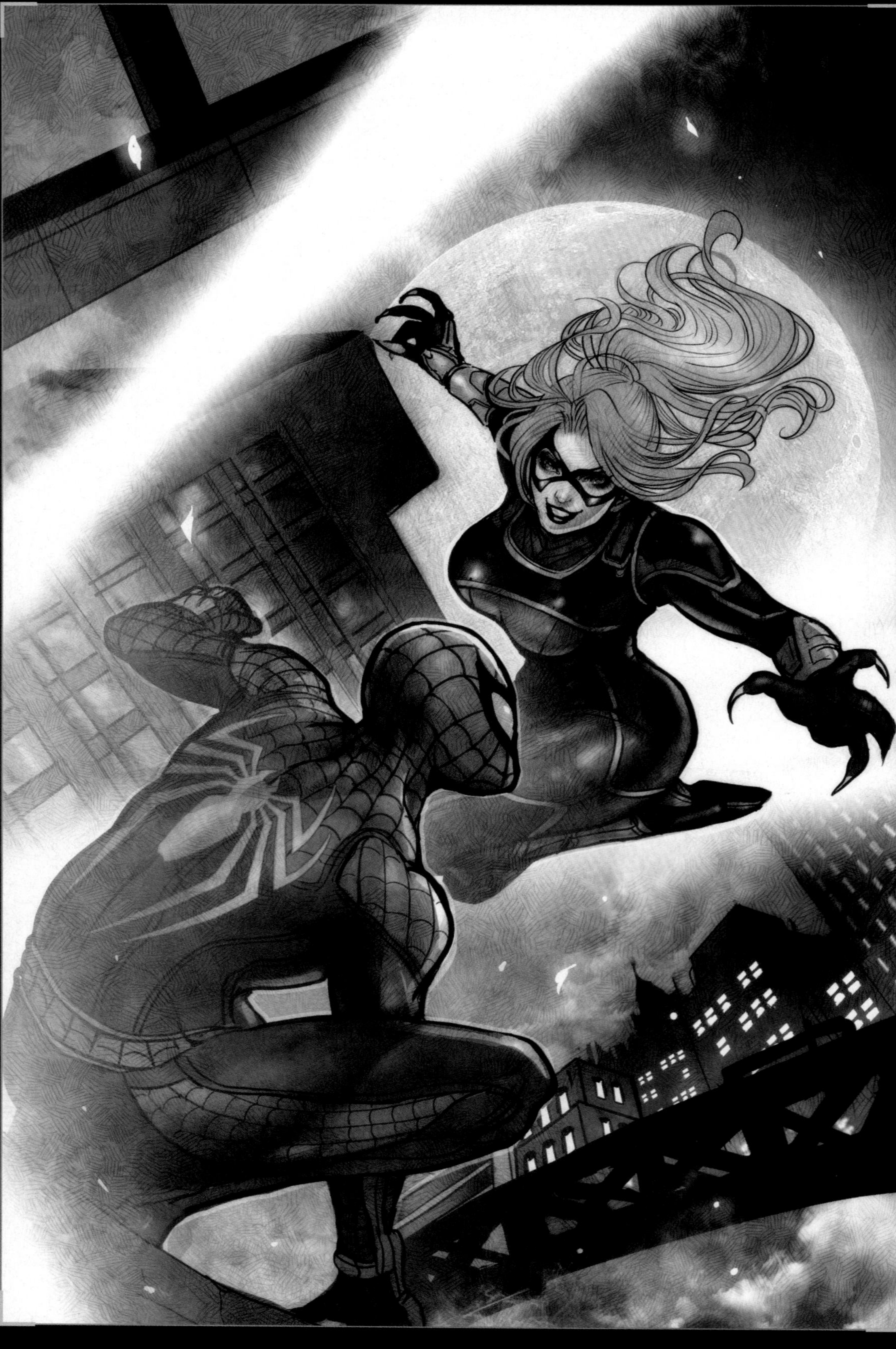

1

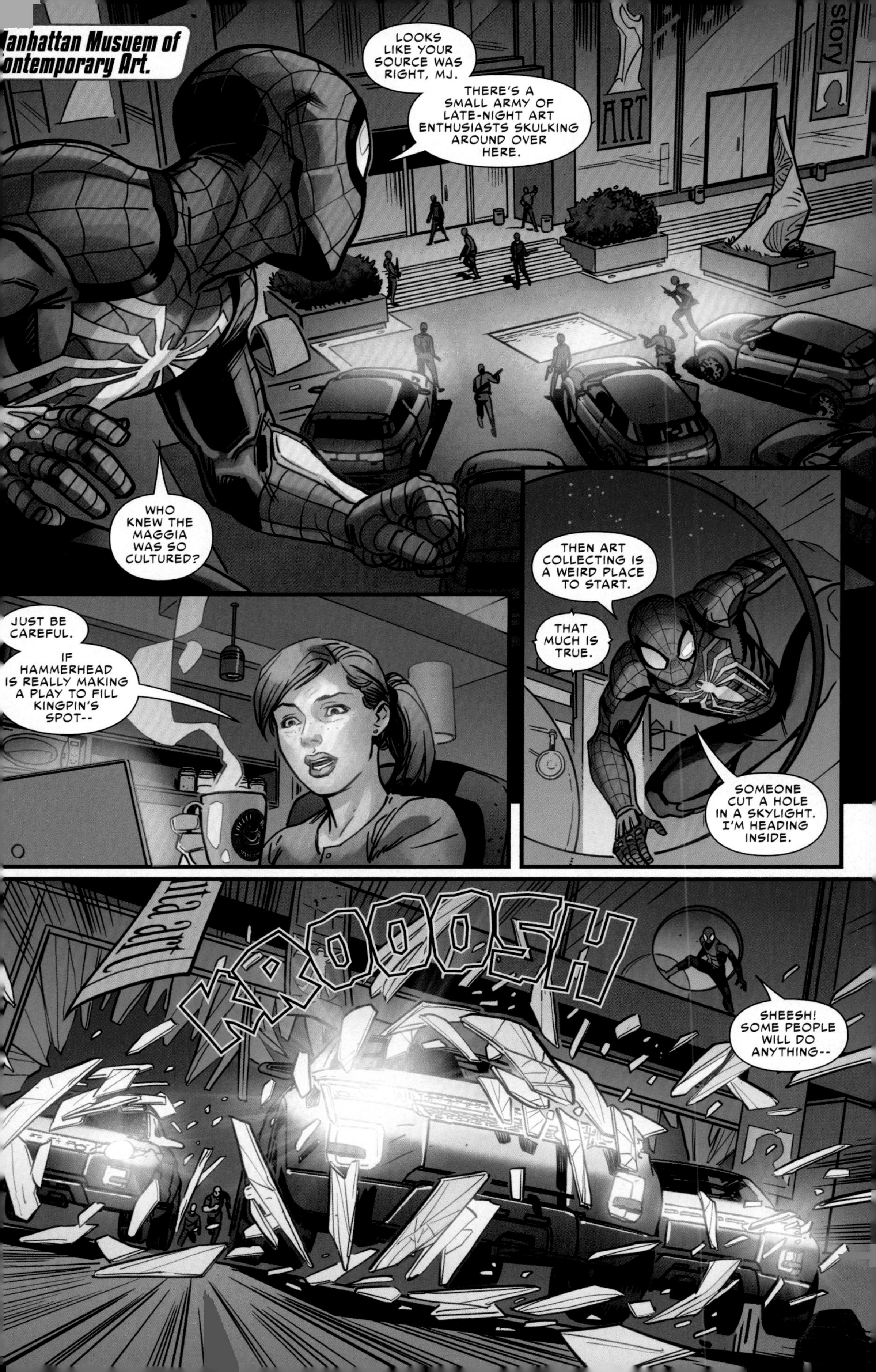

Manhattan Museum of Contemporary Art.
LOOKS LIKE YOUR SOURCE WAS RIGHT, MJ.
THERE'S A SMALL ARMY OF LATE-NIGHT ART ENTHUSIASTS SKULKING AROUND OVER HERE.
WHO KNEW THE MAGGIA WAS SO CULTURED?
ART
JUST BE CAREFUL.
IF HAMMERHEAD IS REALLY MAKING A PLAY TO FILL KINGPIN'S SPOT--
THEN ART COLLECTING IS A WEIRD PLACE TO START.
THAT MUCH IS TRUE.
SOMEONE CUT A HOLE IN A SKYLIGHT. I'M HEADING INSIDE.
KRAOOOSH
SHEESH! SOME PEOPLE WILL DO ANYTHING--

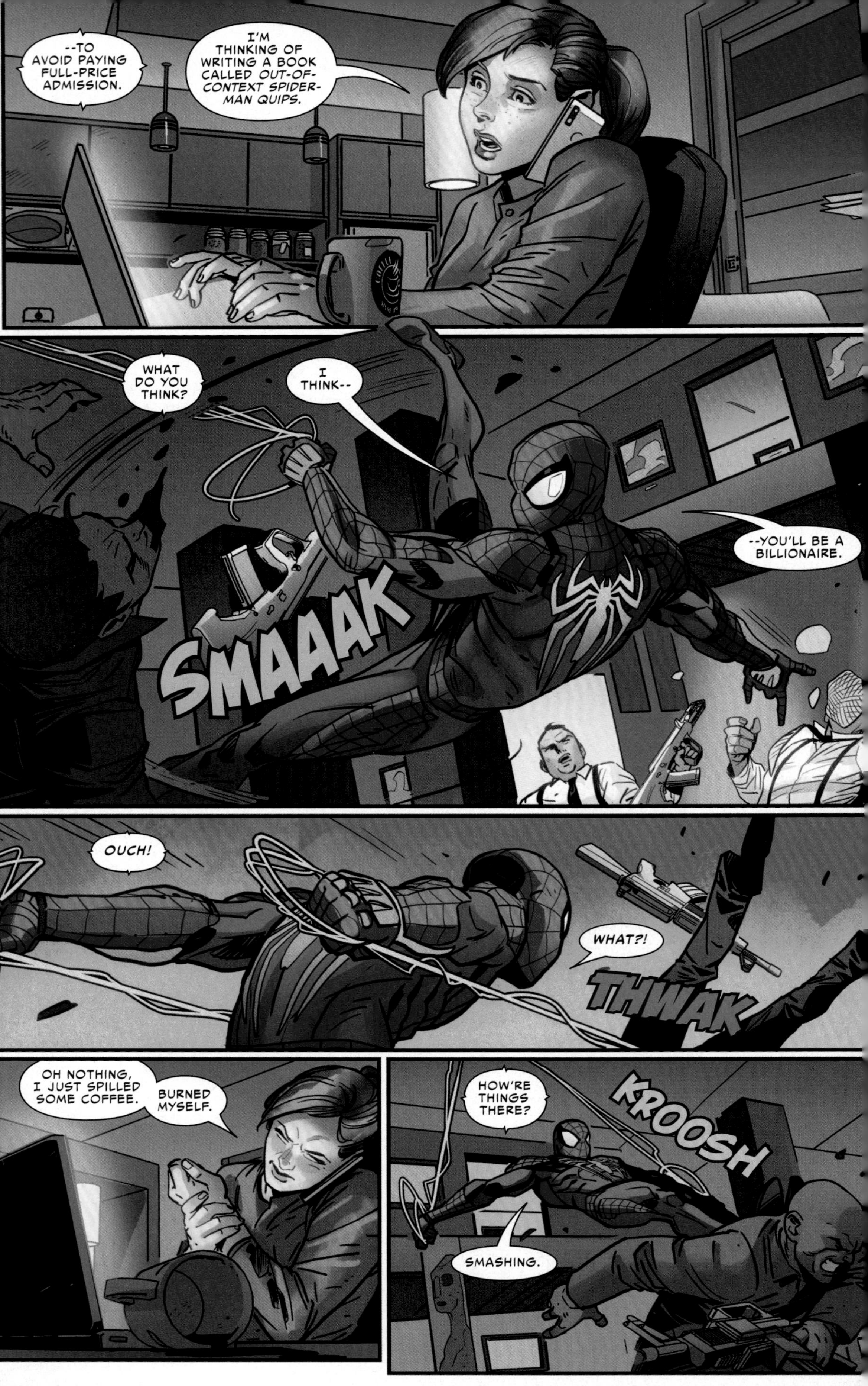
--TO AVOID PAYING FULL-PRICE ADMISSION.
I'M THINKING OF WRITING A BOOK CALLED OUT-OF-CONTEXT SPIDER-MAN QUIPS.
WHAT DO YOU THINK?
I THINK--
--YOU'LL BE A BILLIONAIRE.
SMAAAK
OUCH!
WHAT?!
THWAK
OH NOTHING, I JUST SPILLED SOME COFFEE.
BURNED MYSELF.
HOW'RE THINGS THERE?
KROOSH
SMASHING.

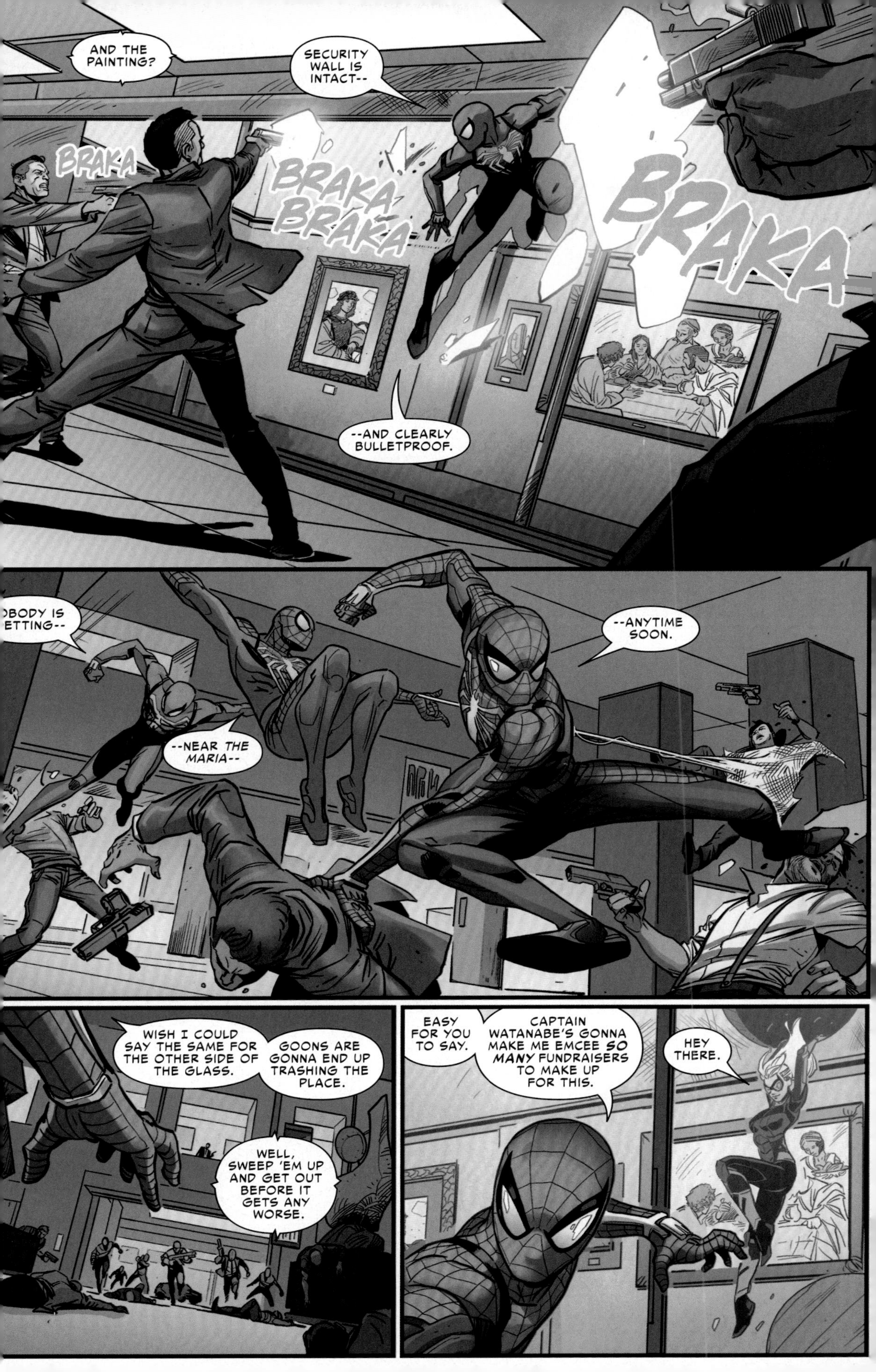

AND THE PAINTING?
SECURITY WALL IS INTACT--
BRAKA
BRAKA BRAKA
BRAKA
--AND CLEARLY BULLETPROOF.
OBODY IS ETTING--
--NEAR THE MARIA--
--ANYTIME SOON.
WISH I COULD SAY THE SAME FOR THE OTHER SIDE OF THE GLASS.
GOONS ARE GONNA END UP TRASHING THE PLACE.
WELL, SWEEP 'EM UP AND GET OUT BEFORE IT GETS ANY WORSE.
EASY FOR YOU TO SAY.
CAPTAIN WATANABE'S GONNA MAKE ME EMCEE *SO MANY* FUNDRAISERS TO MAKE UP FOR THIS.
HEY THERE.

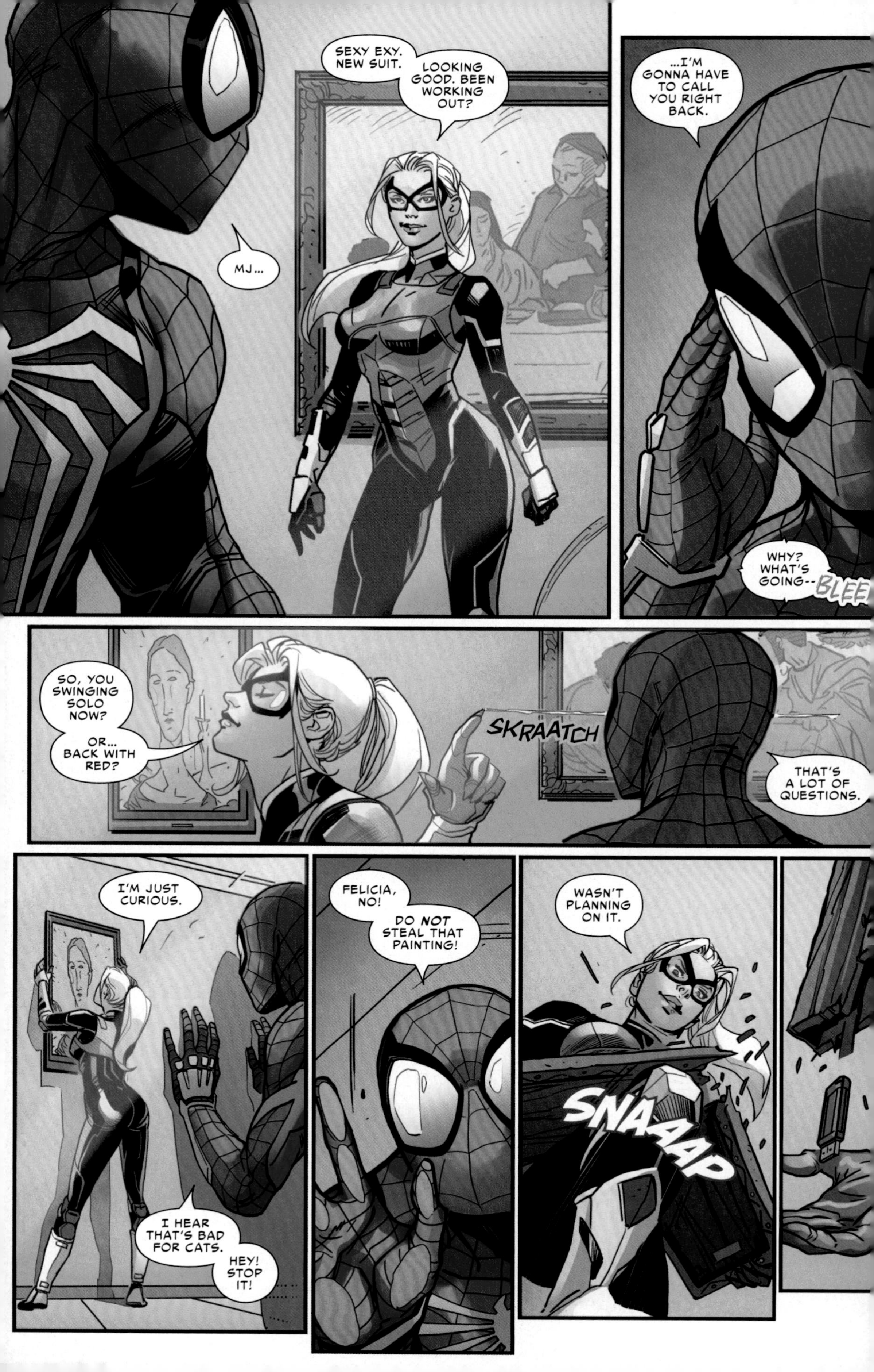
SEXY EXY. NEW SUIT.
LOOKING GOOD. BEEN WORKING OUT?
MJ...
...I'M GONNA HAVE TO CALL YOU RIGHT BACK.
WHY? WHAT'S GOING--BLEE
SO, YOU SWINGING SOLO NOW?
OR... BACK WITH RED?
SKRAATCH
THAT'S A LOT OF QUESTIONS.
I'M JUST CURIOUS.
I HEAR THAT'S BAD FOR CATS.
HEY! STOP IT!
FELICIA, NO!
DO NOT STEAL THAT PAINTING!
WASN'T PLANNING ON IT.
SNAAAP

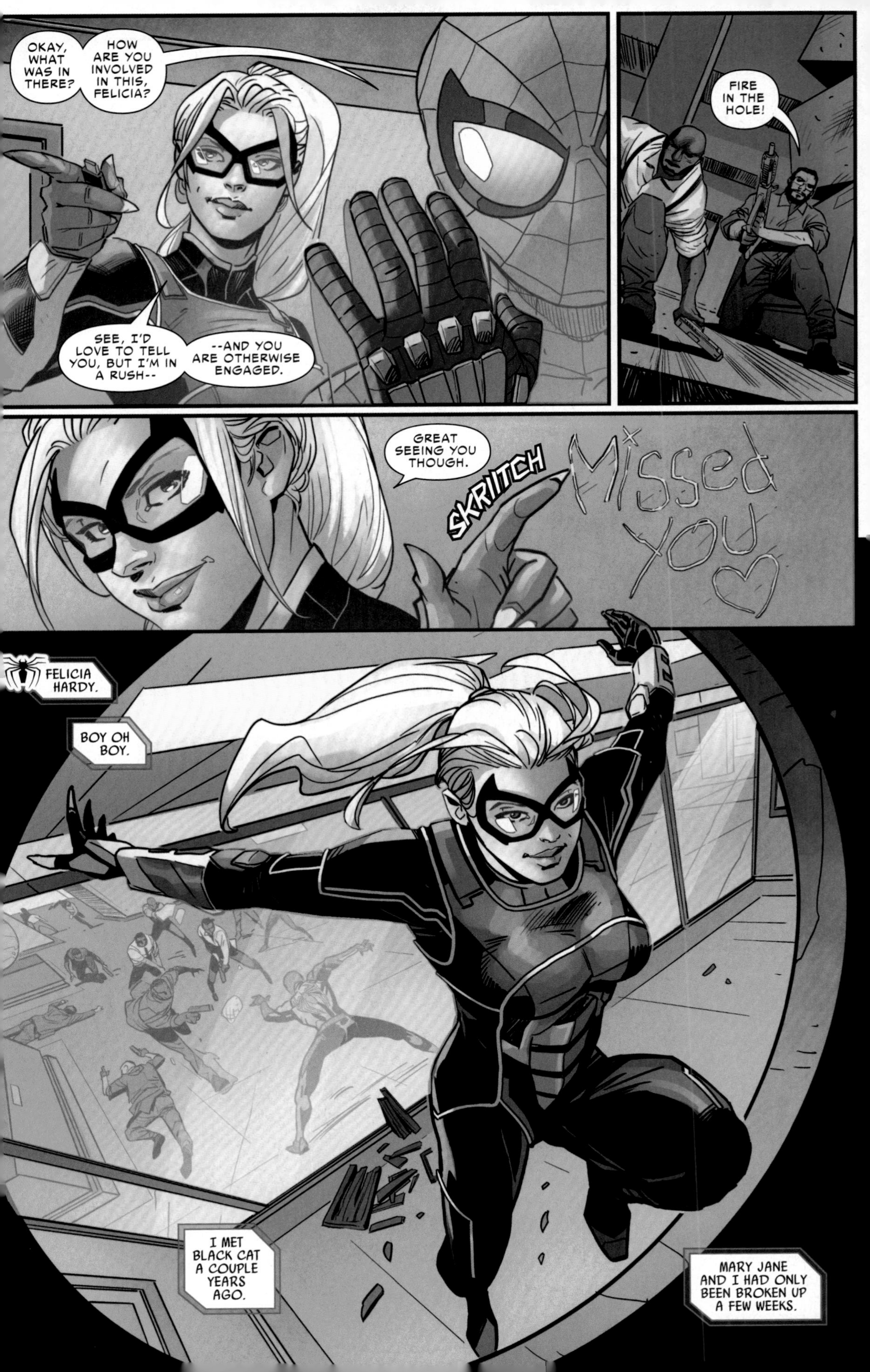

OKAY, WHAT WAS IN THERE?
HOW ARE YOU INVOLVED IN THIS, FELICIA?
SEE, I'D LOVE TO TELL YOU, BUT I'M IN A RUSH--
--AND YOU ARE OTHERWISE ENGAGED.
FIRE IN THE HOLE!
GREAT SEEING YOU THOUGH.
SKRIITCH
Missed you
FELICIA HARDY.
BOY OH BOY.
I MET BLACK CAT A COUPLE YEARS AGO.
MARY JANE AND I HAD ONLY BEEN BROKEN UP A FEW WEEKS.

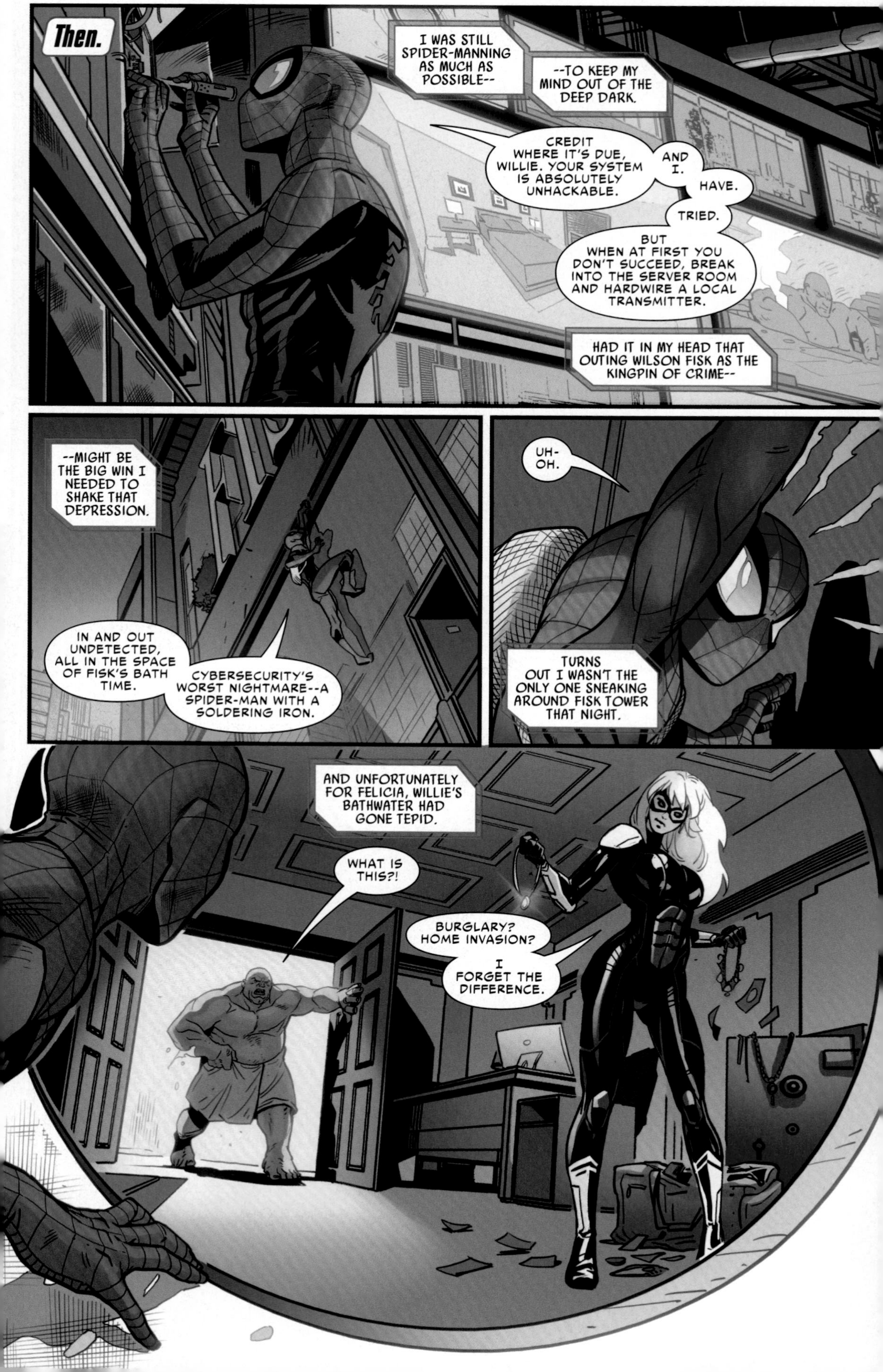

Then.
I WAS STILL SPIDER-MANNING AS MUCH AS POSSIBLE--
--TO KEEP MY MIND OUT OF THE DEEP DARK.
CREDIT WHERE IT'S DUE, WILLIE. YOUR SYSTEM IS ABSOLUTELY UNHACKABLE.
AND I.
HAVE.
TRIED.
BUT WHEN AT FIRST YOU DON'T SUCCEED, BREAK INTO THE SERVER ROOM AND HARDWIRE A LOCAL TRANSMITTER.
HAD IT IN MY HEAD THAT OUTING WILSON FISK AS THE KINGPIN OF CRIME--
--MIGHT BE THE BIG WIN I NEEDED TO SHAKE THAT DEPRESSION.
IN AND OUT UNDETECTED, ALL IN THE SPACE OF FISK'S BATH TIME.
CYBERSECURITY'S WORST NIGHTMARE--A SPIDER-MAN WITH A SOLDERING IRON.
UH-OH.
TURNS OUT I WASN'T THE ONLY ONE SNEAKING AROUND FISK TOWER THAT NIGHT.
AND UNFORTUNATELY FOR FELICIA, WILLIE'S BATHWATER HAD GONE TEPID.
WHAT IS THIS?!
BURGLARY? HOME INVASION?
I FORGET THE DIFFERENCE.

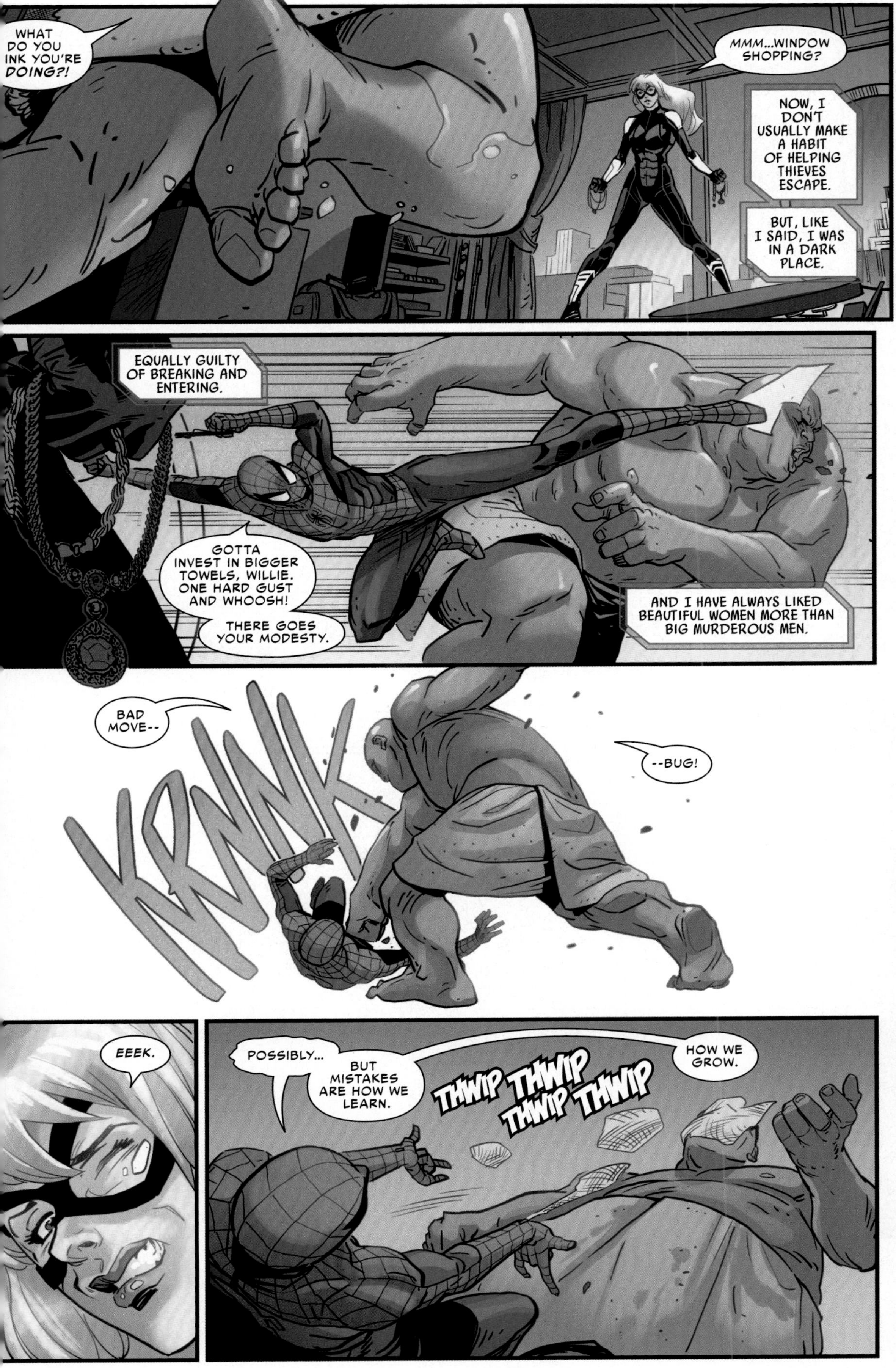
WHAT DO YOU INK YOU'RE DOING?!
MMM...WINDOW SHOPPING?
NOW, I DON'T USUALLY MAKE A HABIT OF HELPING THIEVES ESCAPE.
BUT, LIKE I SAID, I WAS IN A DARK PLACE.
EQUALLY GUILTY OF BREAKING AND ENTERING.
GOTTA INVEST IN BIGGER TOWELS, WILLIE. ONE HARD GUST AND WHOOSH!
THERE GOES YOUR MODESTY.
AND I HAVE ALWAYS LIKED BEAUTIFUL WOMEN MORE THAN BIG MURDEROUS MEN.
BAD MOVE--
KRNNK
--BUG!
EEEK.
POSSIBLY... BUT MISTAKES ARE HOW WE LEARN.
THWIP THWIP THWIP THWIP
HOW WE GROW.

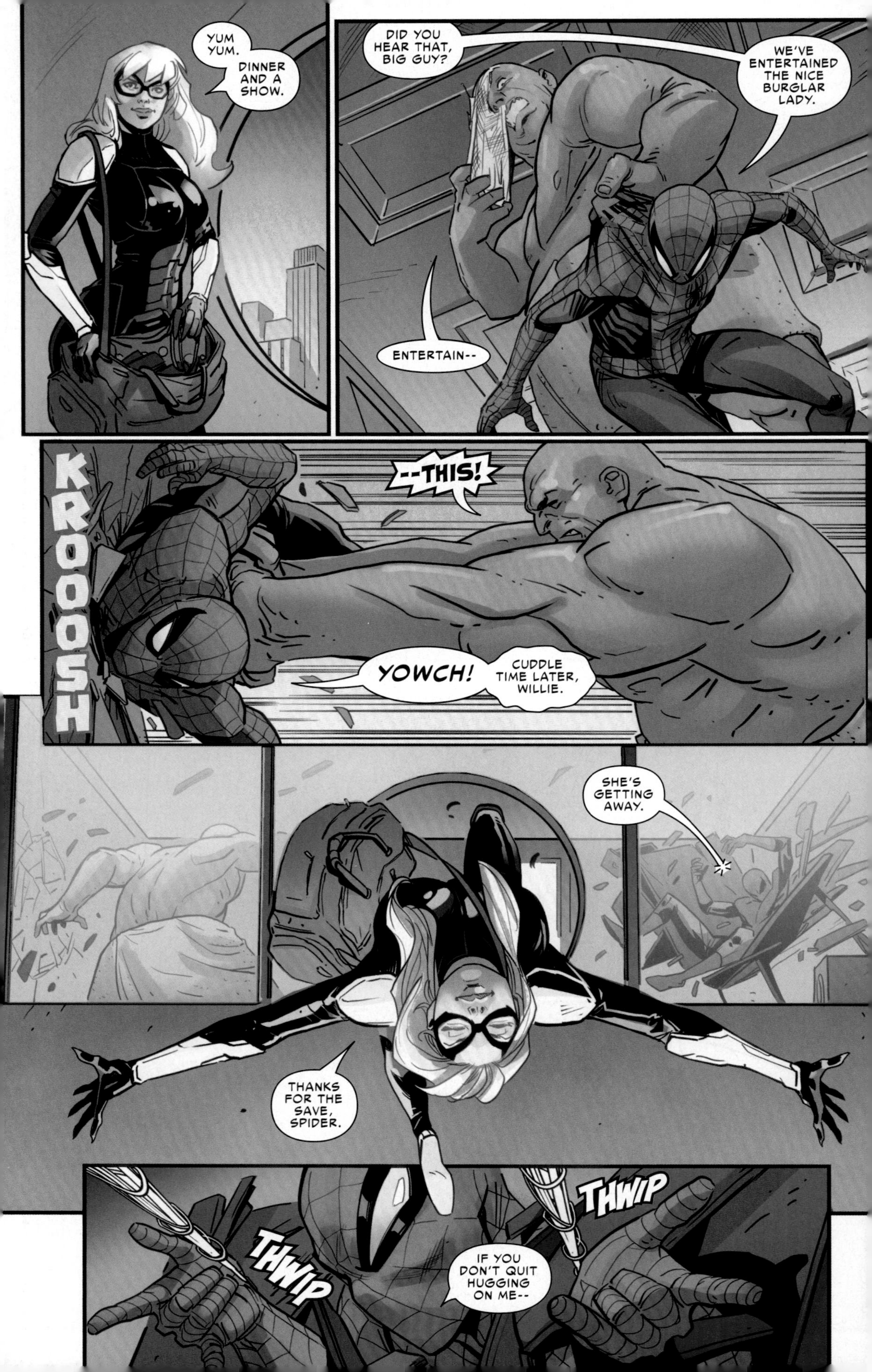
YUM YUM.
DINNER AND A SHOW.
DID YOU HEAR THAT, BIG GUY?
WE'VE ENTERTAINED THE NICE BURGLAR LADY.
ENTERTAIN--
KROOOOSH
--THIS!
YOWCH!
CUDDLE TIME LATER, WILLIE.
SHE'S GETTING AWAY.
THANKS FOR THE SAVE, SPIDER.
THWIP
THWIP
IF YOU DON'T QUIT HUGGING ON ME--

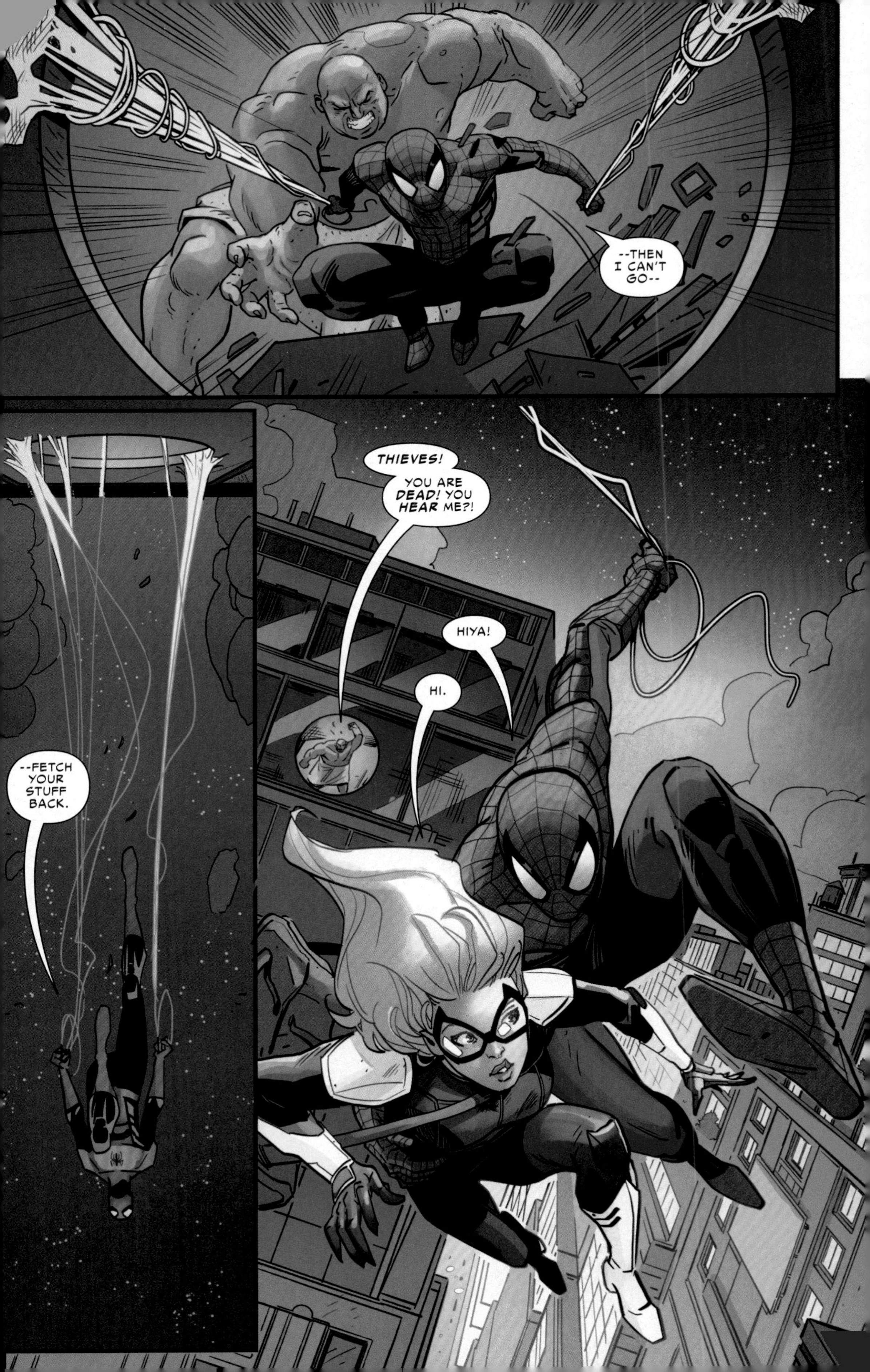
--THEN I CAN'T GO--
--FETCH YOUR STUFF BACK.
THIEVES!
YOU ARE DEAD! YOU HEAR ME?!
HIYA!
HI.

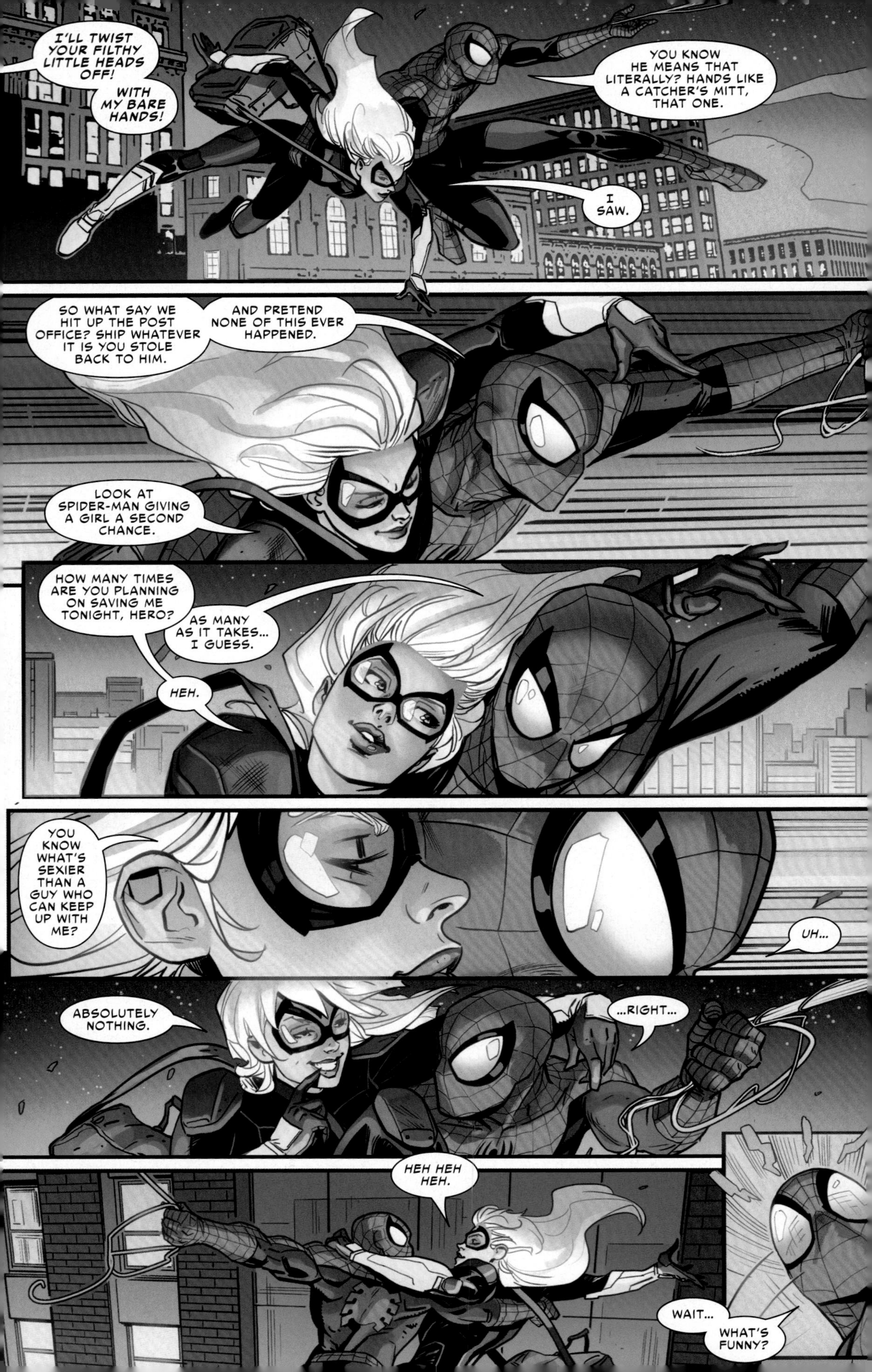
I'LL TWIST YOUR FILTHY LITTLE HEADS OFF!
WITH MY BARE HANDS!
YOU KNOW HE MEANS THAT LITERALLY? HANDS LIKE A CATCHER'S MITT, THAT ONE.
I SAW.
SO WHAT SAY WE HIT UP THE POST OFFICE? SHIP WHATEVER IT IS YOU STOLE BACK TO HIM.
AND PRETEND NONE OF THIS EVER HAPPENED.
LOOK AT SPIDER-MAN GIVING A GIRL A SECOND CHANCE.
HOW MANY TIMES ARE YOU PLANNING ON SAVING ME TONIGHT, HERO?
AS MANY AS IT TAKES... I GUESS.
HEH.
YOU KNOW WHAT'S SEXIER THAN A GUY WHO CAN KEEP UP WITH ME?
UH...
ABSOLUTELY NOTHING.
...RIGHT...
HEH HEH HEH.
WAIT...
WHAT'S FUNNY?

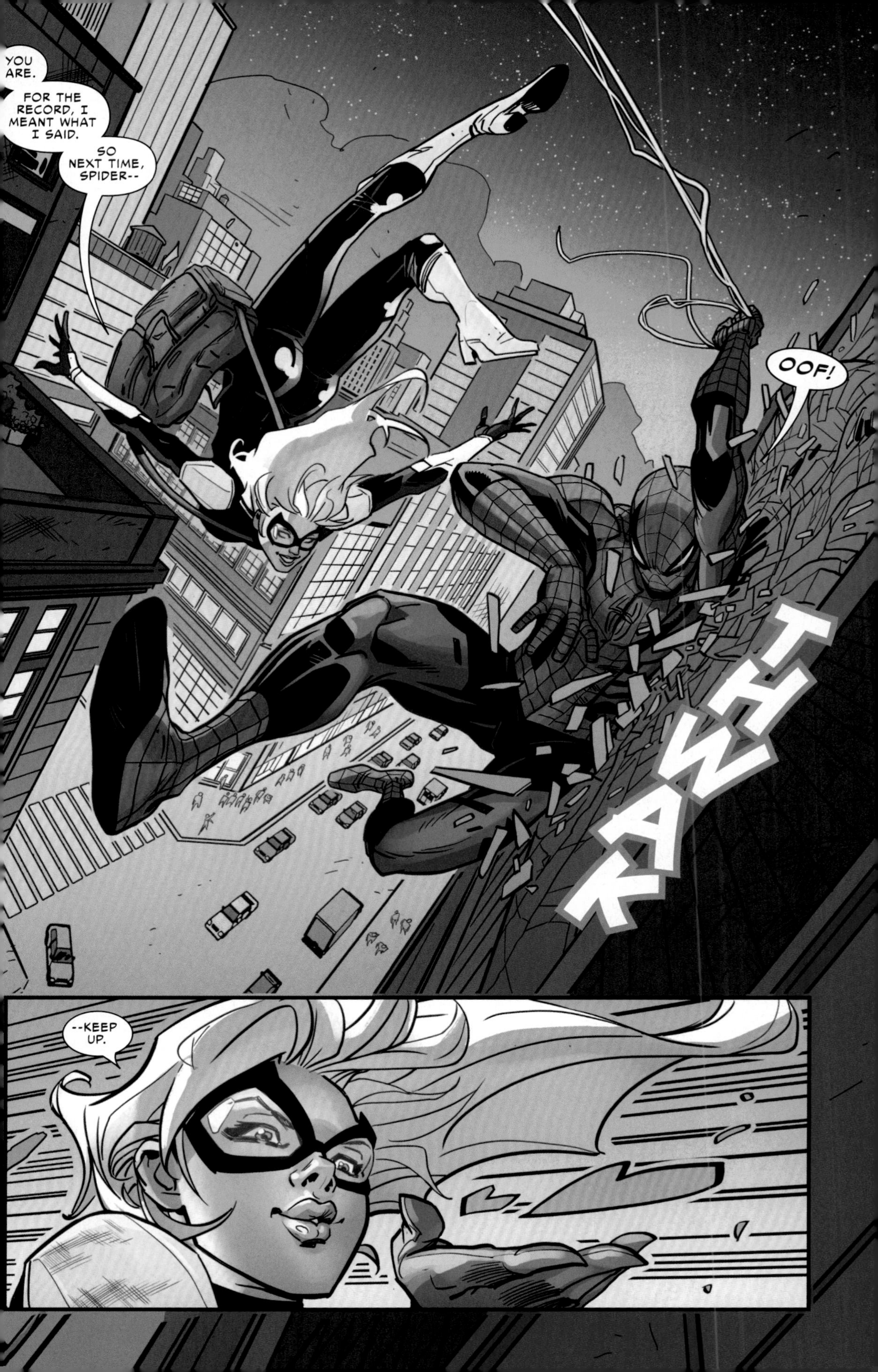
YOU ARE.
FOR THE RECORD, I MEANT WHAT I SAID.
SO NEXT TIME, SPIDER--
OOF!
THWAK
--KEEP UP.

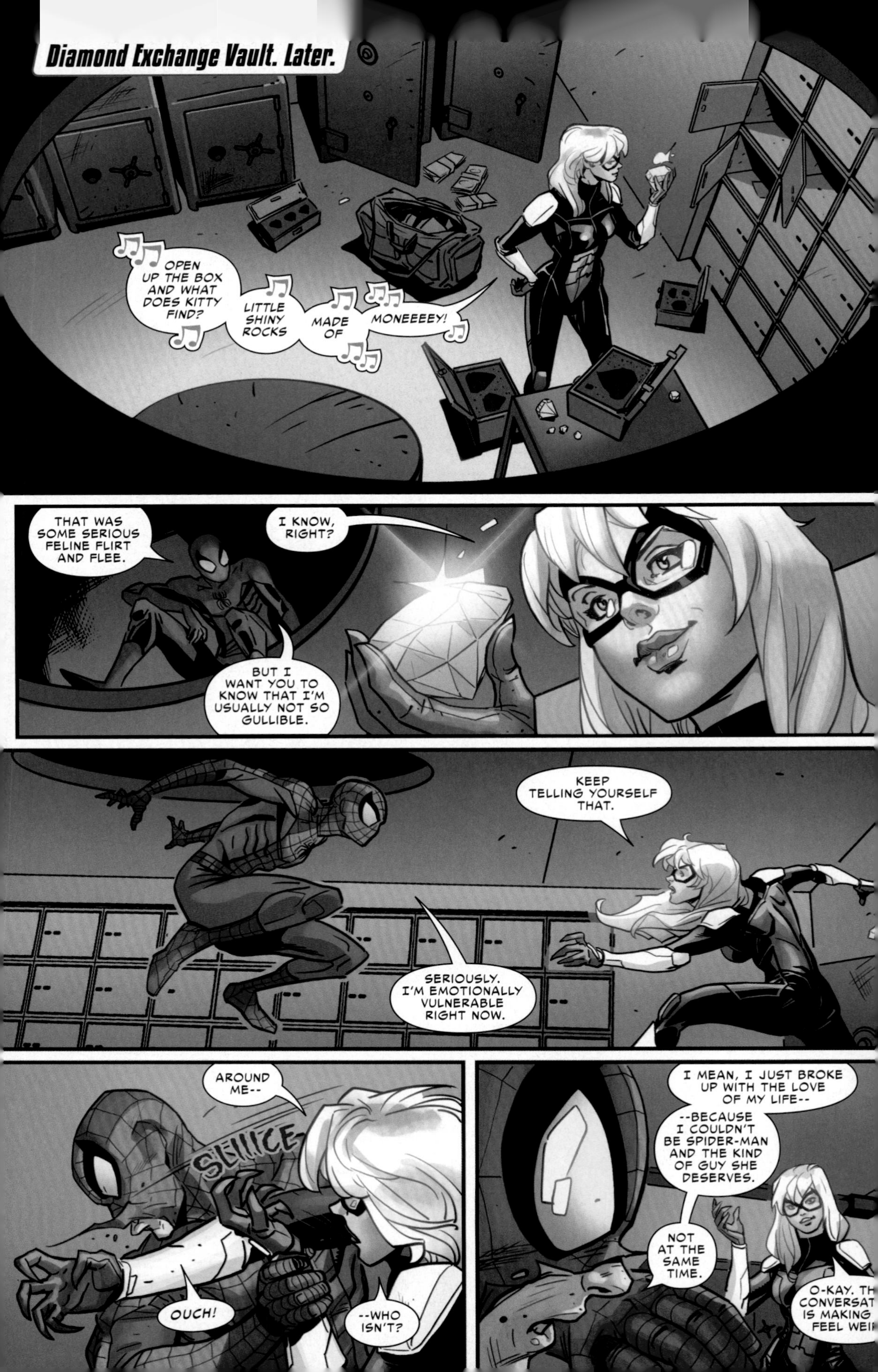

Diamond Exchange Vault. Later.
OPEN UP THE BOX AND WHAT DOES KITTY FIND?
LITTLE SHINY ROCKS
MADE OF
MONEEEEY!
THAT WAS SOME SERIOUS FELINE FLIRT AND FLEE.
I KNOW, RIGHT?
BUT I WANT YOU TO KNOW THAT I'M USUALLY NOT SO GULLIBLE.
KEEP TELLING YOURSELF THAT.
SERIOUSLY. I'M EMOTIONALLY VULNERABLE RIGHT NOW.
AROUND ME--
SLIIICE
OUCH!
--WHO ISN'T?
I MEAN, I JUST BROKE UP WITH THE LOVE OF MY LIFE--
--BECAUSE I COULDN'T BE SPIDER-MAN AND THE KIND OF GUY SHE DESERVES.
NOT AT THE SAME TIME.
O-KAY. TH CONVERSAT IS MAKING FEEL WEI

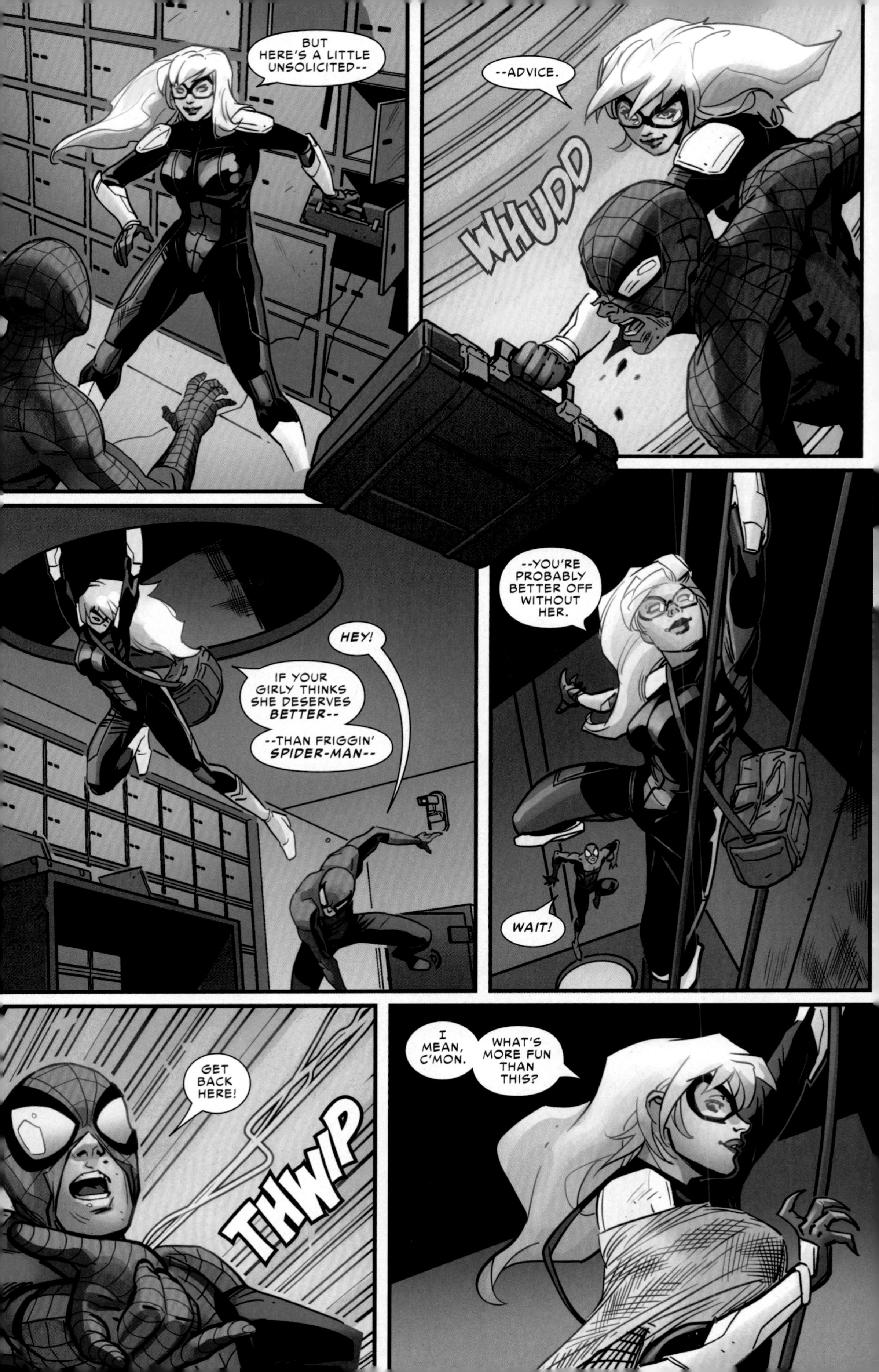
BUT HERE'S A LITTLE UNSOLICITED--
--ADVICE.
WHUDD
HEY!
IF YOUR GIRLY THINKS SHE DESERVES BETTER--
--THAN FRIGGIN' SPIDER-MAN--
--YOU'RE PROBABLY BETTER OFF WITHOUT HER.
WAIT!
GET BACK HERE!
THWIP
I MEAN, C'MON.
WHAT'S MORE FUN THAN THIS?

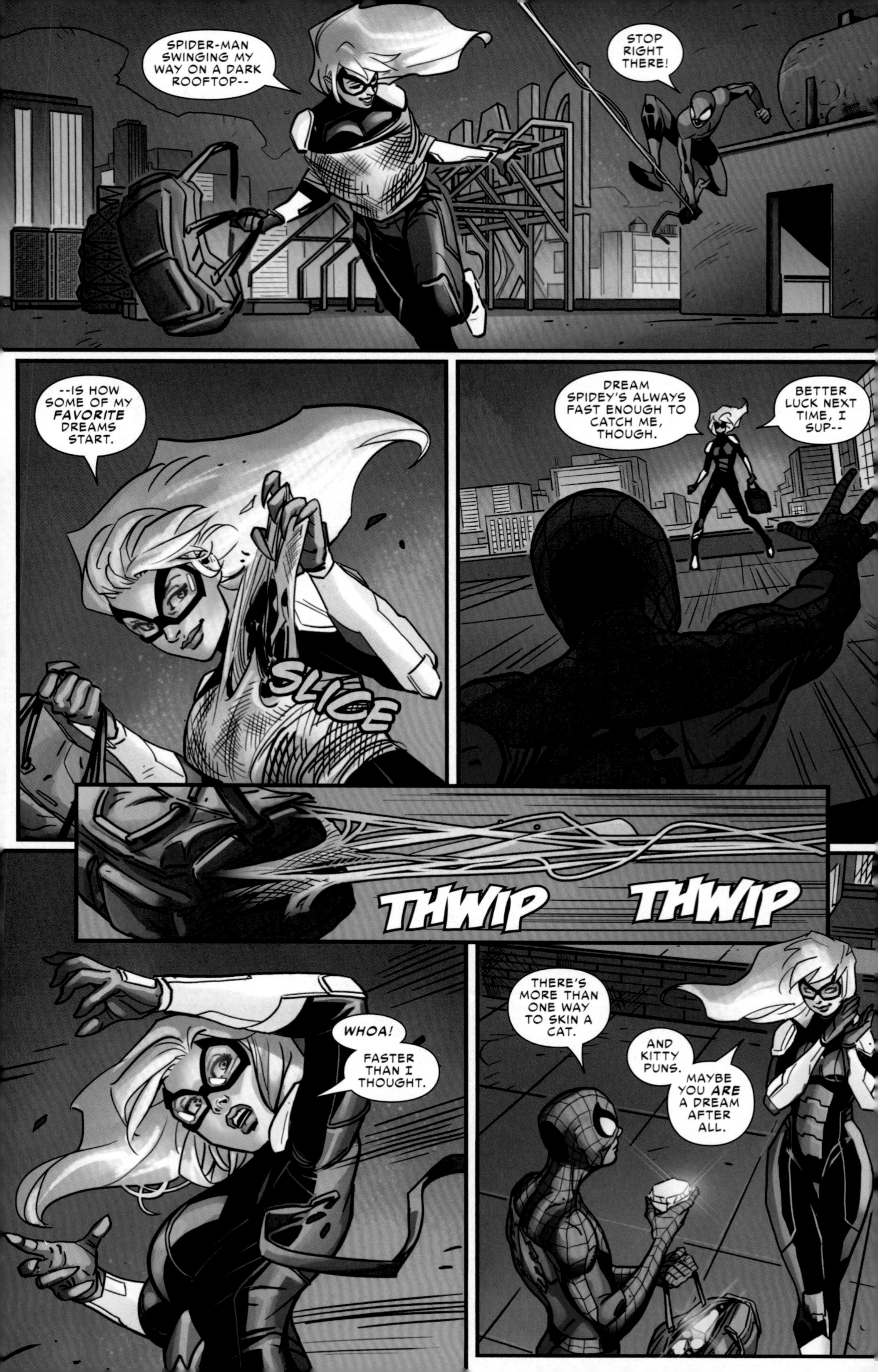
SPIDER-MAN SWINGING MY WAY ON A DARK ROOFTOP--
STOP RIGHT THERE!
--IS HOW SOME OF MY FAVORITE DREAMS START.
SLICE
DREAM SPIDEY'S ALWAYS FAST ENOUGH TO CATCH ME, THOUGH.
BETTER LUCK NEXT TIME, I SUP--
THWIP THWIP
WHOA!
FASTER THAN I THOUGHT.
THERE'S MORE THAN ONE WAY TO SKIN A CAT.
AND KITTY PUNS.
MAYBE YOU ARE A DREAM AFTER ALL.

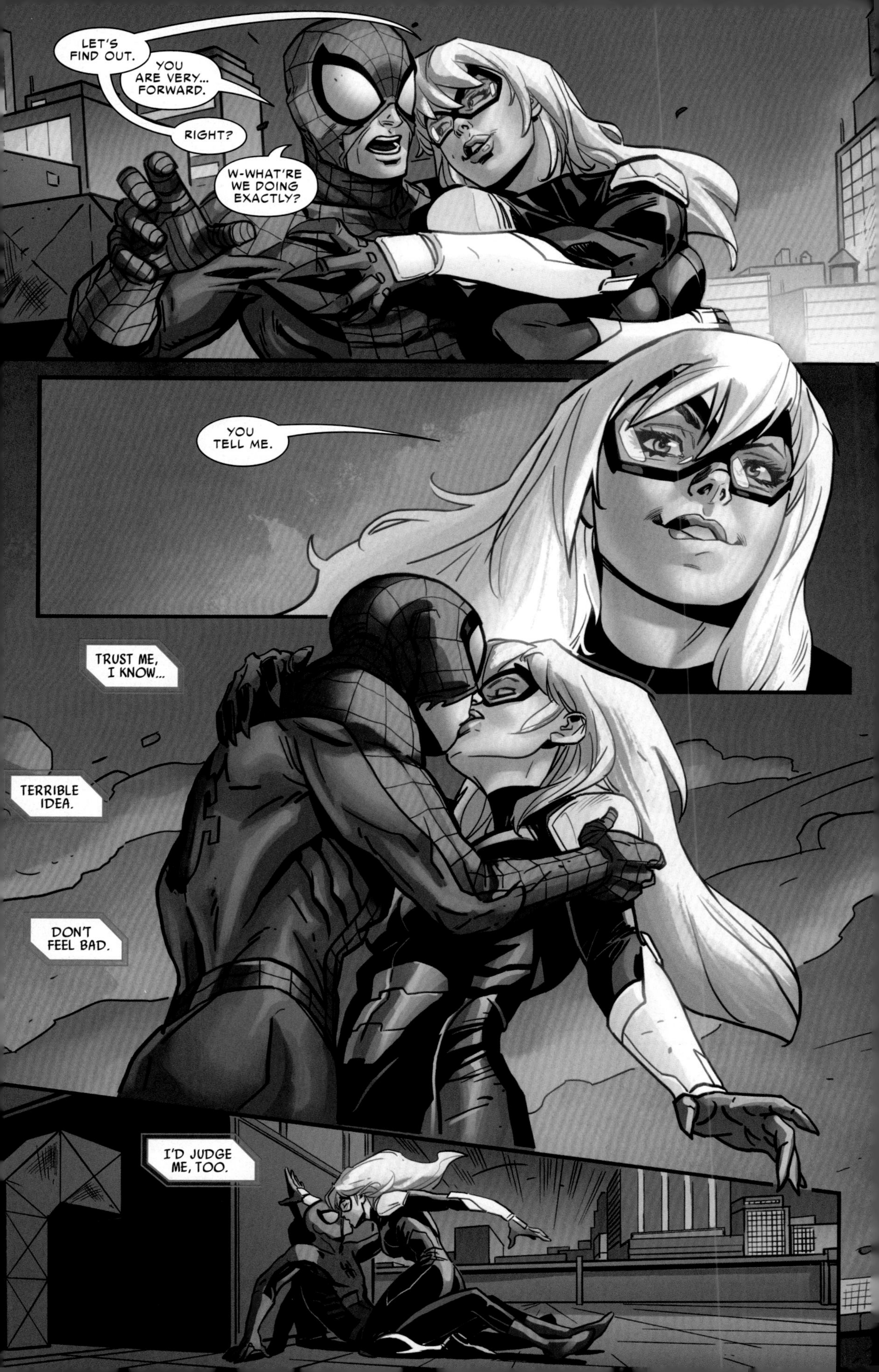

LET'S FIND OUT.
YOU ARE VERY... FORWARD.
RIGHT?
W-WHAT'RE WE DOING EXACTLY?
YOU TELL ME.
TRUST ME, I KNOW...
TERRIBLE IDEA.
DON'T FEEL BAD.
I'D JUDGE ME, TOO.

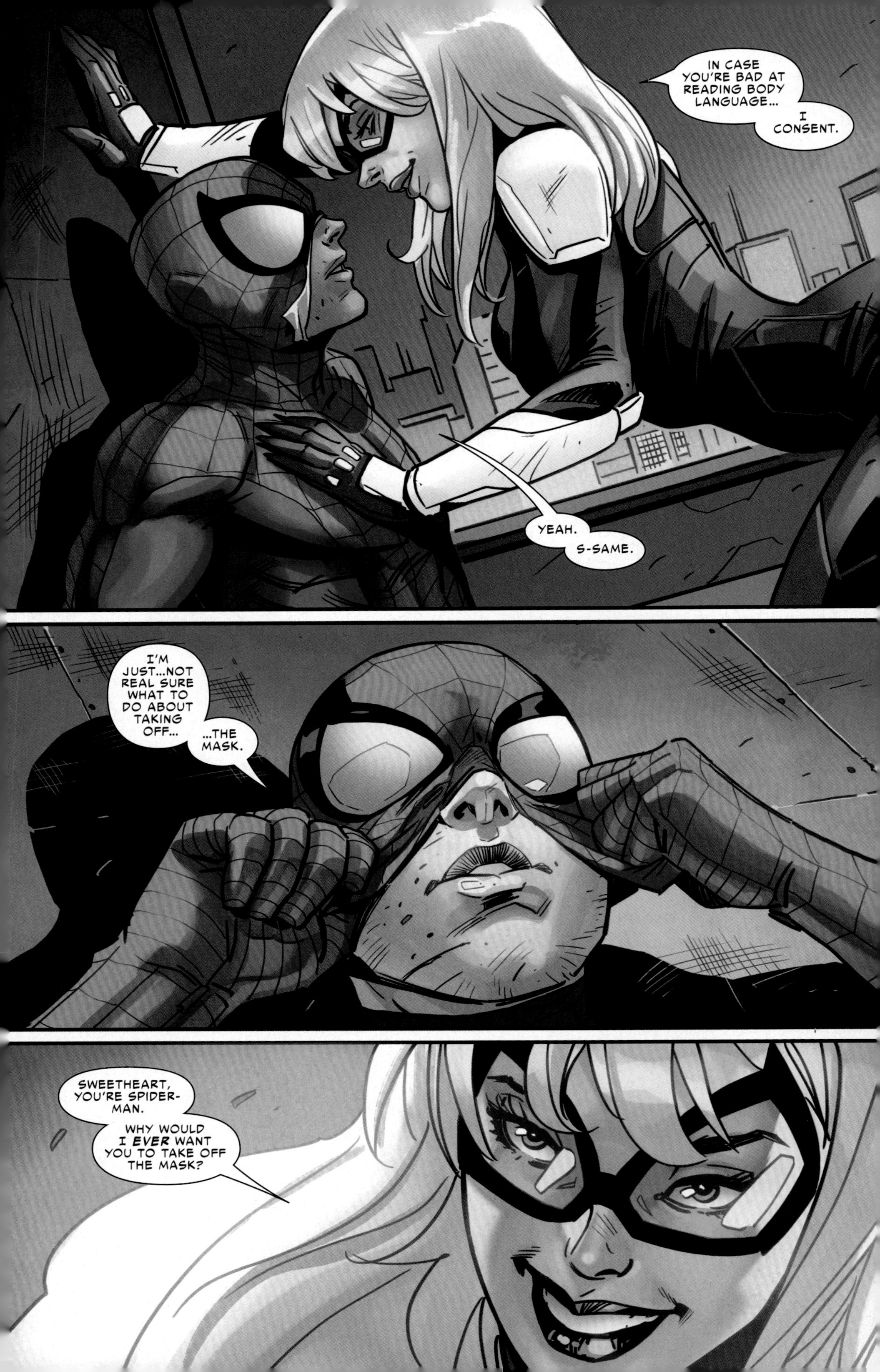
IN CASE YOU'RE BAD AT READING BODY LANGUAGE...
I CONSENT.
YEAH.
S-SAME.
I'M JUST...NOT REAL SURE WHAT TO DO ABOUT TAKING OFF...
...THE MASK.
SWEETHEART, YOU'RE SPIDER-MAN.
WHY WOULD I *EVER* WANT YOU TO TAKE OFF THE MASK?

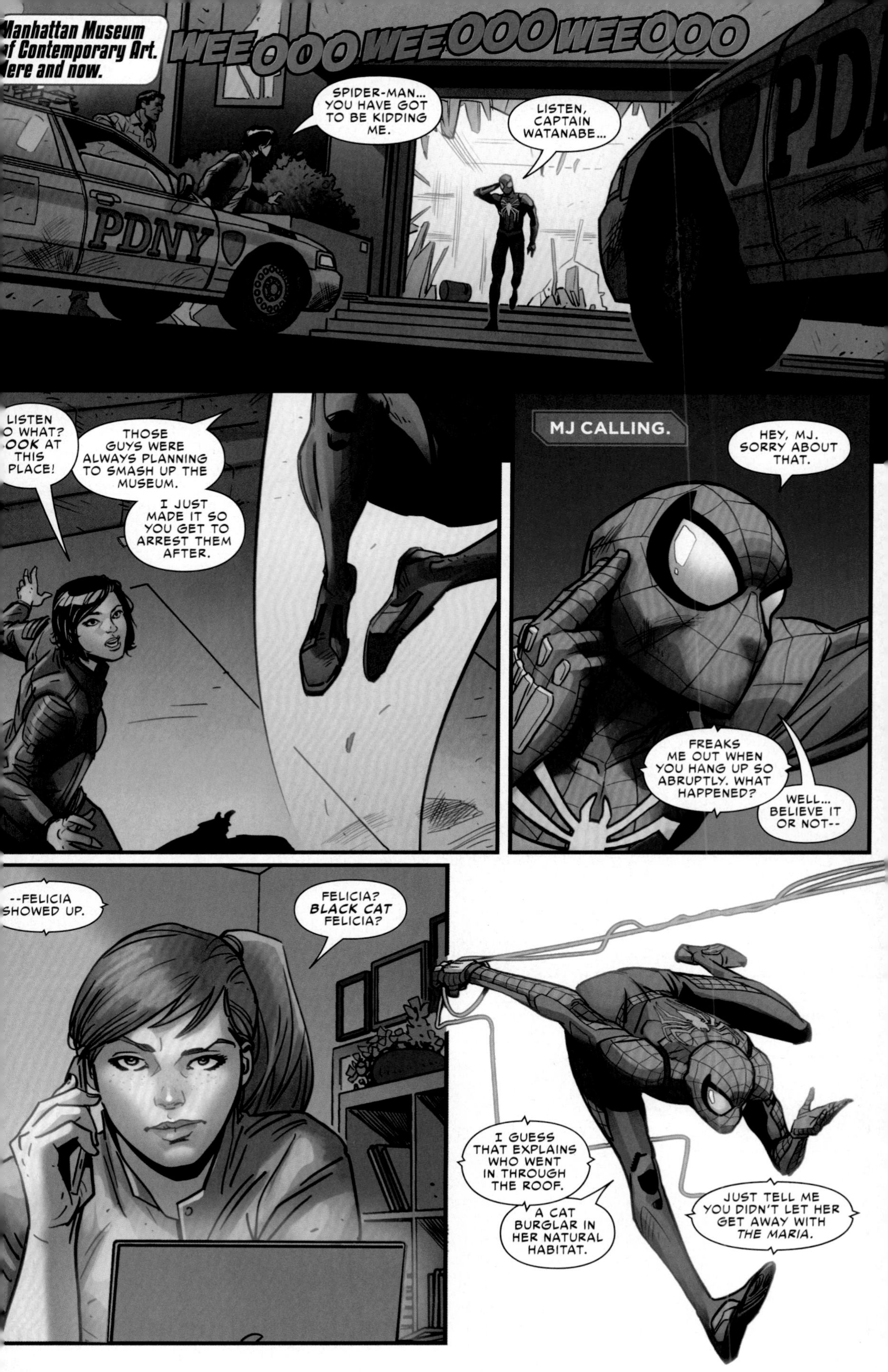

Manhattan Museum of Contemporary Art. Here and now.
WEEOOOWEEOOOWEEOOO
SPIDER-MAN... YOU HAVE GOT TO BE KIDDING ME.
LISTEN, CAPTAIN WATANABE...
PDNY
LISTEN TO WHAT? LOOK AT THIS PLACE!
THOSE GUYS WERE ALWAYS PLANNING TO SMASH UP THE MUSEUM.
I JUST MADE IT SO YOU GET TO ARREST THEM AFTER.
MJ CALLING.
HEY, MJ. SORRY ABOUT THAT.
FREAKS ME OUT WHEN YOU HANG UP SO ABRUPTLY. WHAT HAPPENED?
WELL... BELIEVE IT OR NOT--
--FELICIA SHOWED UP.
FELICIA? BLACK CAT FELICIA?
I GUESS THAT EXPLAINS WHO WENT IN THROUGH THE ROOF.
A CAT BURGLAR IN HER NATURAL HABITAT.
JUST TELL ME YOU DIDN'T LET HER GET AWAY WITH THE MARIA.

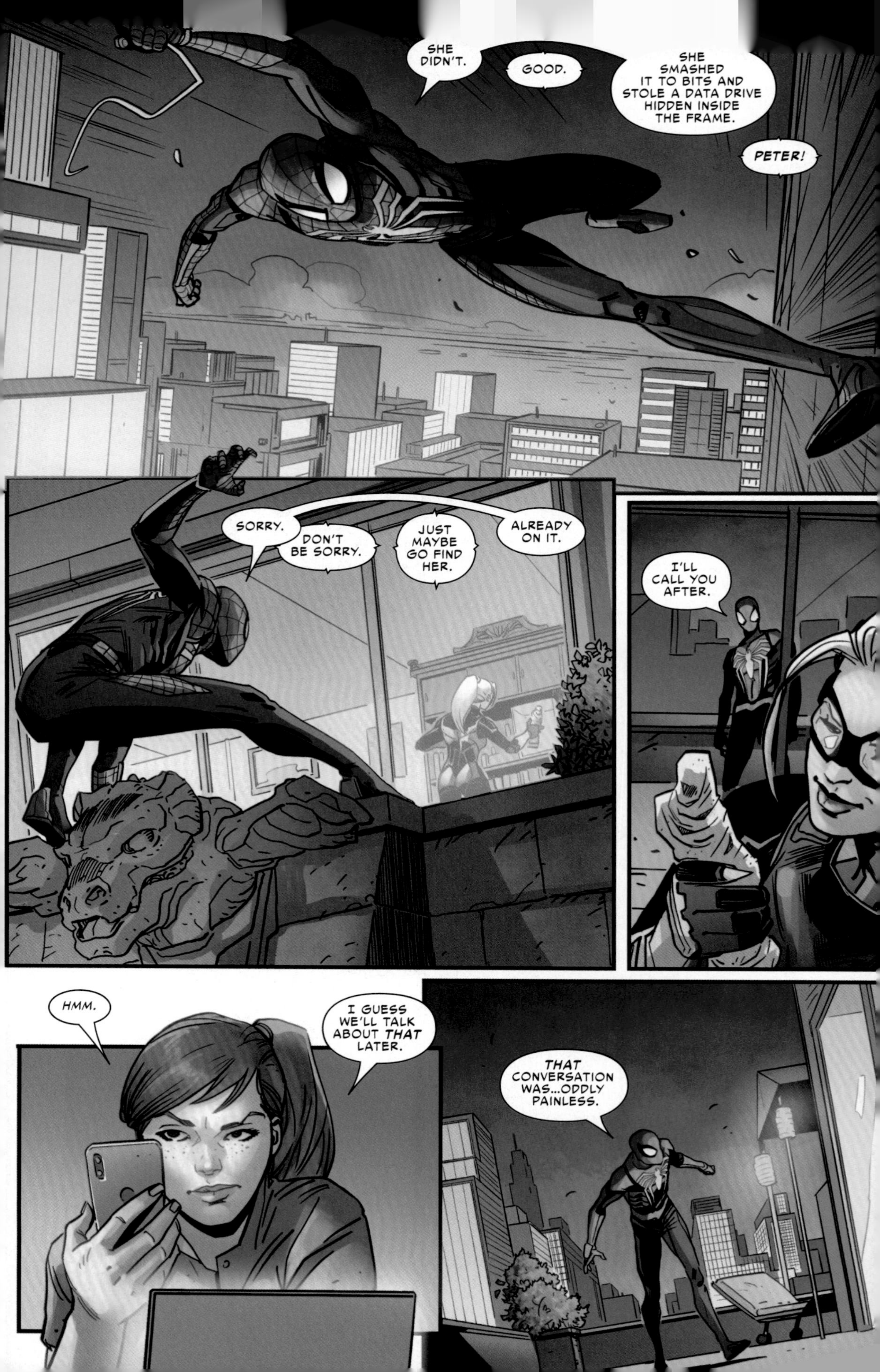

SHE DIDN'T.
GOOD.
SHE SMASHED IT TO BITS AND STOLE A DATA DRIVE HIDDEN INSIDE THE FRAME.
PETER!
SORRY.
DON'T BE SORRY.
JUST MAYBE GO FIND HER.
ALREADY ON IT.
I'LL CALL YOU AFTER.
HMM.
I GUESS WE'LL TALK ABOUT THAT LATER.
THAT CONVERSATION WAS...ODDLY PAINLESS.

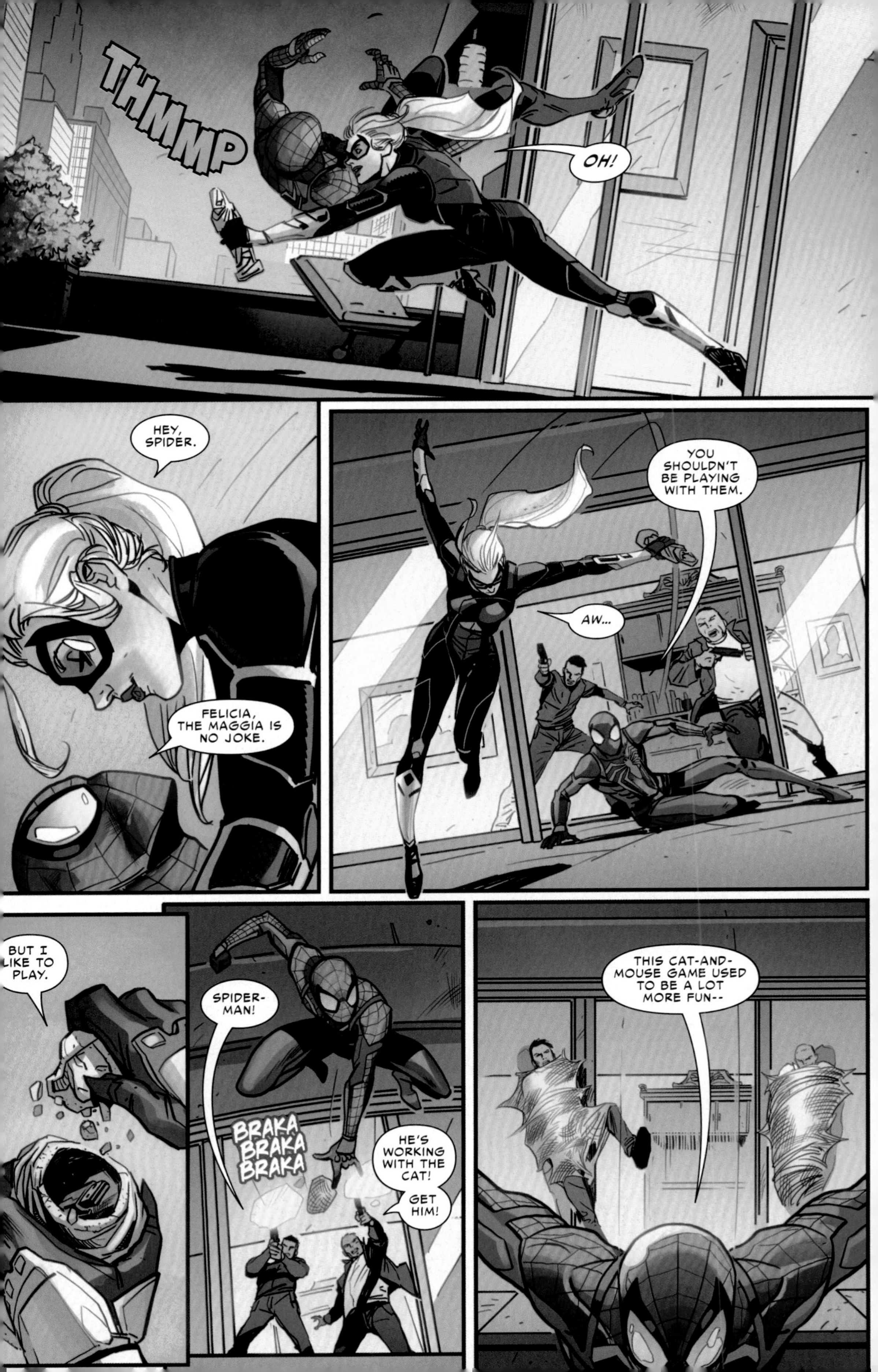
THMMMP
OH!
HEY, SPIDER.
FELICIA, THE MAGGIA IS NO JOKE.
YOU SHOULDN'T BE PLAYING WITH THEM.
AW...
BUT I LIKE TO PLAY.
SPIDER-MAN!
BRAKA BRAKA BRAKA
HE'S WORKING WITH THE CAT!
GET HIM!
THIS CAT-AND-MOUSE GAME USED TO BE A LOT MORE FUN--

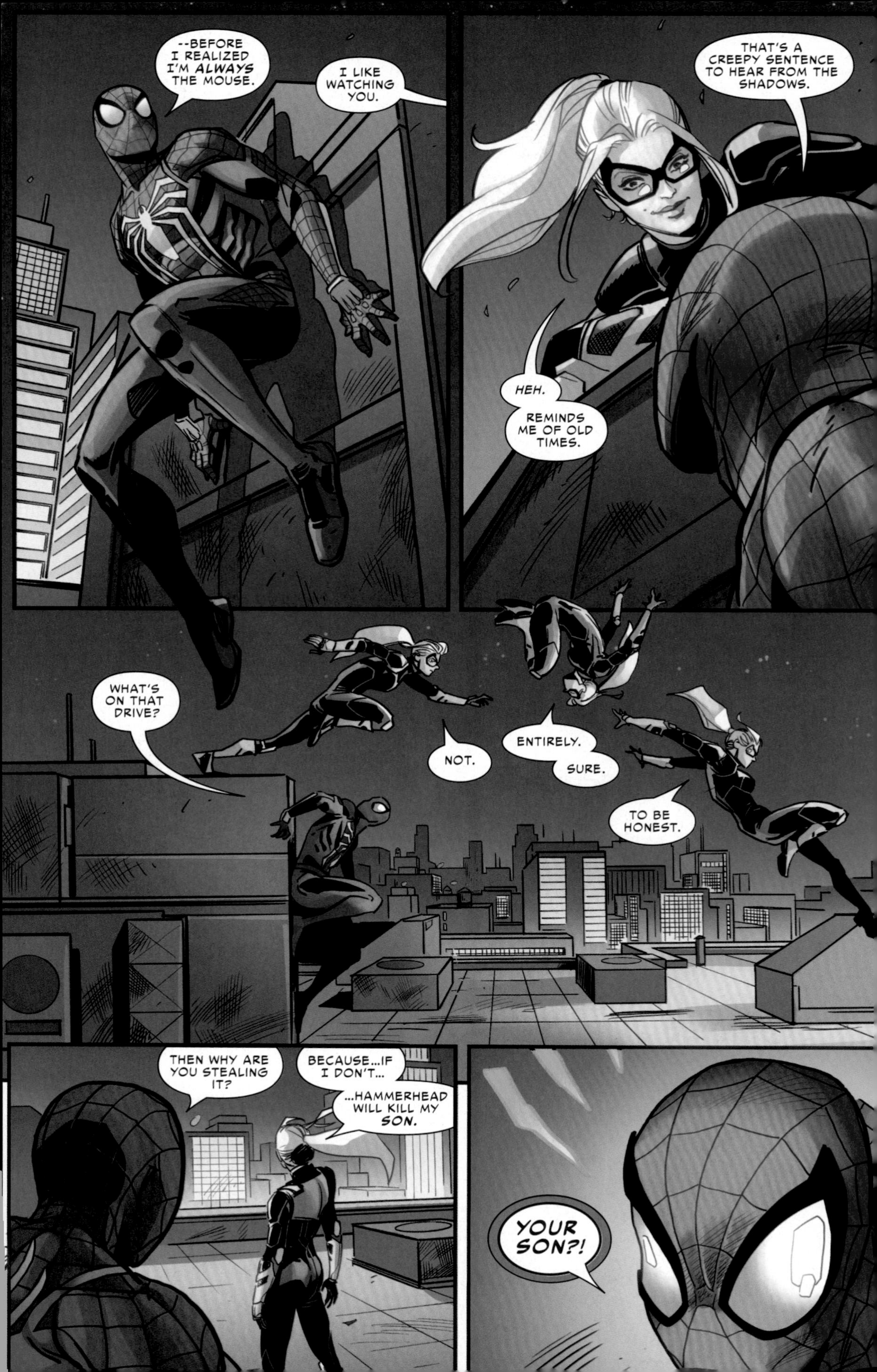
--BEFORE I REALIZED I'M ALWAYS THE MOUSE.
I LIKE WATCHING YOU.
THAT'S A CREEPY SENTENCE TO HEAR FROM THE SHADOWS.
HEH.
REMINDS ME OF OLD TIMES.
WHAT'S ON THAT DRIVE?
NOT.
ENTIRELY.
SURE.
TO BE HONEST.
THEN WHY ARE YOU STEALING IT?
BECAUSE...IF I DON'T...
...HAMMERHEAD WILL KILL MY SON.
YOUR SON?!

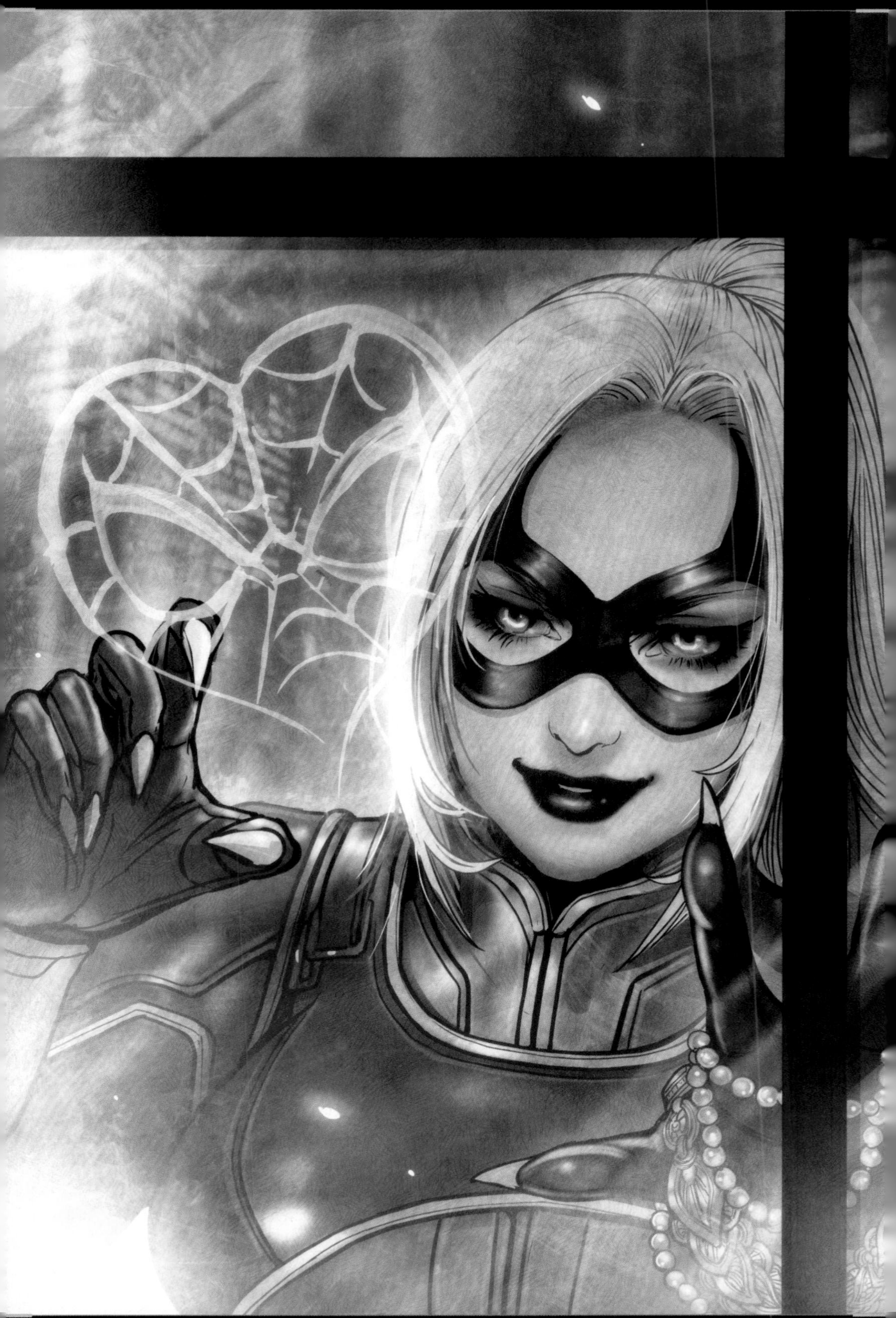

2

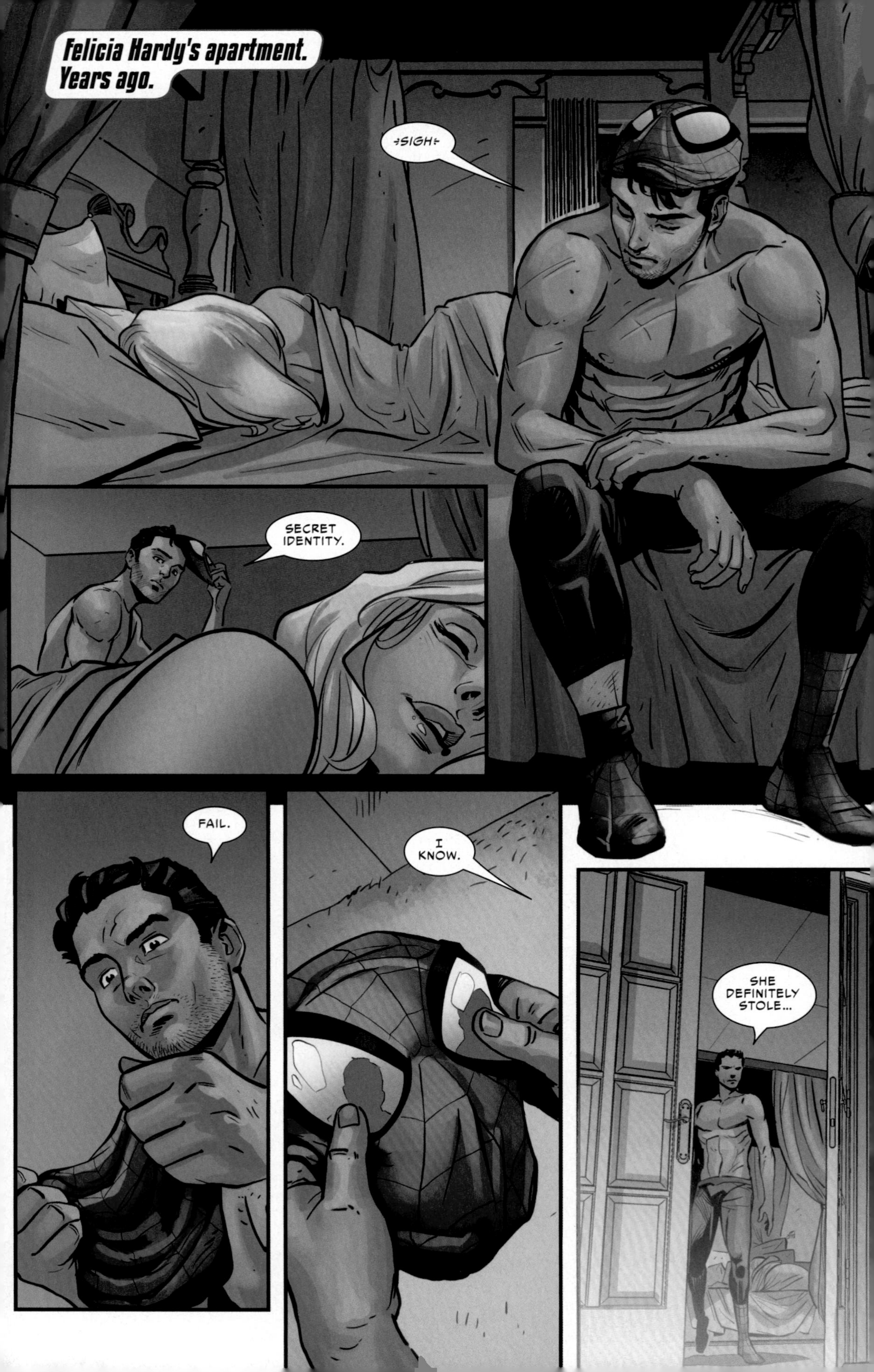
Felicia Hardy's apartment. Years ago.
⇌SIGH⇌
SECRET IDENTITY.
FAIL.
I KNOW.
SHE DEFINITELY STOLE...

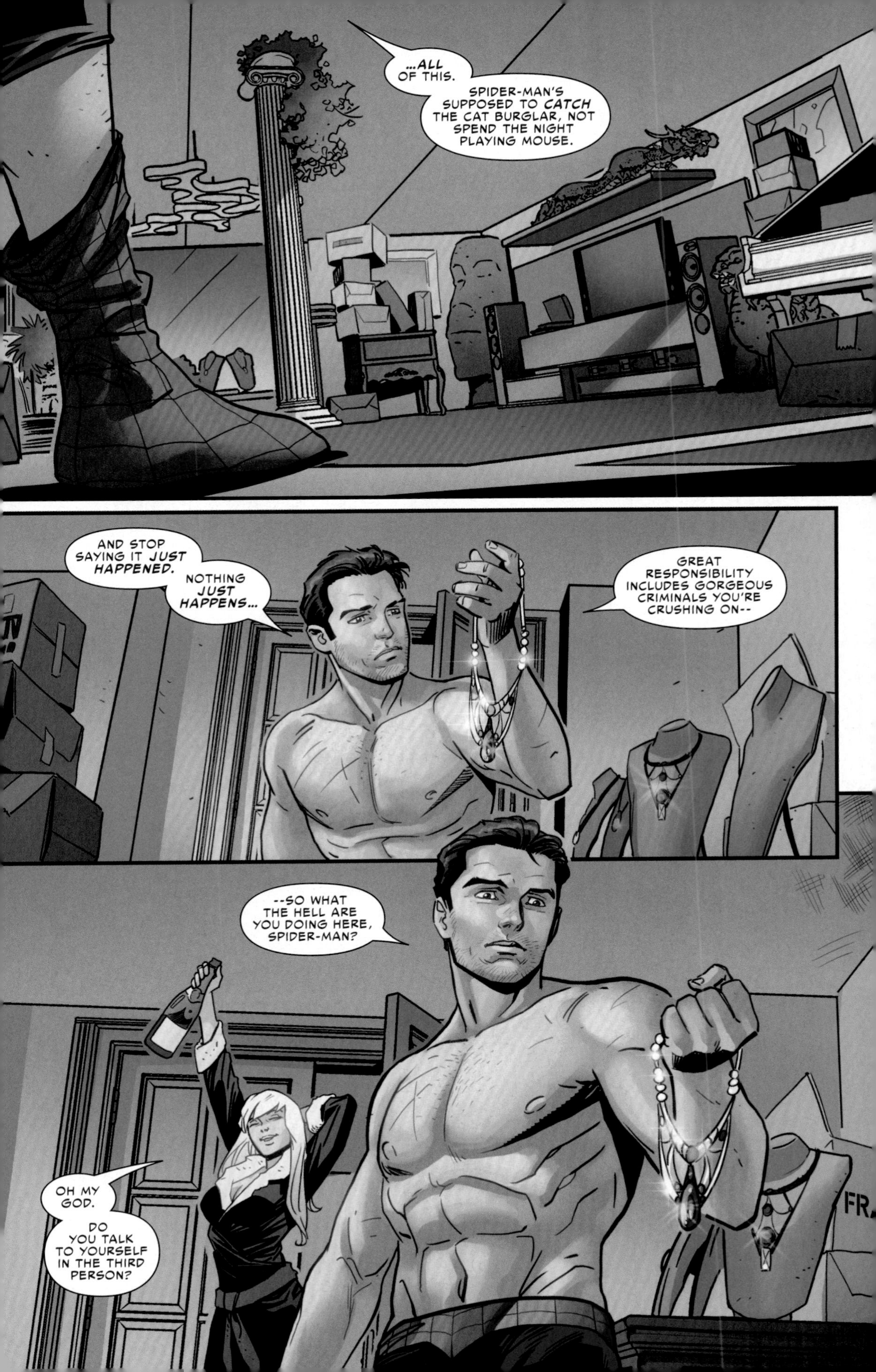
...ALL OF THIS.
SPIDER-MAN'S SUPPOSED TO CATCH THE CAT BURGLAR, NOT SPEND THE NIGHT PLAYING MOUSE.
AND STOP SAYING IT JUST HAPPENED.
NOTHING JUST HAPPENS...
GREAT RESPONSIBILITY INCLUDES GORGEOUS CRIMINALS YOU'RE CRUSHING ON--
--SO WHAT THE HELL ARE YOU DOING HERE, SPIDER-MAN?
OH MY GOD.
DO YOU TALK TO YOURSELF IN THE THIRD PERSON?

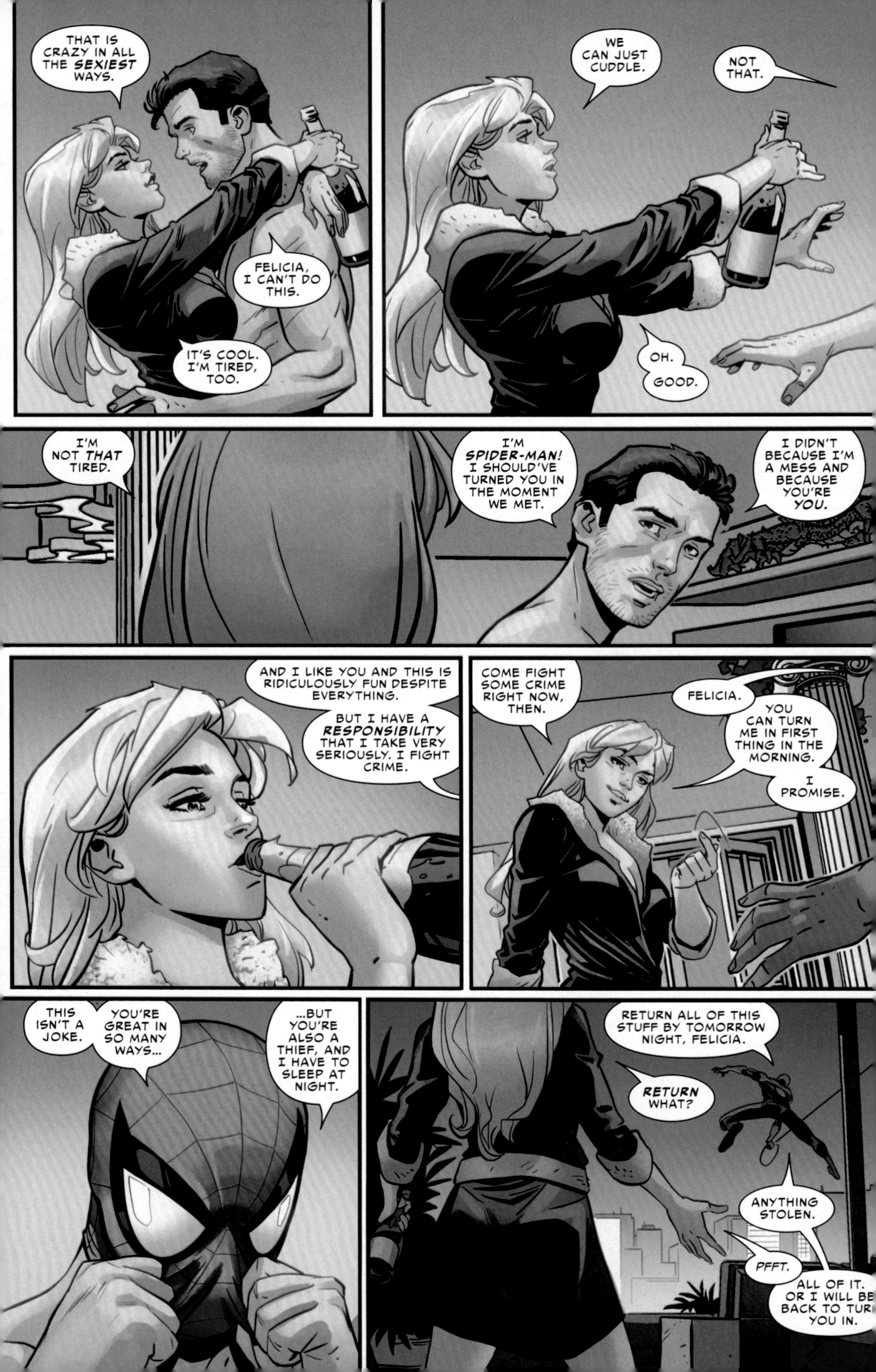

THAT IS CRAZY IN ALL THE *SEXIEST* WAYS.
FELICIA, I CAN'T DO THIS.
IT'S COOL. I'M TIRED, TOO.
WE CAN JUST CUDDLE.
NOT THAT.
OH.
GOOD.
I'M NOT *THAT* TIRED.
I'M *SPIDER-MAN!* I SHOULD'VE TURNED YOU IN THE MOMENT WE MET.
I DIDN'T BECAUSE I'M A MESS AND BECAUSE YOU'RE *YOU.*
AND I LIKE YOU AND THIS IS RIDICULOUSLY FUN DESPITE EVERYTHING.
BUT I HAVE A *RESPONSIBILITY* THAT I TAKE VERY SERIOUSLY. I FIGHT CRIME.
COME FIGHT SOME CRIME RIGHT NOW, THEN.
FELICIA.
YOU CAN TURN ME IN FIRST THING IN THE MORNING.
I PROMISE.
THIS ISN'T A JOKE.
YOU'RE GREAT IN SO MANY WAYS...
...BUT YOU'RE ALSO A THIEF, AND I HAVE TO SLEEP AT NIGHT.
RETURN ALL OF THIS STUFF BY TOMORROW NIGHT, FELICIA.
RETURN WHAT?
ANYTHING STOLEN.
PFFT.
ALL OF IT. OR I WILL BE BACK TO TURN YOU IN.

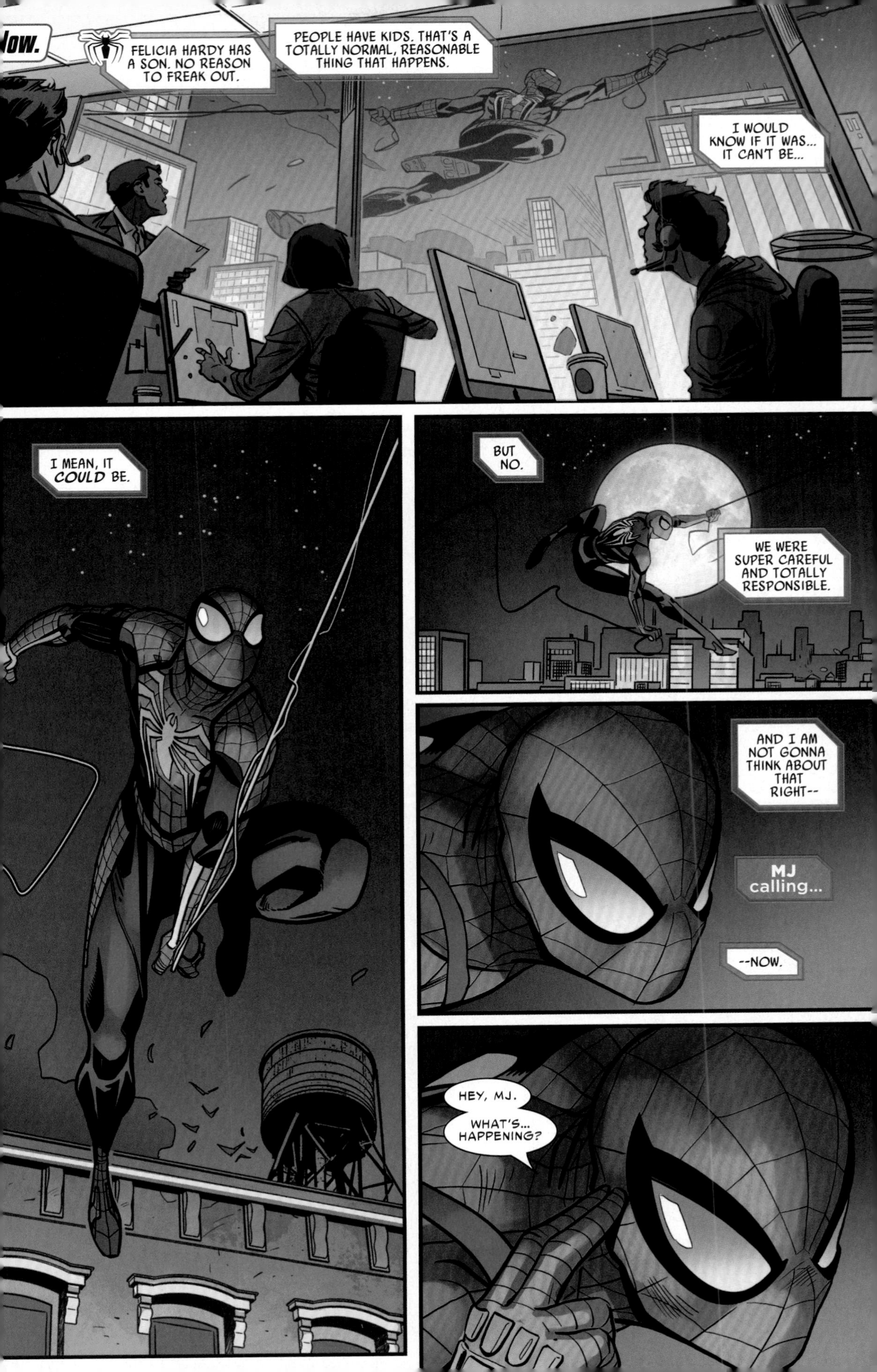
Now.
FELICIA HARDY HAS A SON. NO REASON TO FREAK OUT.
PEOPLE HAVE KIDS. THAT'S A TOTALLY NORMAL, REASONABLE THING THAT HAPPENS.
I WOULD KNOW IF IT WAS... IT CAN'T BE...
I MEAN, IT COULD BE.
BUT NO.
WE WERE SUPER CAREFUL AND TOTALLY RESPONSIBLE.
AND I AM NOT GONNA THINK ABOUT THAT RIGHT--
MJ calling...
--NOW.
HEY, MJ.
WHAT'S... HAPPENING?

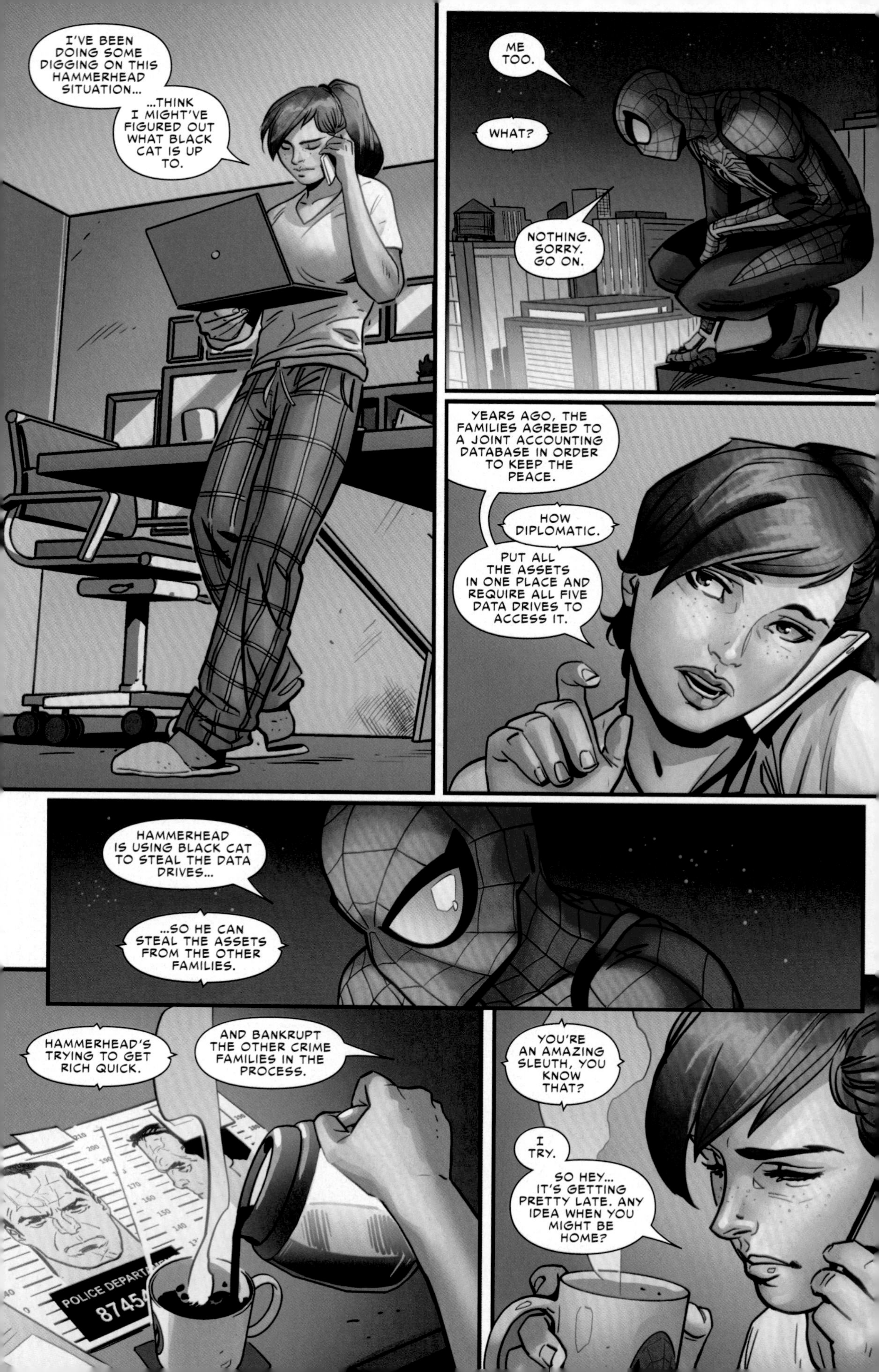
I'VE BEEN DOING SOME DIGGING ON THIS HAMMERHEAD SITUATION...
...THINK I MIGHT'VE FIGURED OUT WHAT BLACK CAT IS UP TO.
ME TOO.
WHAT?
NOTHING. SORRY. GO ON.
YEARS AGO, THE FAMILIES AGREED TO A JOINT ACCOUNTING DATABASE IN ORDER TO KEEP THE PEACE.
HOW DIPLOMATIC.
PUT ALL THE ASSETS IN ONE PLACE AND REQUIRE ALL FIVE DATA DRIVES TO ACCESS IT.
HAMMERHEAD IS USING BLACK CAT TO STEAL THE DATA DRIVES...
...SO HE CAN STEAL THE ASSETS FROM THE OTHER FAMILIES.
HAMMERHEAD'S TRYING TO GET RICH QUICK.
AND BANKRUPT THE OTHER CRIME FAMILIES IN THE PROCESS.
POLICE DEPARTME
8745
YOU'RE AN AMAZING SLEUTH, YOU KNOW THAT?
I TRY.
SO HEY... IT'S GETTING PRETTY LATE. ANY IDEA WHEN YOU MIGHT BE HOME?

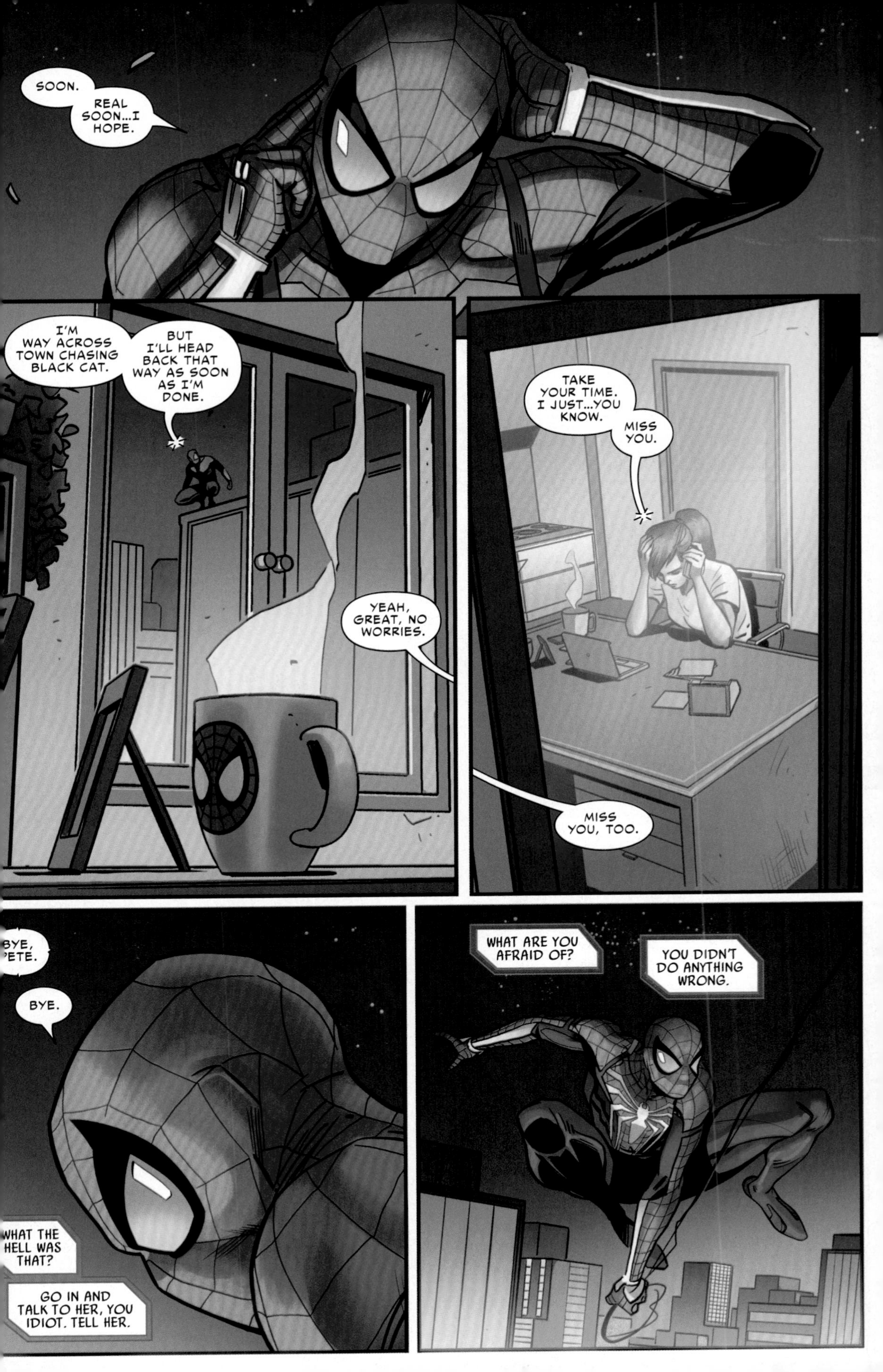
SOON.
REAL SOON...I HOPE.
I'M WAY ACROSS TOWN CHASING BLACK CAT.
BUT I'LL HEAD BACK THAT WAY AS SOON AS I'M DONE.
YEAH, GREAT, NO WORRIES.
TAKE YOUR TIME. I JUST...YOU KNOW.
MISS YOU.
MISS YOU, TOO.
BYE, PETE.
BYE.
WHAT THE HELL WAS THAT?
GO IN AND TALK TO HER, YOU IDIOT. TELL HER.
WHAT ARE YOU AFRAID OF?
YOU DIDN'T DO ANYTHING WRONG.

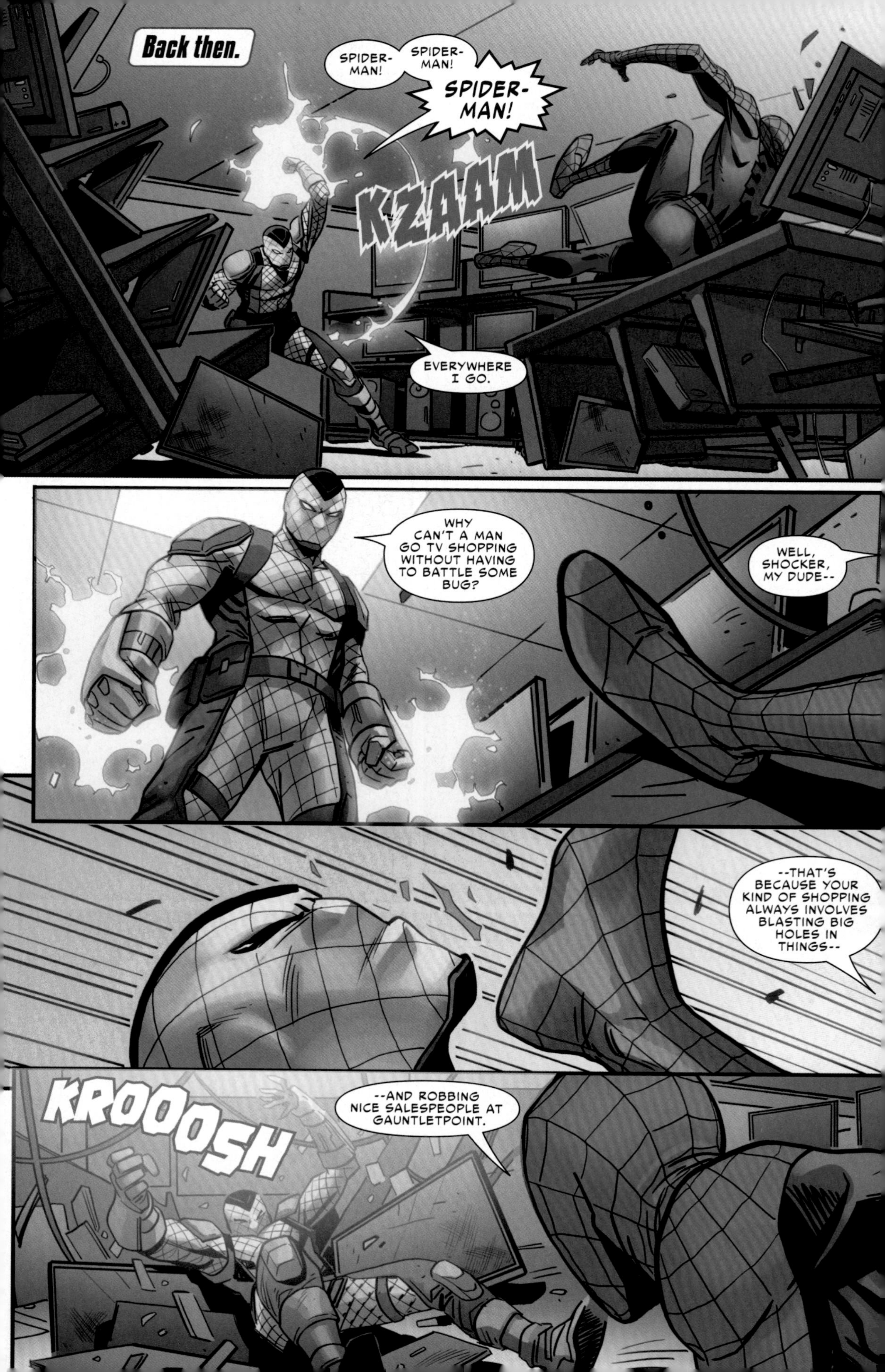
Back then.
SPIDER-MAN!
SPIDER-MAN!
SPIDER-MAN!
KZAAM
EVERYWHERE I GO.
WHY CAN'T A MAN GO TV SHOPPING WITHOUT HAVING TO BATTLE SOME BUG?
WELL, SHOCKER, MY DUDE--
--THAT'S BECAUSE YOUR KIND OF SHOPPING ALWAYS INVOLVES BLASTING BIG HOLES IN THINGS--
KROOOSH
--AND ROBBING NICE SALESPEOPLE AT GAUNTLETPOINT.

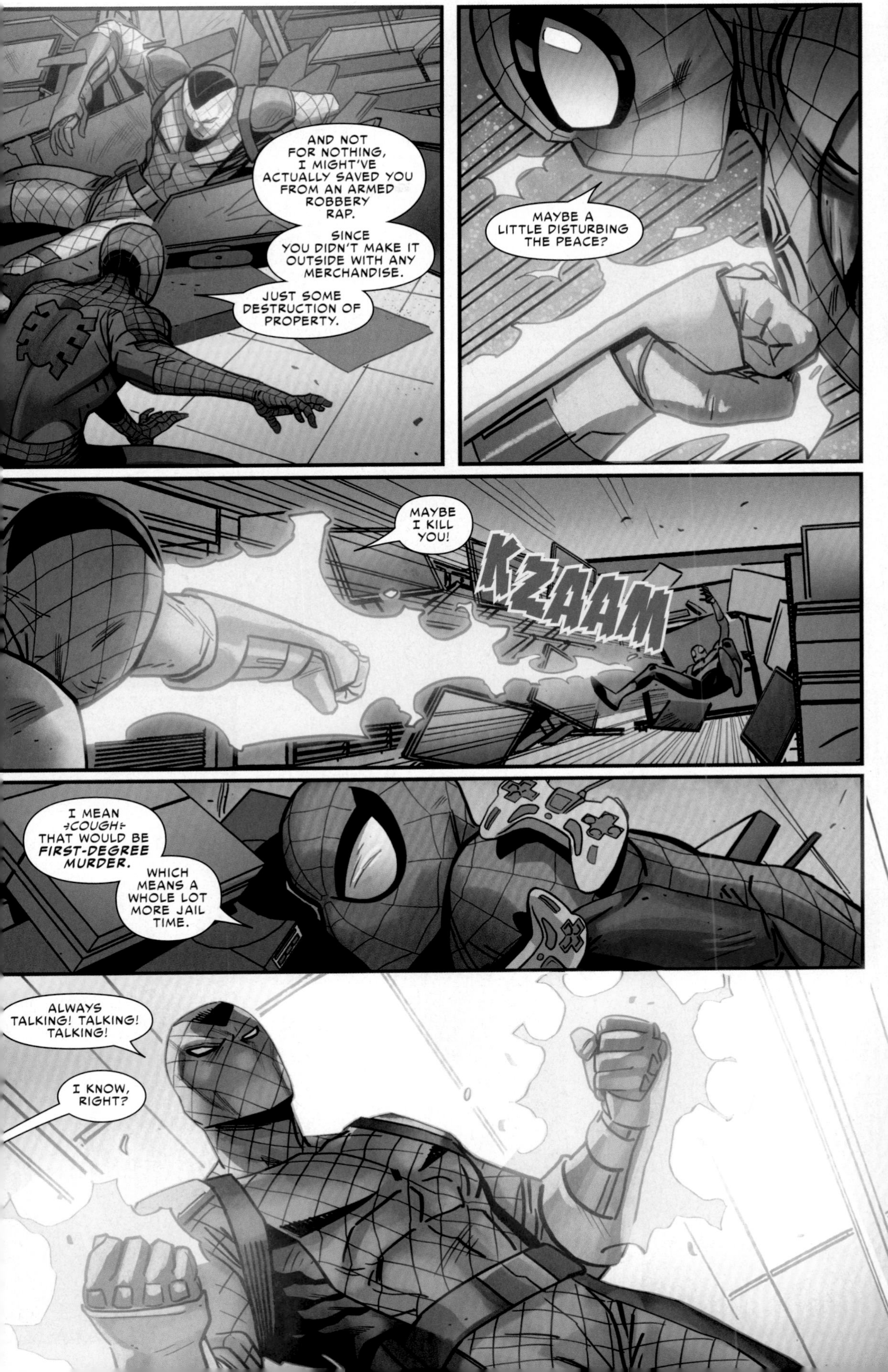
AND NOT FOR NOTHING, I MIGHT'VE ACTUALLY SAVED YOU FROM AN ARMED ROBBERY RAP.
SINCE YOU DIDN'T MAKE IT OUTSIDE WITH ANY MERCHANDISE.
JUST SOME DESTRUCTION OF PROPERTY.
MAYBE A LITTLE DISTURBING THE PEACE?
MAYBE I KILL YOU!
KZAAM
I MEAN *COUGH* THAT WOULD BE FIRST-DEGREE MURDER.
WHICH MEANS A WHOLE LOT MORE JAIL TIME.
ALWAYS TALKING! TALKING! TALKING!
I KNOW, RIGHT?

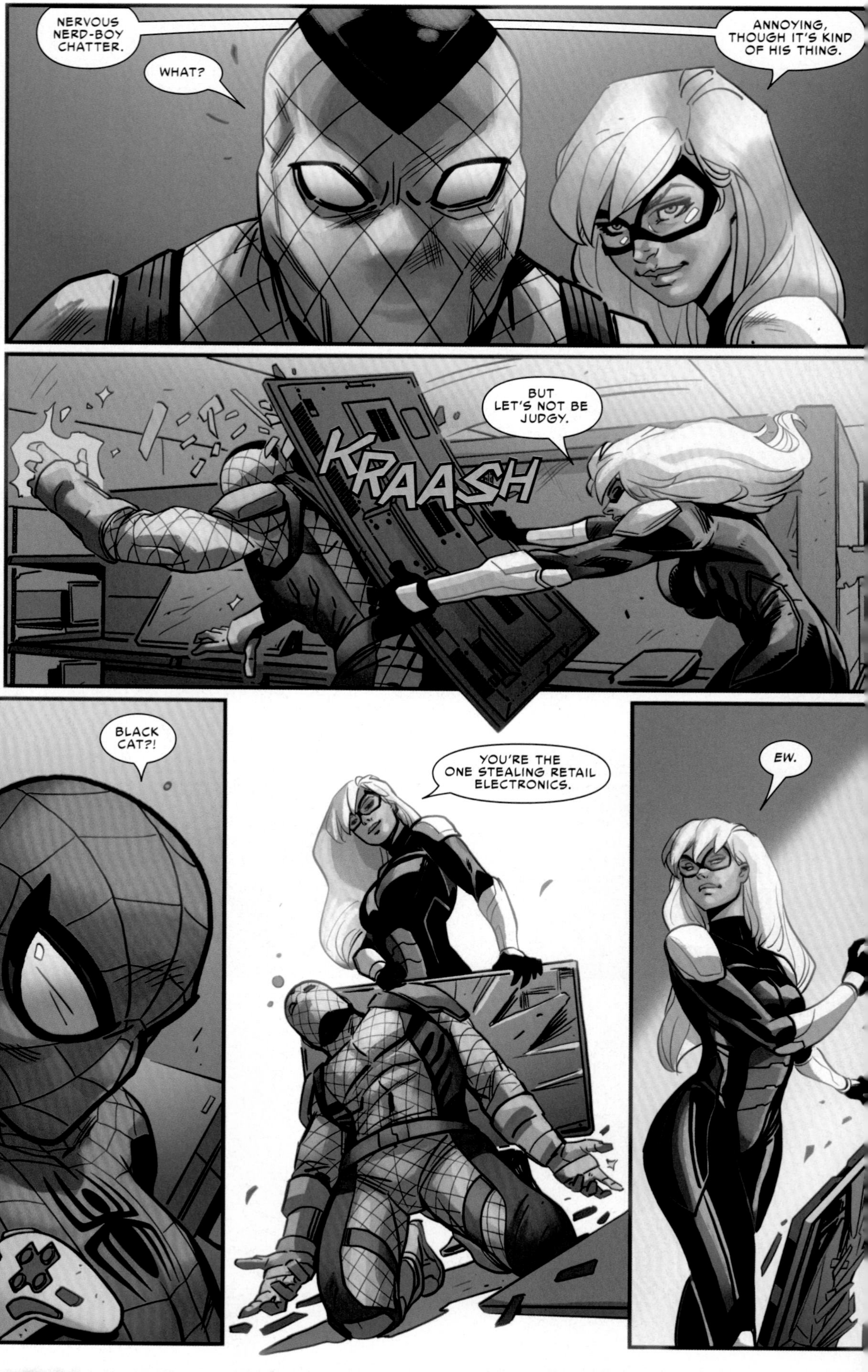
NERVOUS NERD-BOY CHATTER.
ANNOYING, THOUGH IT'S KIND OF HIS THING.
WHAT?
BUT LET'S NOT BE JUDGY.
KRAASH
BLACK CAT?!
YOU'RE THE ONE STEALING RETAIL ELECTRONICS.
EW.

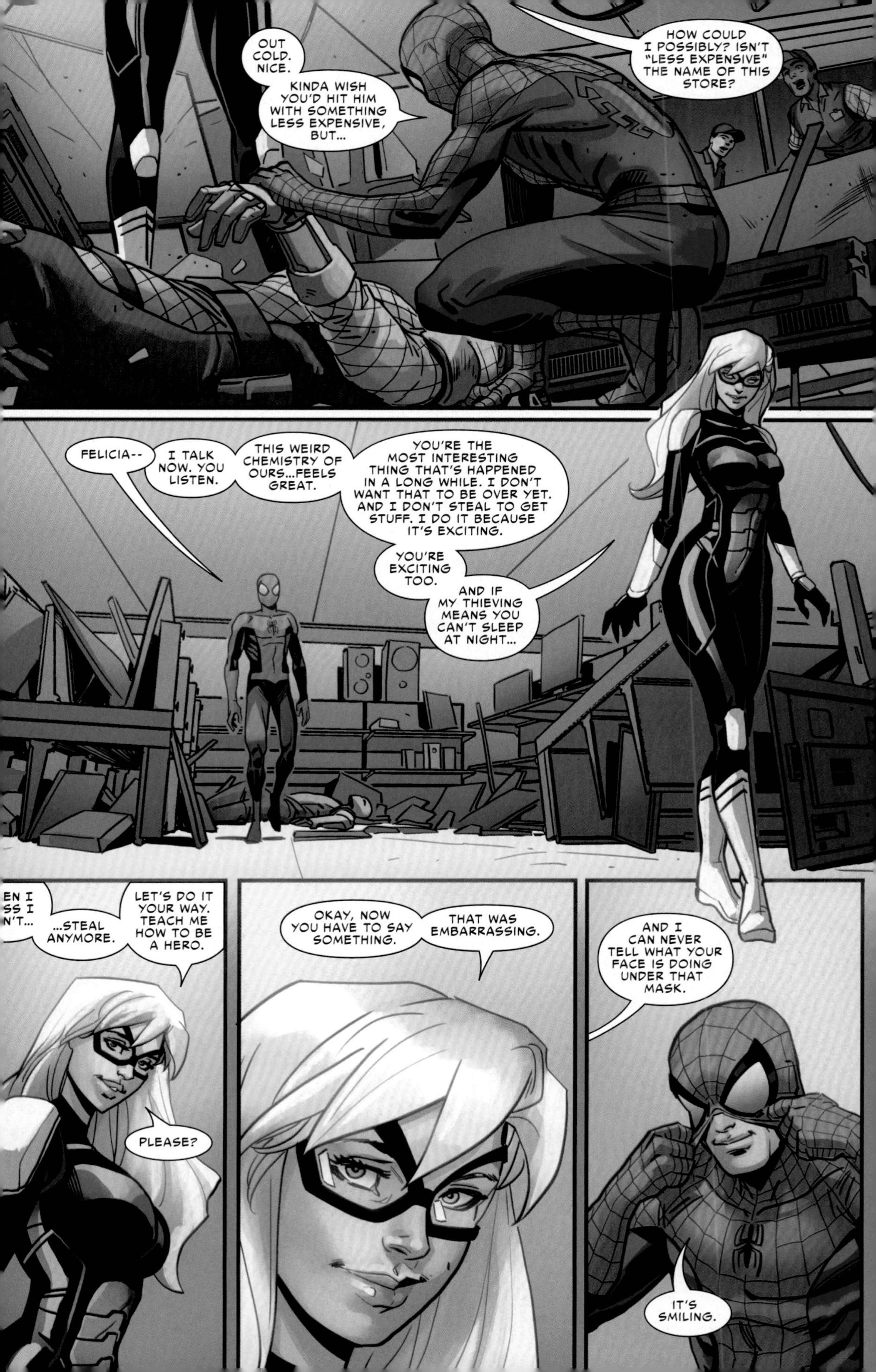
OUT COLD. NICE.
KINDA WISH YOU'D HIT HIM WITH SOMETHING LESS EXPENSIVE, BUT...
HOW COULD I POSSIBLY? ISN'T "LESS EXPENSIVE" THE NAME OF THIS STORE?
FELICIA--
I TALK NOW. YOU LISTEN.
THIS WEIRD CHEMISTRY OF OURS...FEELS GREAT.
YOU'RE THE MOST INTERESTING THING THAT'S HAPPENED IN A LONG WHILE. I DON'T WANT THAT TO BE OVER YET. AND I DON'T STEAL TO GET STUFF. I DO IT BECAUSE IT'S EXCITING.
YOU'RE EXCITING TOO.
AND IF MY THIEVING MEANS YOU CAN'T SLEEP AT NIGHT...
...STEAL ANYMORE.
LET'S DO IT YOUR WAY. TEACH ME HOW TO BE A HERO.
PLEASE?
OKAY, NOW YOU HAVE TO SAY SOMETHING.
THAT WAS EMBARRASSING.
AND I CAN NEVER TELL WHAT YOUR FACE IS DOING UNDER THAT MASK.
IT'S SMILING.

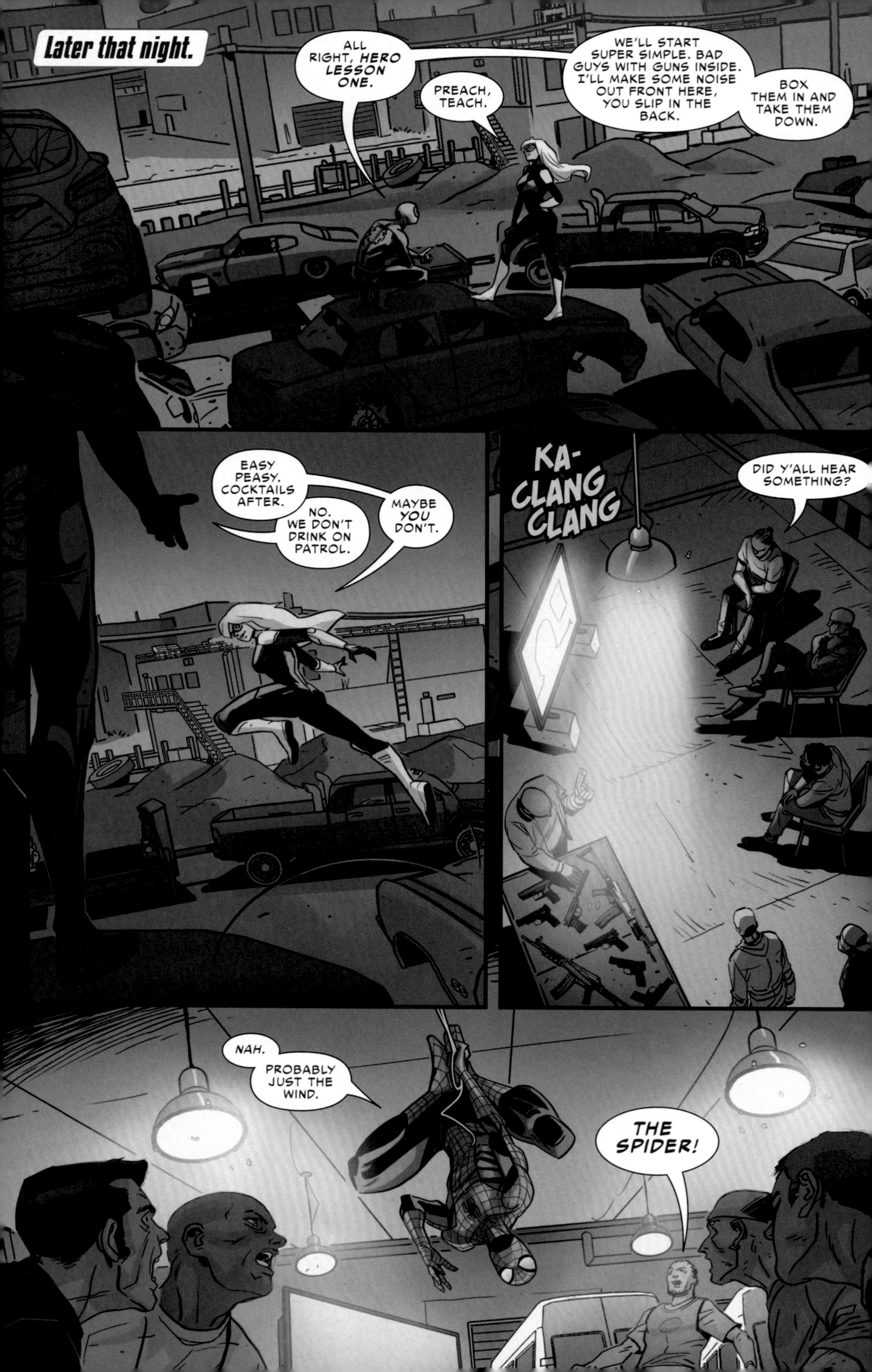
Later that night.
ALL RIGHT, HERO LESSON ONE.
PREACH, TEACH.
WE'LL START SUPER SIMPLE. BAD GUYS WITH GUNS INSIDE. I'LL MAKE SOME NOISE OUT FRONT HERE, YOU SLIP IN THE BACK.
BOX THEM IN AND TAKE THEM DOWN.
EASY PEASY. COCKTAILS AFTER.
NO. WE DON'T DRINK ON PATROL.
MAYBE YOU DON'T.
KA-CLANG CLANG
DID Y'ALL HEAR SOMETHING?
NAH.
PROBABLY JUST THE WIND.
THE SPIDER!

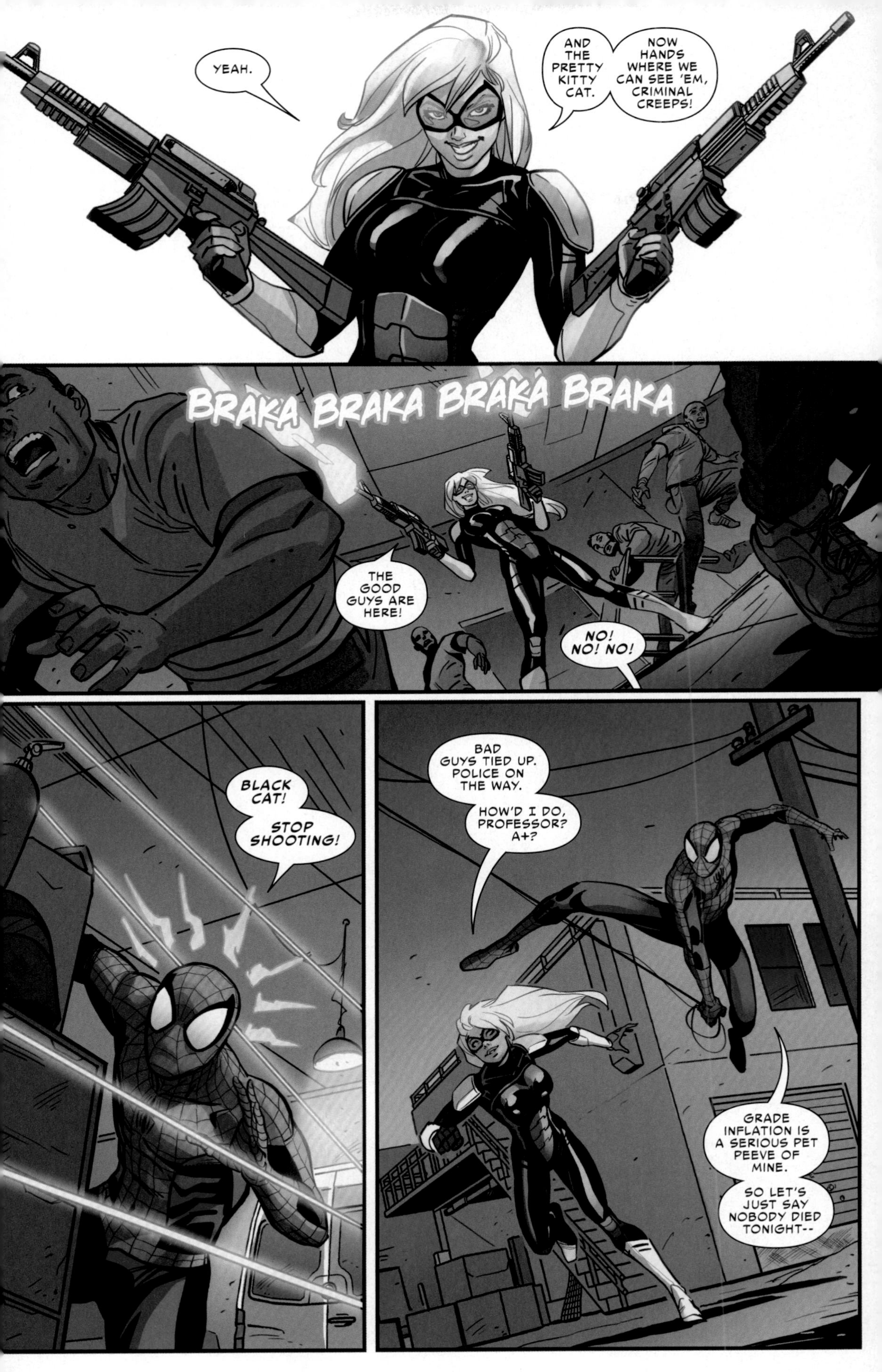
YEAH.
AND THE PRETTY KITTY CAT.
NOW HANDS WHERE WE CAN SEE 'EM, CRIMINAL CREEPS!
BRAKA BRAKA BRAKA BRAKA
THE GOOD GUYS ARE HERE!
NO! NO! NO!
BLACK CAT!
STOP SHOOTING!
BAD GUYS TIED UP. POLICE ON THE WAY.
HOW'D I DO, PROFESSOR? A+?
GRADE INFLATION IS A SERIOUS PET PEEVE OF MINE.
SO LET'S JUST SAY NOBODY DIED TONIGHT--

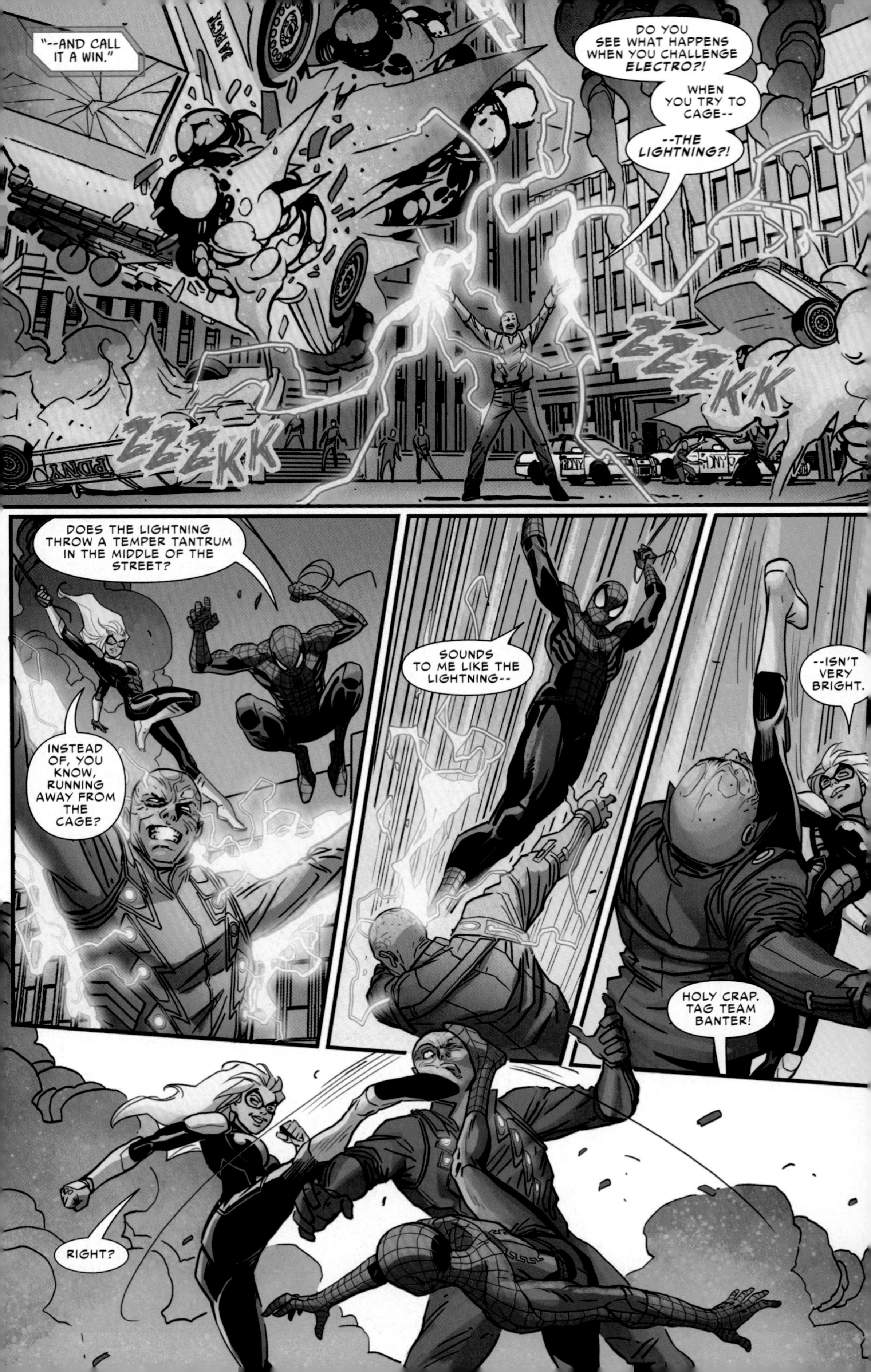
"--AND CALL IT A WIN."
DO YOU SEE WHAT HAPPENS WHEN YOU CHALLENGE *ELECTRO?!*
WHEN YOU TRY TO CAGE--
--*THE LIGHTNING?!*
ZZZKK
ZZZKK
DOES THE LIGHTNING THROW A TEMPER TANTRUM IN THE MIDDLE OF THE STREET?
INSTEAD OF, YOU KNOW, RUNNING AWAY FROM THE CAGE?
SOUNDS TO ME LIKE THE LIGHTNING--
--ISN'T VERY BRIGHT.
HOLY CRAP. TAG TEAM BANTER!
RIGHT?

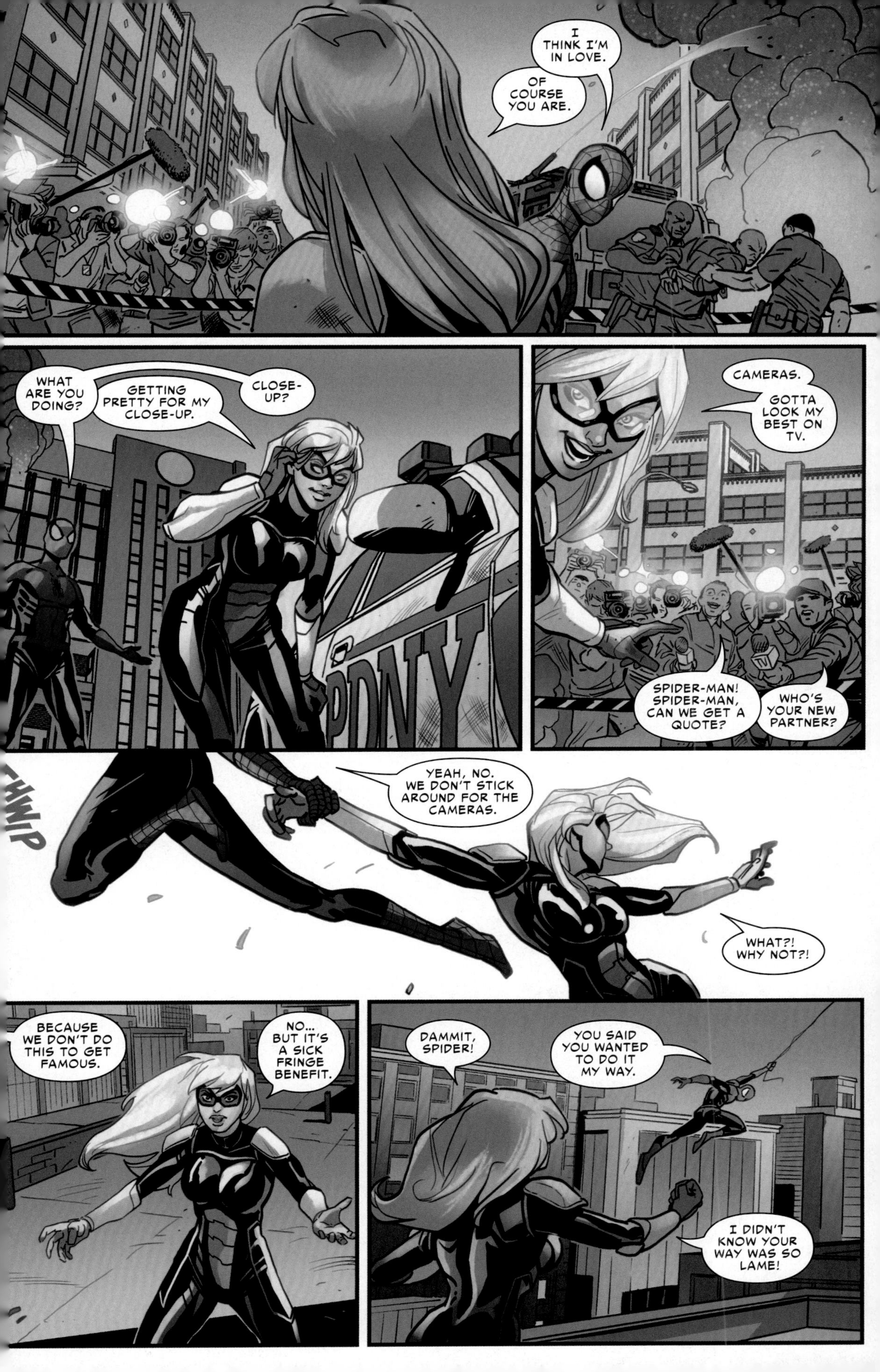
I THINK I'M IN LOVE.
OF COURSE YOU ARE.
WHAT ARE YOU DOING?
GETTING PRETTY FOR MY CLOSE-UP.
CLOSE-UP?
CAMERAS.
GOTTA LOOK MY BEST ON TV.
SPIDER-MAN! SPIDER-MAN, CAN WE GET A QUOTE?
WHO'S YOUR NEW PARTNER?
THWIP
YEAH, NO. WE DON'T STICK AROUND FOR THE CAMERAS.
WHAT?! WHY NOT?!
BECAUSE WE DON'T DO THIS TO GET FAMOUS.
NO... BUT IT'S A SICK FRINGE BENEFIT.
DAMMIT, SPIDER!
YOU SAID YOU WANTED TO DO IT MY WAY.
I DIDN'T KNOW YOUR WAY WAS SO LAME!

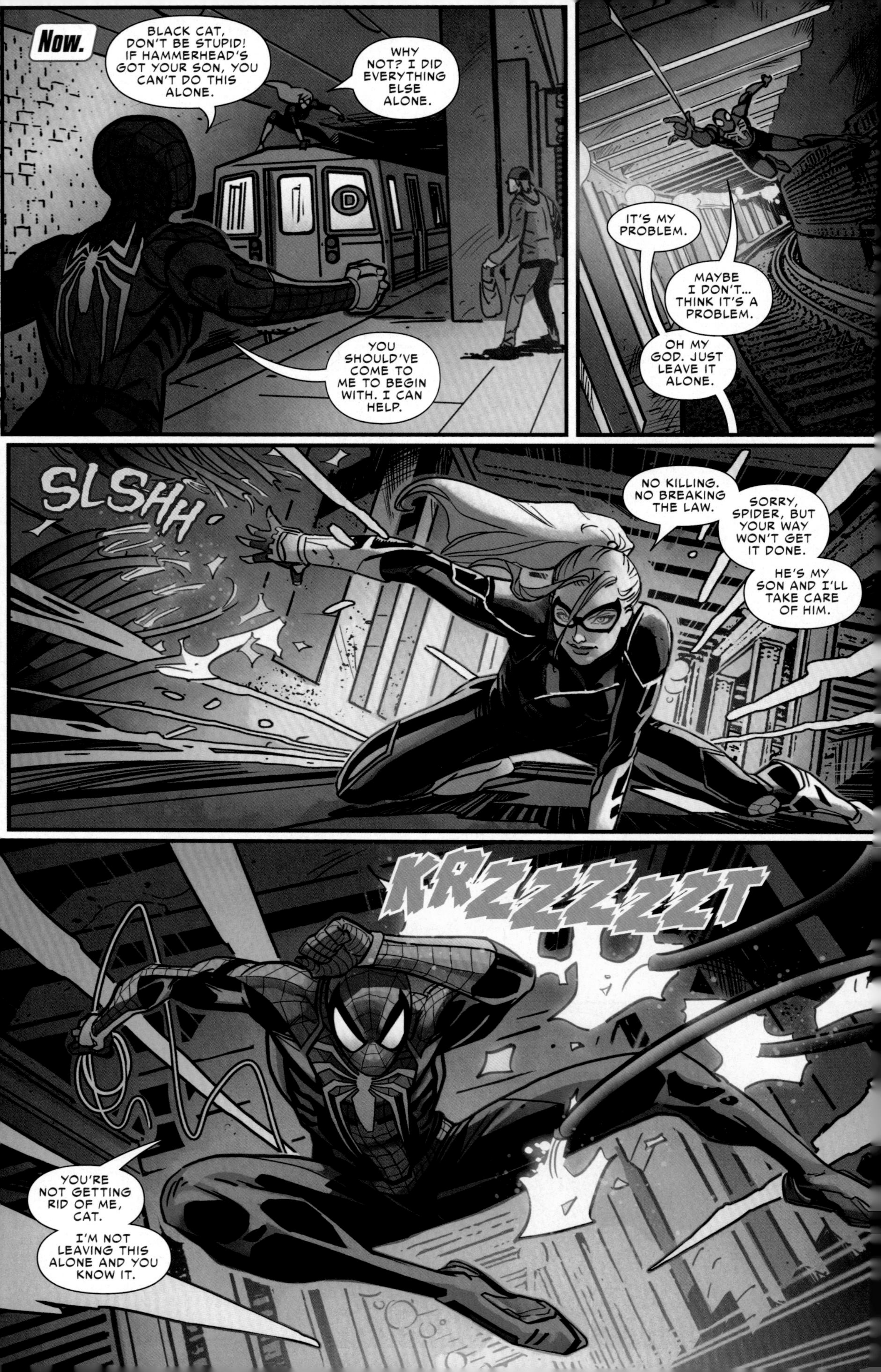
Now.
BLACK CAT, DON'T BE STUPID! IF HAMMERHEAD'S GOT YOUR SON, YOU CAN'T DO THIS ALONE.
WHY NOT? I DID EVERYTHING ELSE ALONE.
YOU SHOULD'VE COME TO ME TO BEGIN WITH. I CAN HELP.
IT'S MY PROBLEM.
MAYBE I DON'T... THINK IT'S A PROBLEM.
OH MY GOD. JUST LEAVE IT ALONE.
SLSHH
NO KILLING. NO BREAKING THE LAW.
SORRY, SPIDER, BUT YOUR WAY WON'T GET IT DONE.
HE'S MY SON AND I'LL TAKE CARE OF HIM.
KRZZZZZZT
YOU'RE NOT GETTING RID OF ME, CAT.
I'M NOT LEAVING THIS ALONE AND YOU KNOW IT.

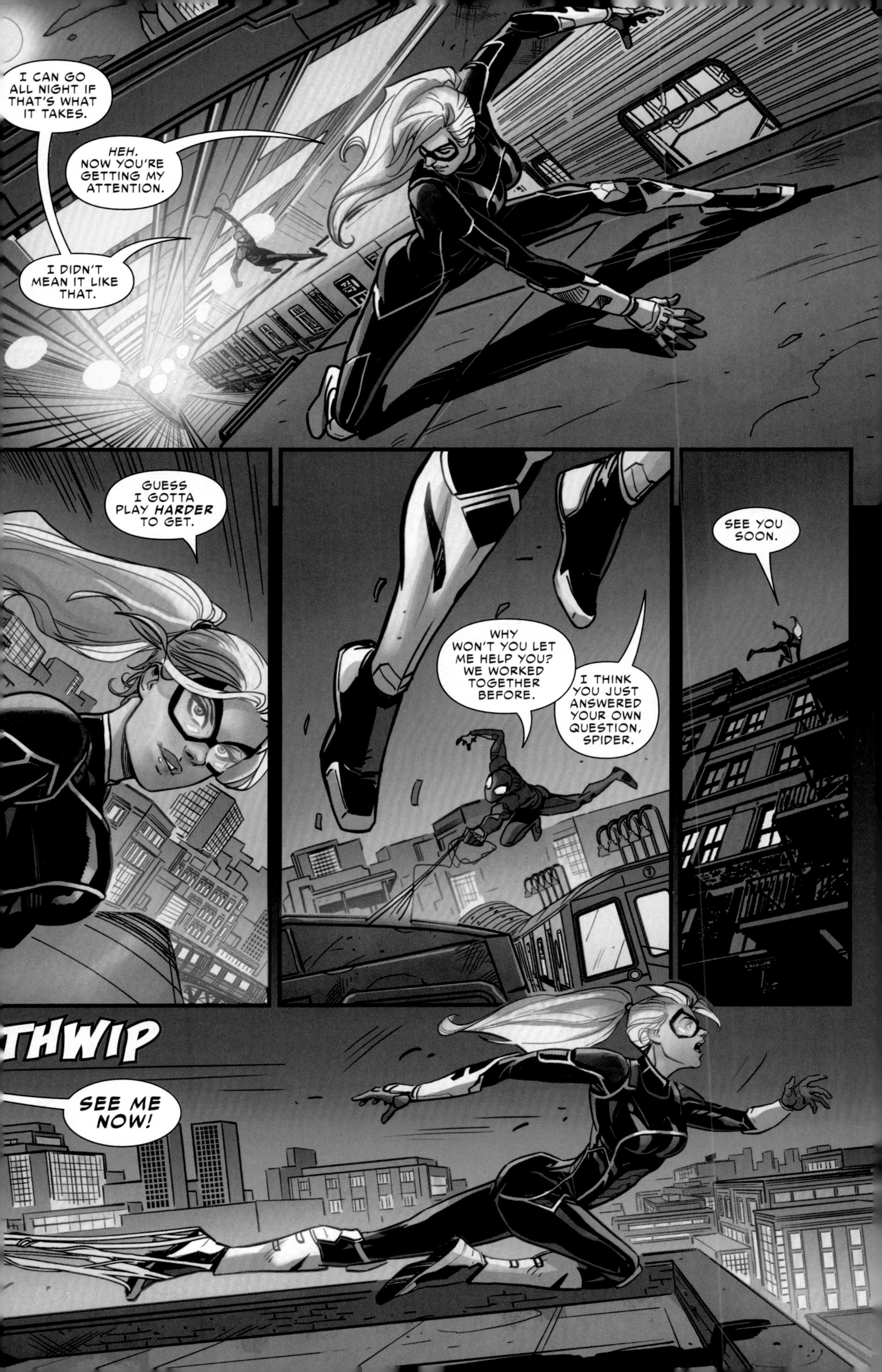
I CAN GO ALL NIGHT IF THAT'S WHAT IT TAKES.
HEH. NOW YOU'RE GETTING MY ATTENTION.
I DIDN'T MEAN IT LIKE THAT.
GUESS I GOTTA PLAY HARDER TO GET.
WHY WON'T YOU LET ME HELP YOU? WE WORKED TOGETHER BEFORE.
I THINK YOU JUST ANSWERED YOUR OWN QUESTION, SPIDER.
SEE YOU SOON.
THWIP
SEE ME NOW!

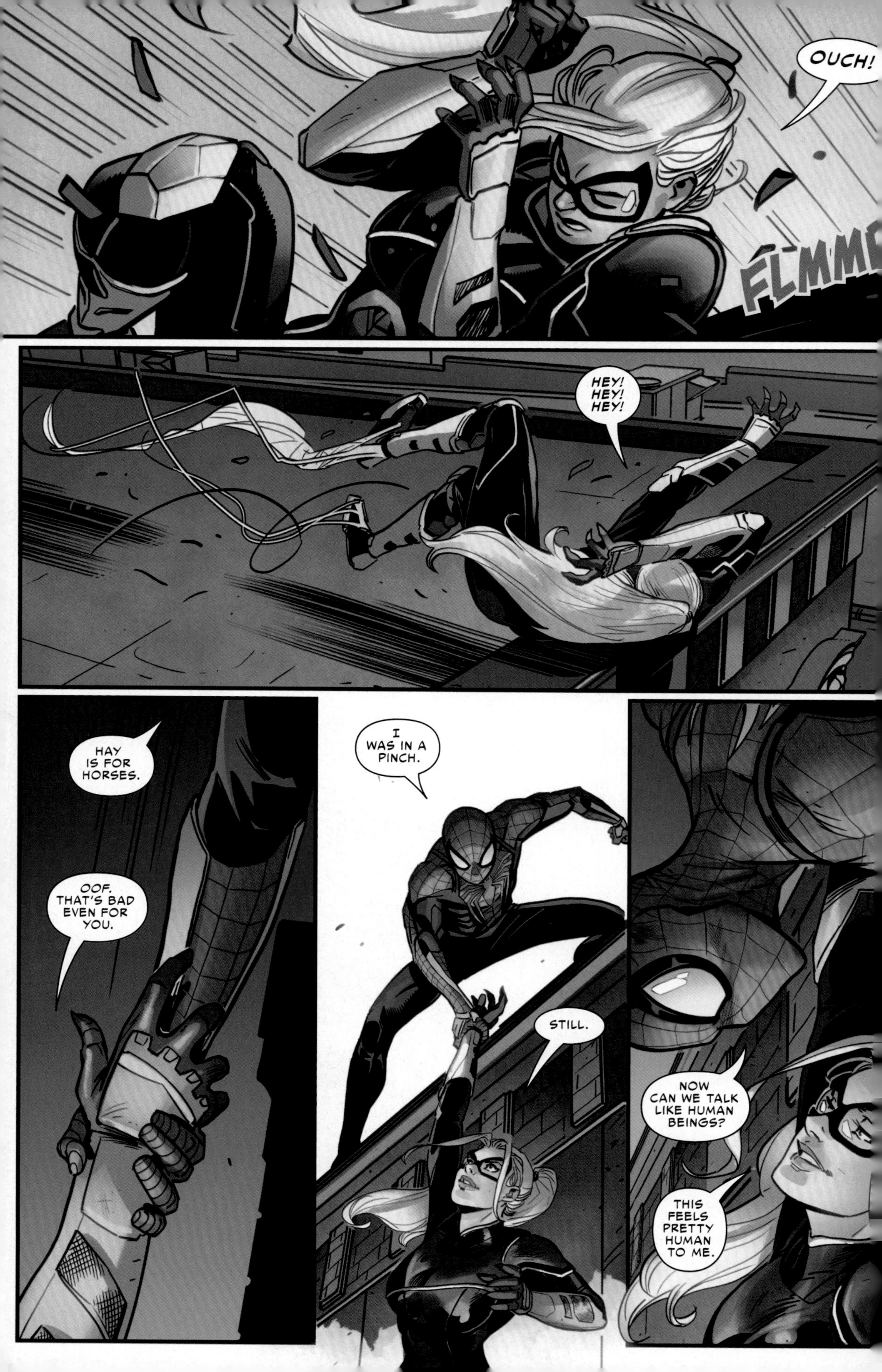
OUCH!
FLMMF
HEY! HEY! HEY!
HAY IS FOR HORSES.
OOF. THAT'S BAD EVEN FOR YOU.
I WAS IN A PINCH.
STILL.
NOW CAN WE TALK LIKE HUMAN BEINGS?
THIS FEELS PRETTY HUMAN TO ME.

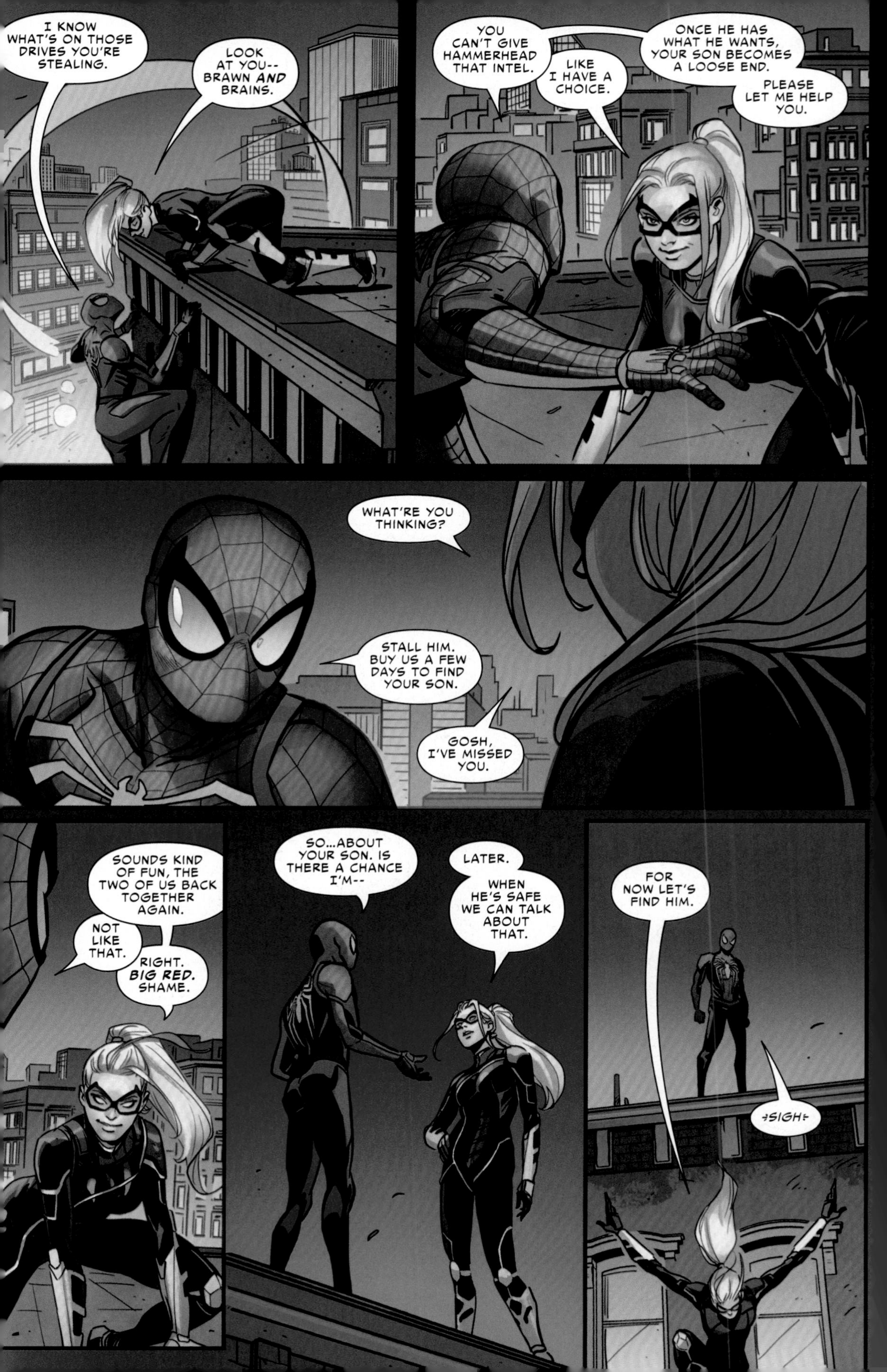

I KNOW WHAT'S ON THOSE DRIVES YOU'RE STEALING.
LOOK AT YOU-- BRAWN *AND* BRAINS.
YOU CAN'T GIVE HAMMERHEAD THAT INTEL.
LIKE I HAVE A CHOICE.
ONCE HE HAS WHAT HE WANTS, YOUR SON BECOMES A LOOSE END.
PLEASE LET ME HELP YOU.
WHAT'RE YOU THINKING?
STALL HIM. BUY US A FEW DAYS TO FIND YOUR SON.
GOSH, I'VE MISSED YOU.
SOUNDS KIND OF FUN, THE TWO OF US BACK TOGETHER AGAIN.
NOT LIKE THAT.
RIGHT. *BIG RED.* SHAME.
SO...ABOUT YOUR SON. IS THERE A CHANCE I'M--
LATER.
WHEN HE'S SAFE WE CAN TALK ABOUT THAT.
FOR NOW LET'S FIND HIM.
SIGH

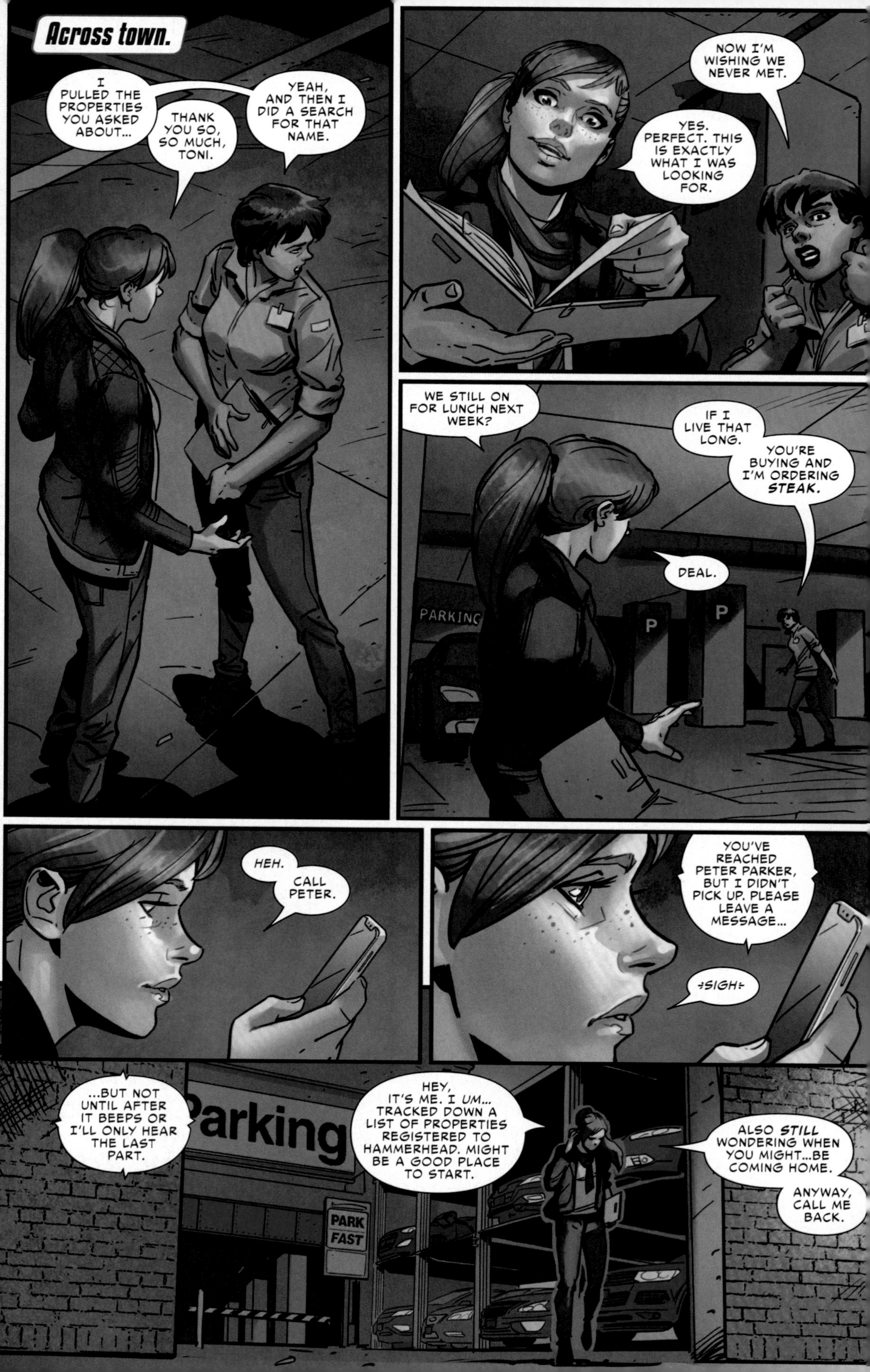
Across town.
I PULLED THE PROPERTIES YOU ASKED ABOUT...
YEAH, AND THEN I DID A SEARCH FOR THAT NAME.
THANK YOU SO, SO MUCH, TONI.
NOW I'M WISHING WE NEVER MET.
YES. PERFECT. THIS IS EXACTLY WHAT I WAS LOOKING FOR.
WE STILL ON FOR LUNCH NEXT WEEK?
IF I LIVE THAT LONG.
YOU'RE BUYING AND I'M ORDERING *STEAK.*
DEAL.
PARKING
P
P
HEH.
CALL PETER.
YOU'VE REACHED PETER PARKER, BUT I DIDN'T PICK UP. PLEASE LEAVE A MESSAGE...
SIGH
...BUT NOT UNTIL AFTER IT BEEPS OR I'LL ONLY HEAR THE LAST PART.
Parking
HEY, IT'S ME. I *UM*... TRACKED DOWN A LIST OF PROPERTIES REGISTERED TO HAMMERHEAD. MIGHT BE A GOOD PLACE TO START.
ALSO *STILL* WONDERING WHEN YOU MIGHT...BE COMING HOME.
ANYWAY, CALL ME BACK.
PARK FAST

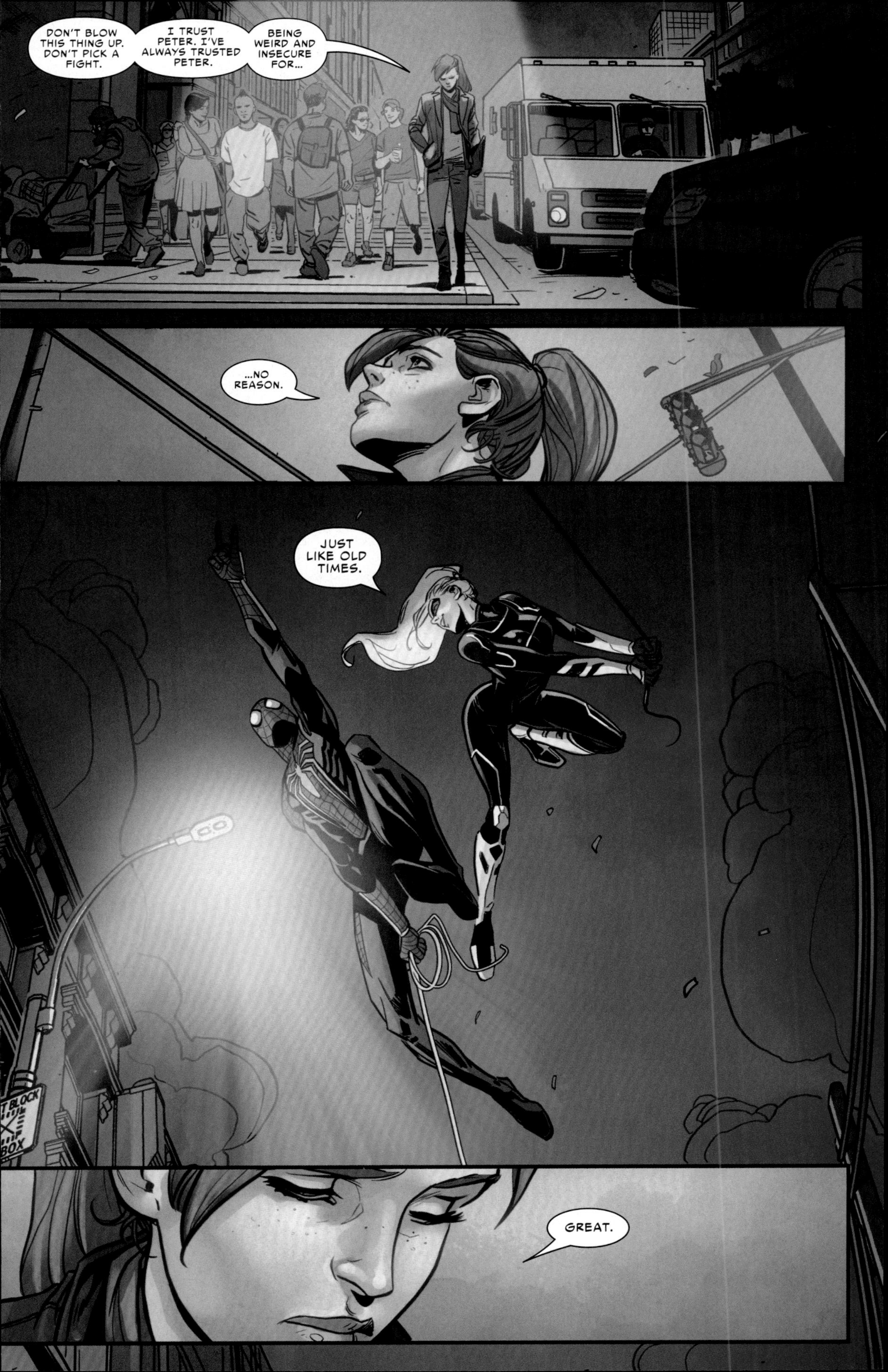
DON'T BLOW THIS THING UP. DON'T PICK A FIGHT.
I TRUST PETER. I'VE ALWAYS TRUSTED PETER.
BEING WEIRD AND INSECURE FOR...
...NO REASON.
JUST LIKE OLD TIMES.
GREAT.

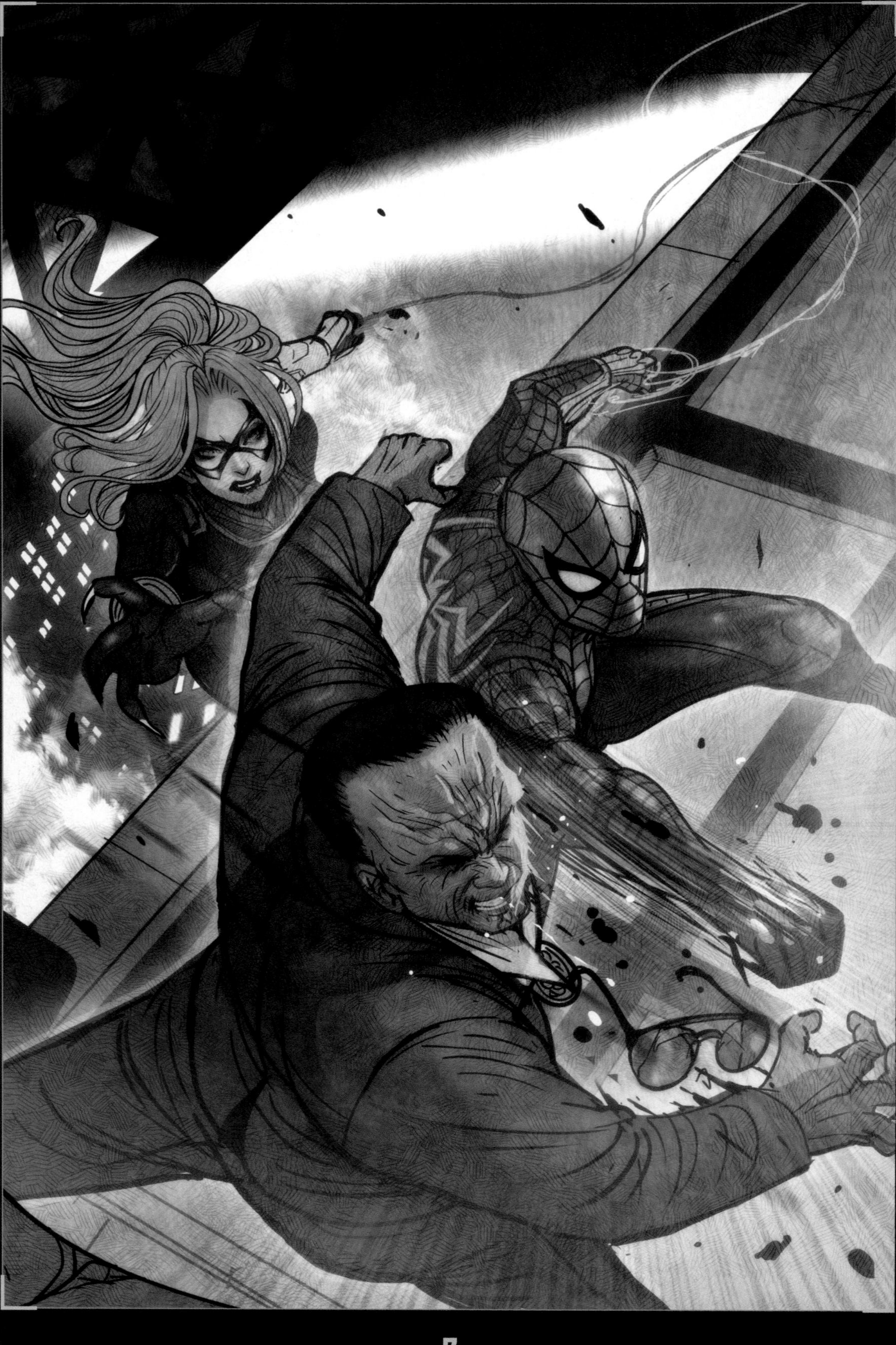

3

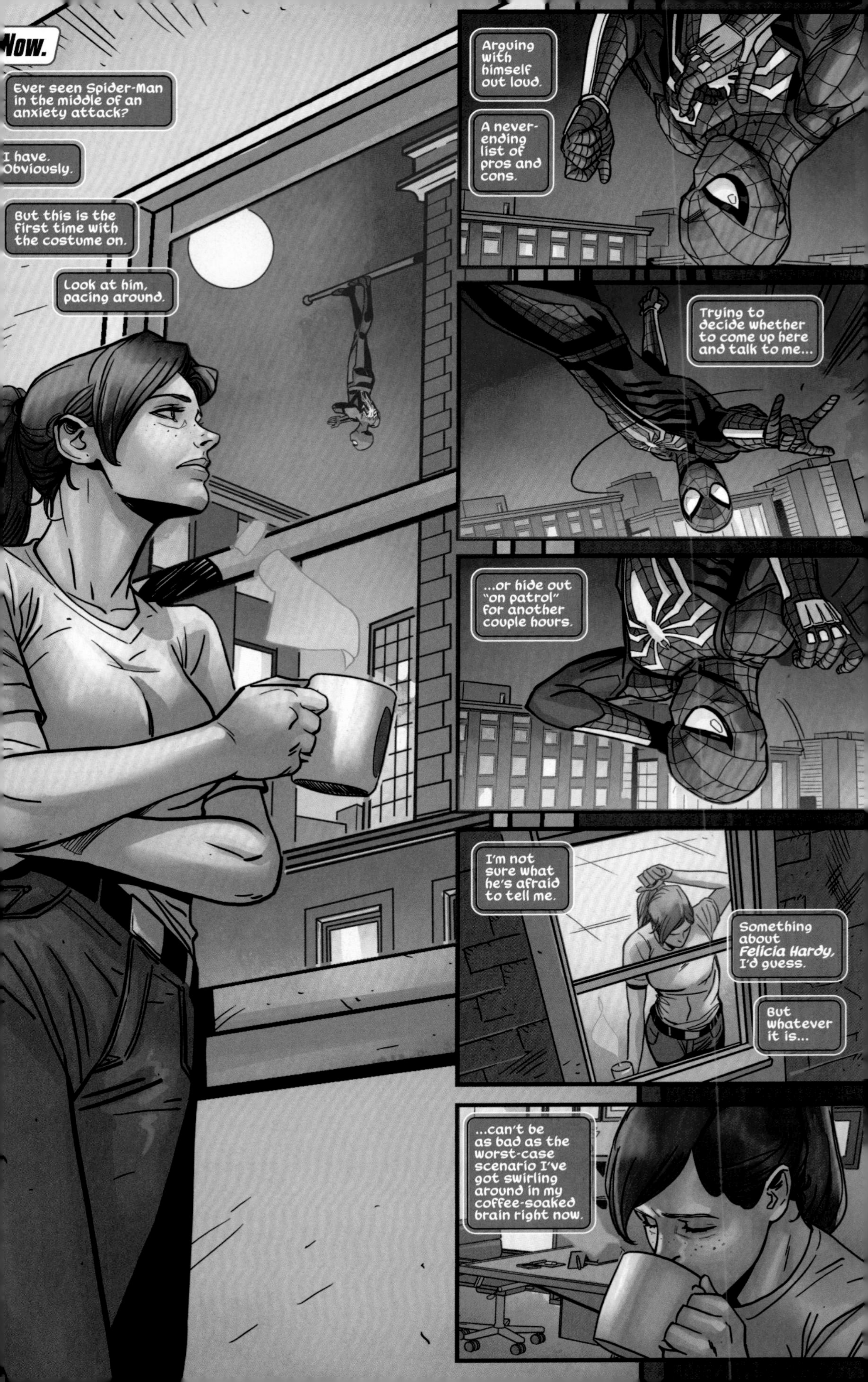

Now.
Ever seen Spider-Man in the middle of an anxiety attack?
I have. Obviously.
But this is the first time with the costume on.
Look at him, pacing around.
Arguing with himself out loud.
A never-ending list of pros and cons.
Trying to decide whether to come up here and talk to me...
...or hide out "on patrol" for another couple hours.
I'm not sure what he's afraid to tell me.
Something about *Felicia Hardy*, I'd guess.
But whatever it is...
...can't be as bad as the worst-case scenario I've got swirling around in my coffee-soaked brain right now.

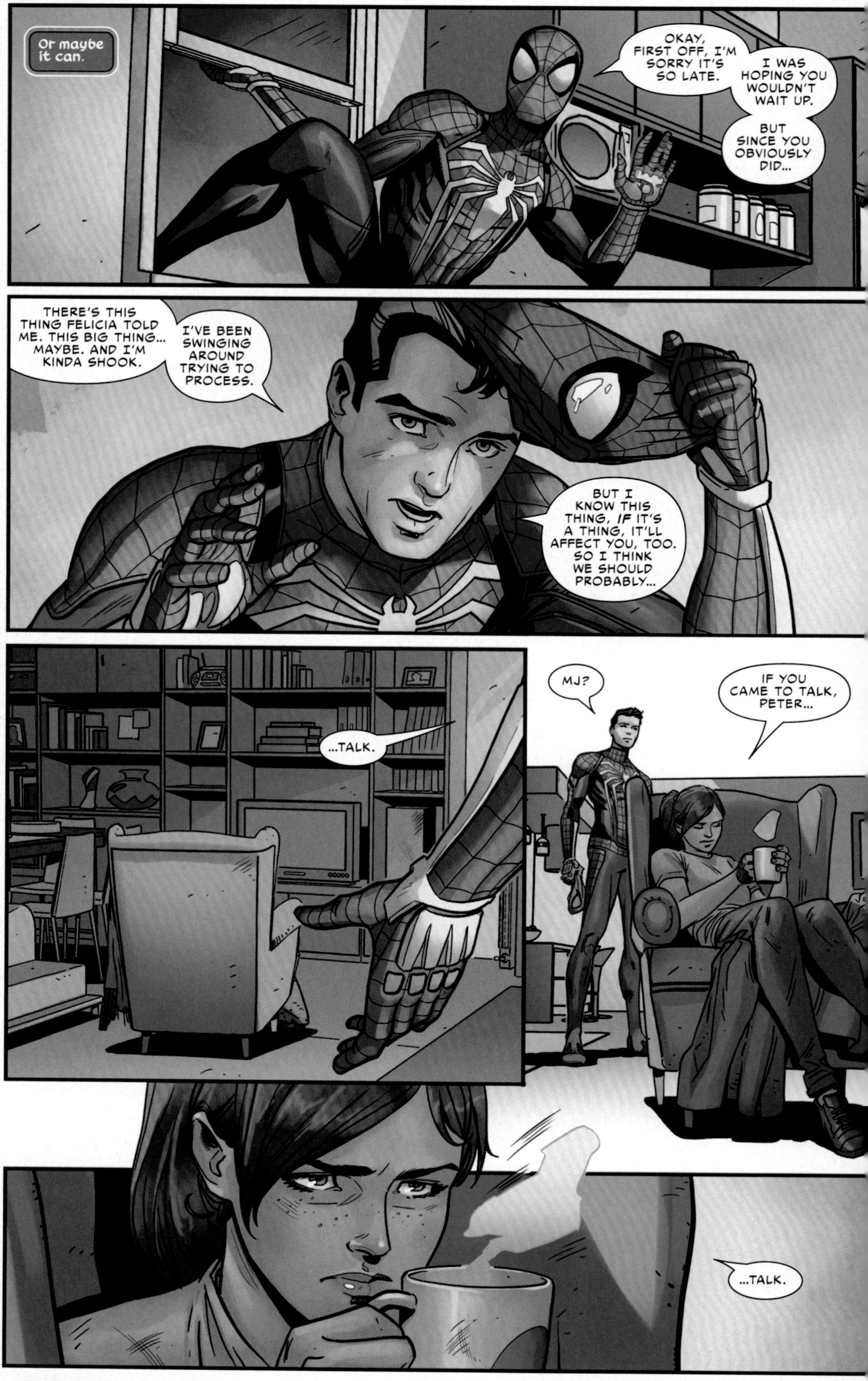
Or maybe it can.
OKAY, FIRST OFF, I'M SORRY IT'S SO LATE.
I WAS HOPING YOU WOULDN'T WAIT UP.
BUT SINCE YOU OBVIOUSLY DID...
THERE'S THIS THING FELICIA TOLD ME. THIS BIG THING... MAYBE. AND I'M KINDA SHOOK.
I'VE BEEN SWINGING AROUND TRYING TO PROCESS.
BUT I KNOW THIS THING, IF IT'S A THING, IT'LL AFFECT YOU, TOO. SO I THINK WE SHOULD PROBABLY...
...TALK.
MJ?
IF YOU CAME TO TALK, PETER...
...TALK.

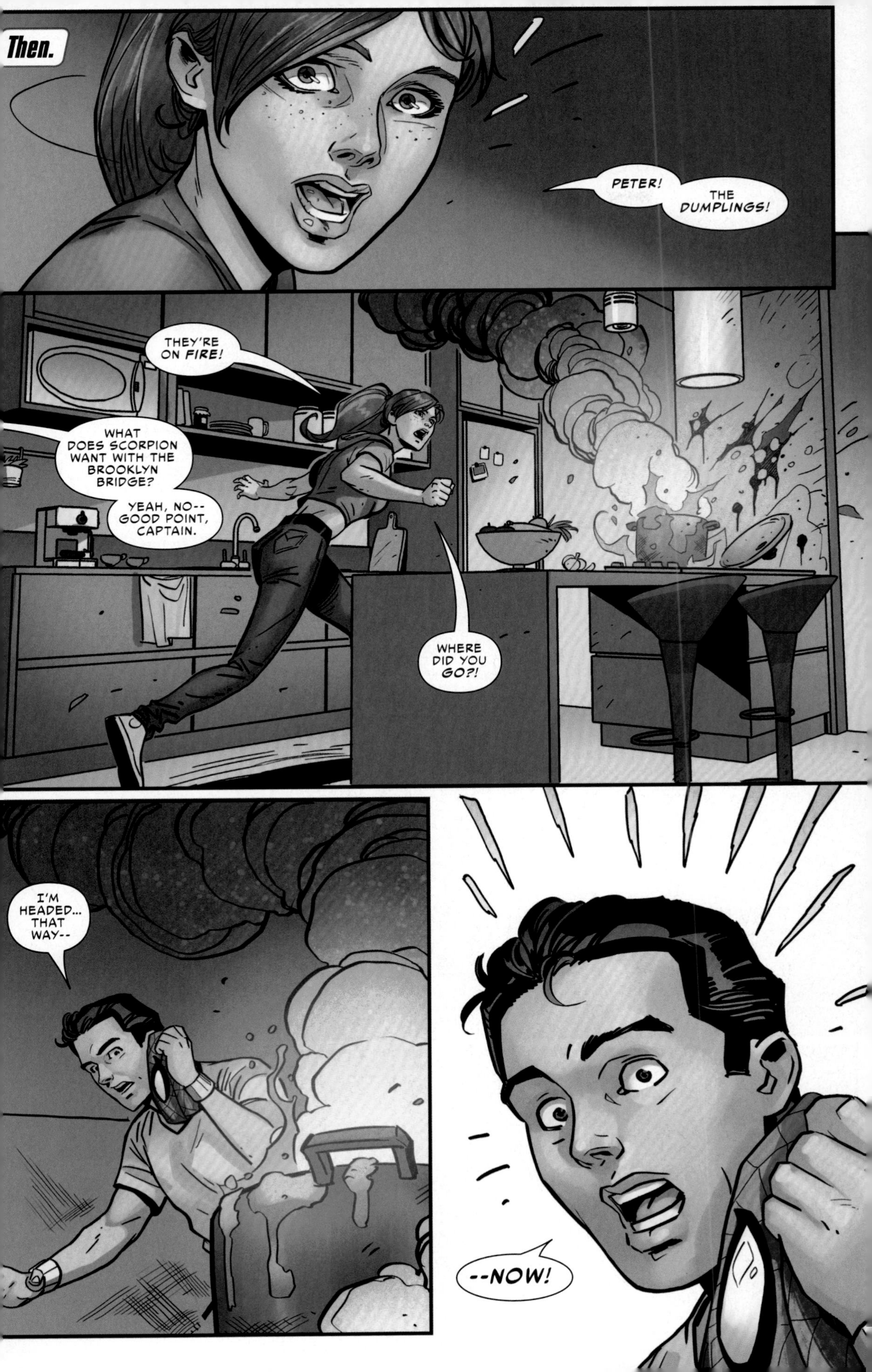
Then.
PETER!
THE DUMPLINGS!
THEY'RE ON FIRE!
WHAT DOES SCORPION WANT WITH THE BROOKLYN BRIDGE?
YEAH, NO-- GOOD POINT, CAPTAIN.
WHERE DID YOU GO?!
I'M HEADED... THAT WAY--
--NOW!

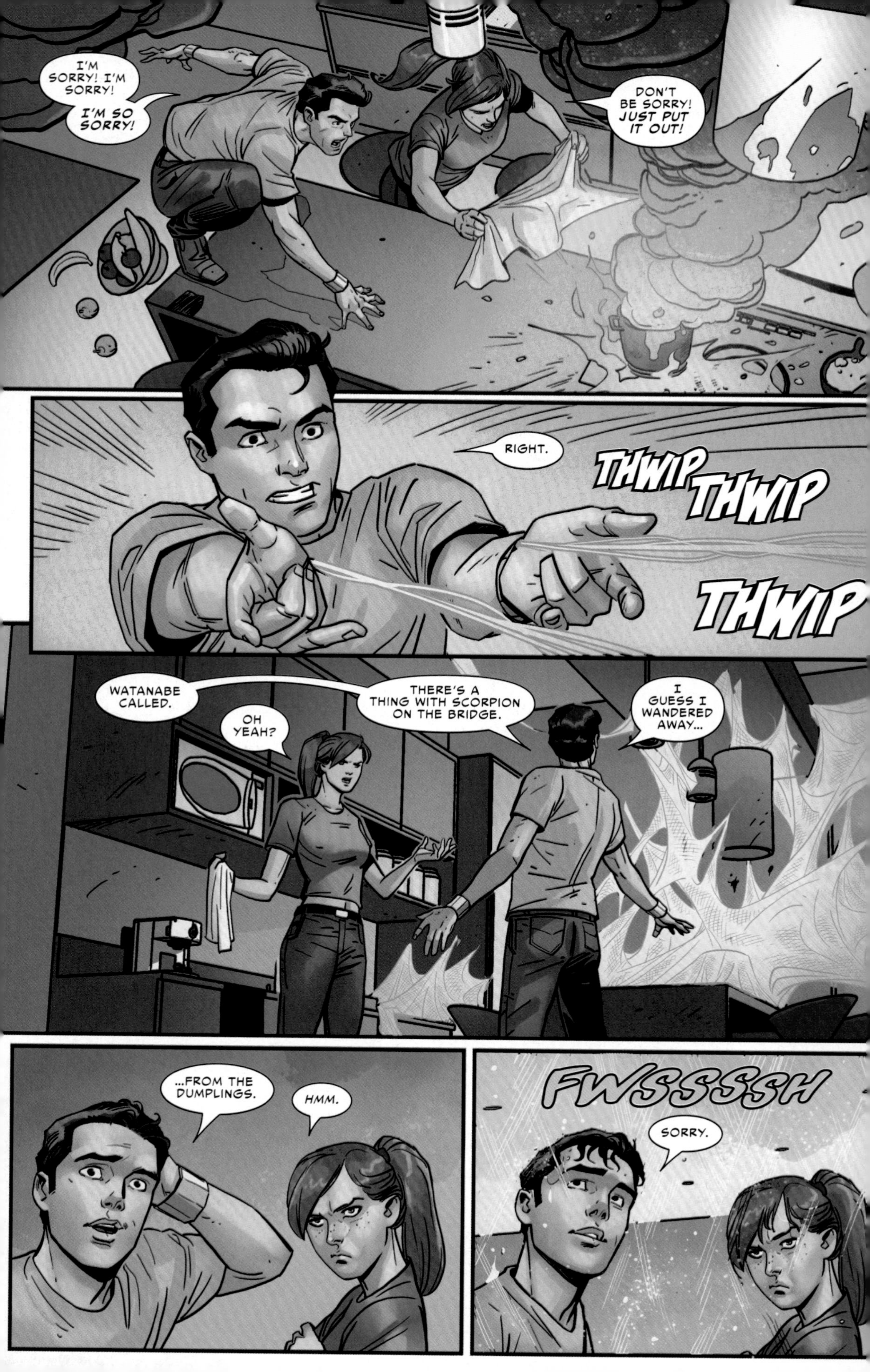
I'M SORRY! I'M SORRY!
I'M SO SORRY!
DON'T BE SORRY! JUST PUT IT OUT!
RIGHT.
THWIP THWIP
THWIP
WATANABE CALLED.
THERE'S A THING WITH SCORPION ON THE BRIDGE.
OH YEAH?
I GUESS I WANDERED AWAY...
...FROM THE DUMPLINGS.
HMM.
FWSSSSH
SORRY.

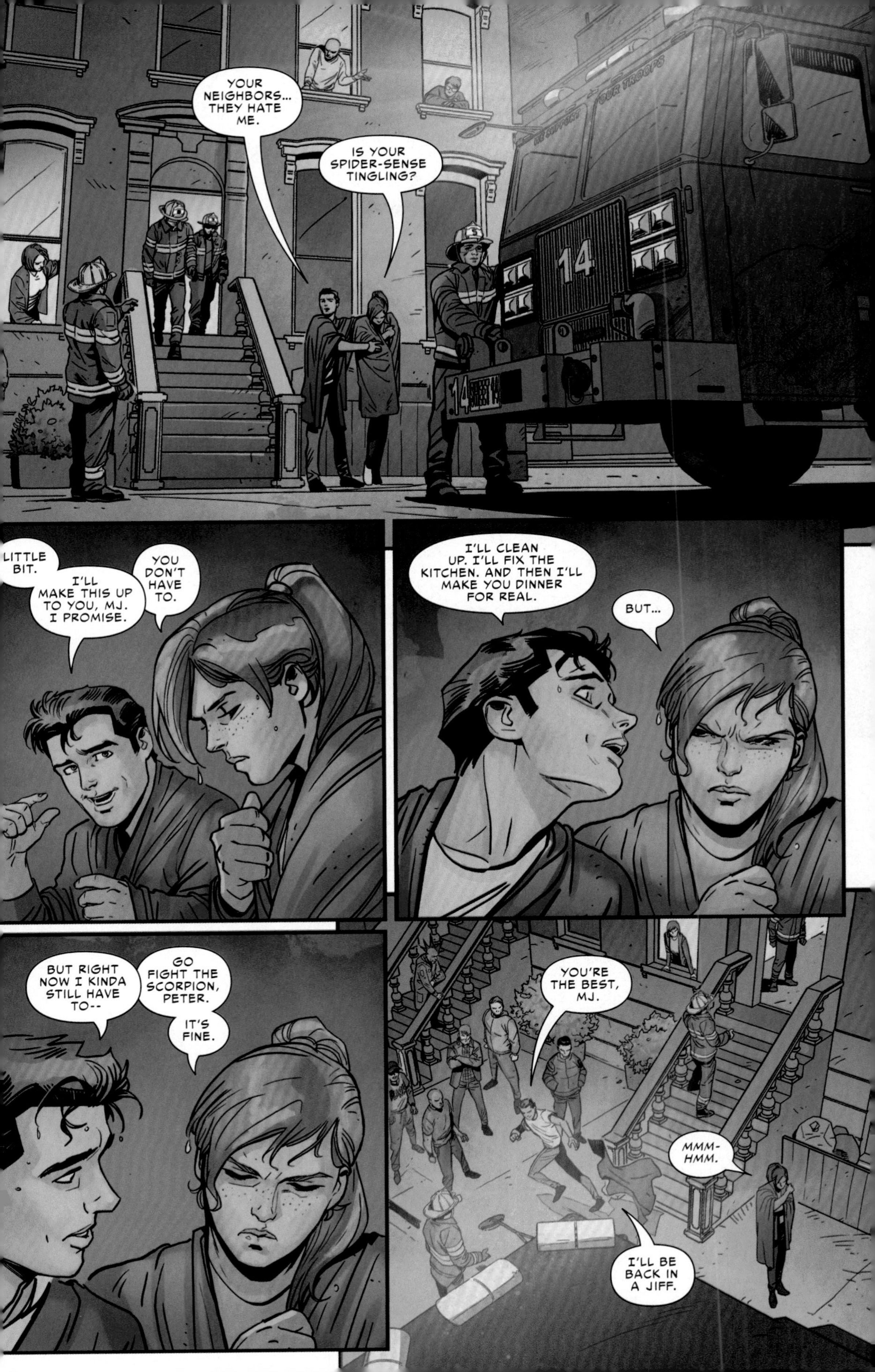
YOUR NEIGHBORS... THEY HATE ME.
IS YOUR SPIDER-SENSE TINGLING?
14
LITTLE BIT.
I'LL MAKE THIS UP TO YOU, MJ. I PROMISE.
YOU DON'T HAVE TO.
I'LL CLEAN UP. I'LL FIX THE KITCHEN. AND THEN I'LL MAKE YOU DINNER FOR REAL.
BUT...
BUT RIGHT NOW I KINDA STILL HAVE TO--
GO FIGHT THE SCORPION, PETER.
IT'S FINE.
YOU'RE THE BEST, MJ.
MMM-HMM.
I'LL BE BACK IN A JIFF.

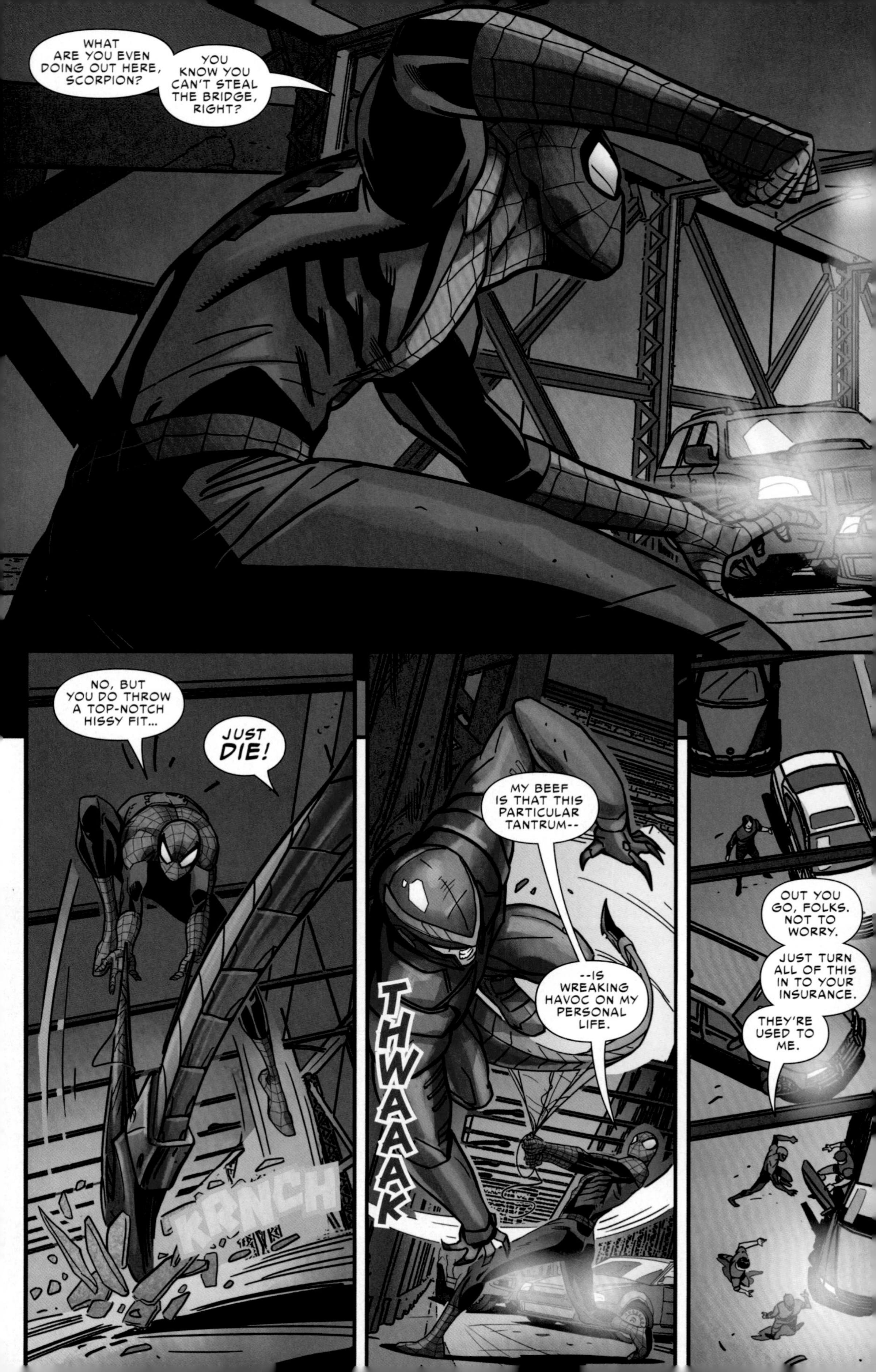
WHAT ARE YOU EVEN DOING OUT HERE, SCORPION?
YOU KNOW YOU CAN'T STEAL THE BRIDGE, RIGHT?
NO, BUT YOU DO THROW A TOP-NOTCH HISSY FIT...
JUST DIE!
KRNCH
MY BEEF IS THAT THIS PARTICULAR TANTRUM--
--IS WREAKING HAVOC ON MY PERSONAL LIFE.
THWAAAK
OUT YOU GO, FOLKS. NOT TO WORRY.
JUST TURN ALL OF THIS IN TO YOUR INSURANCE.
THEY'RE USED TO ME.

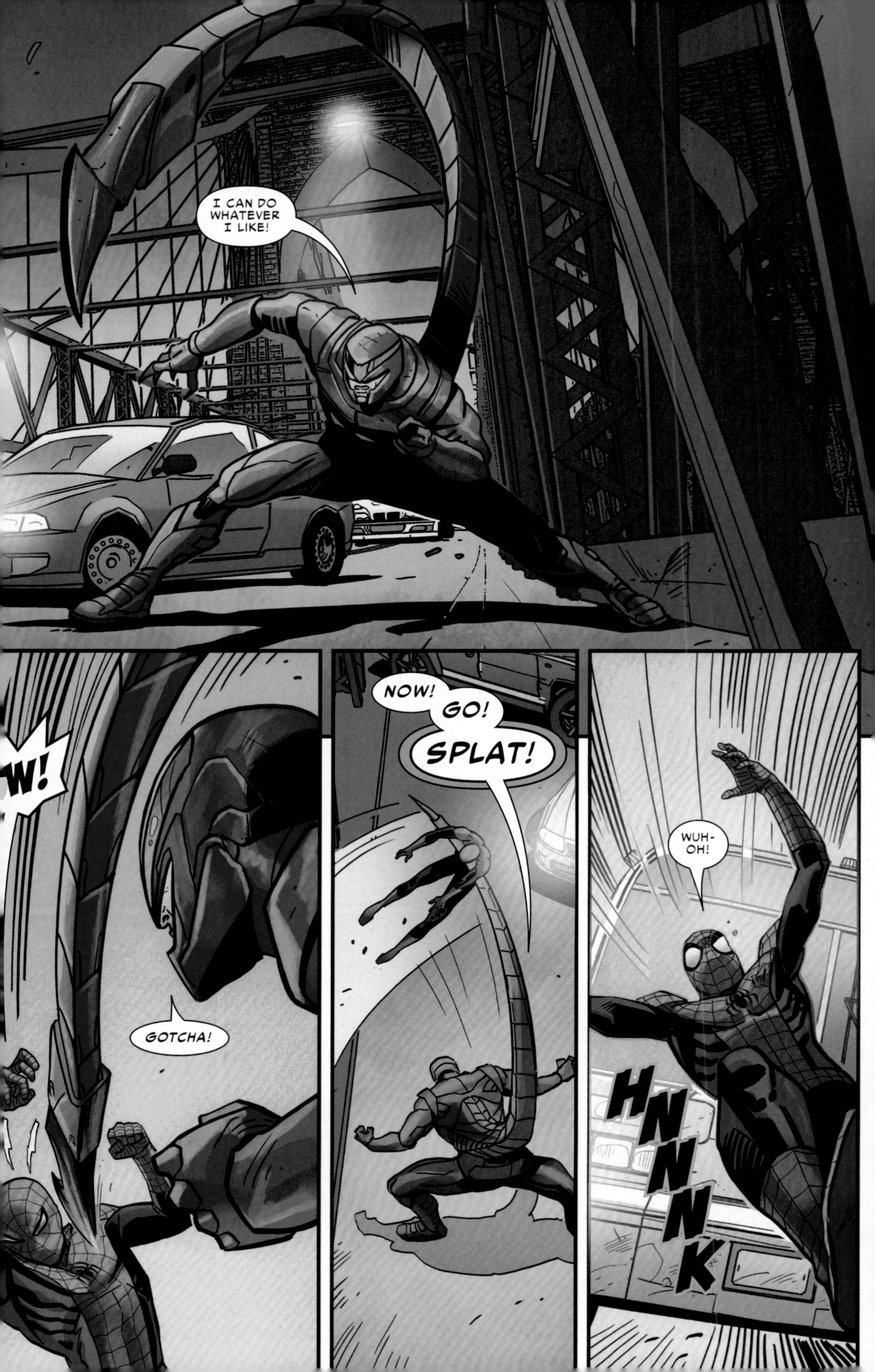
I CAN DO WHATEVER I LIKE!
GOTCHA!
NOW!
GO!
SPLAT!
WUH-OH!
HNNNK

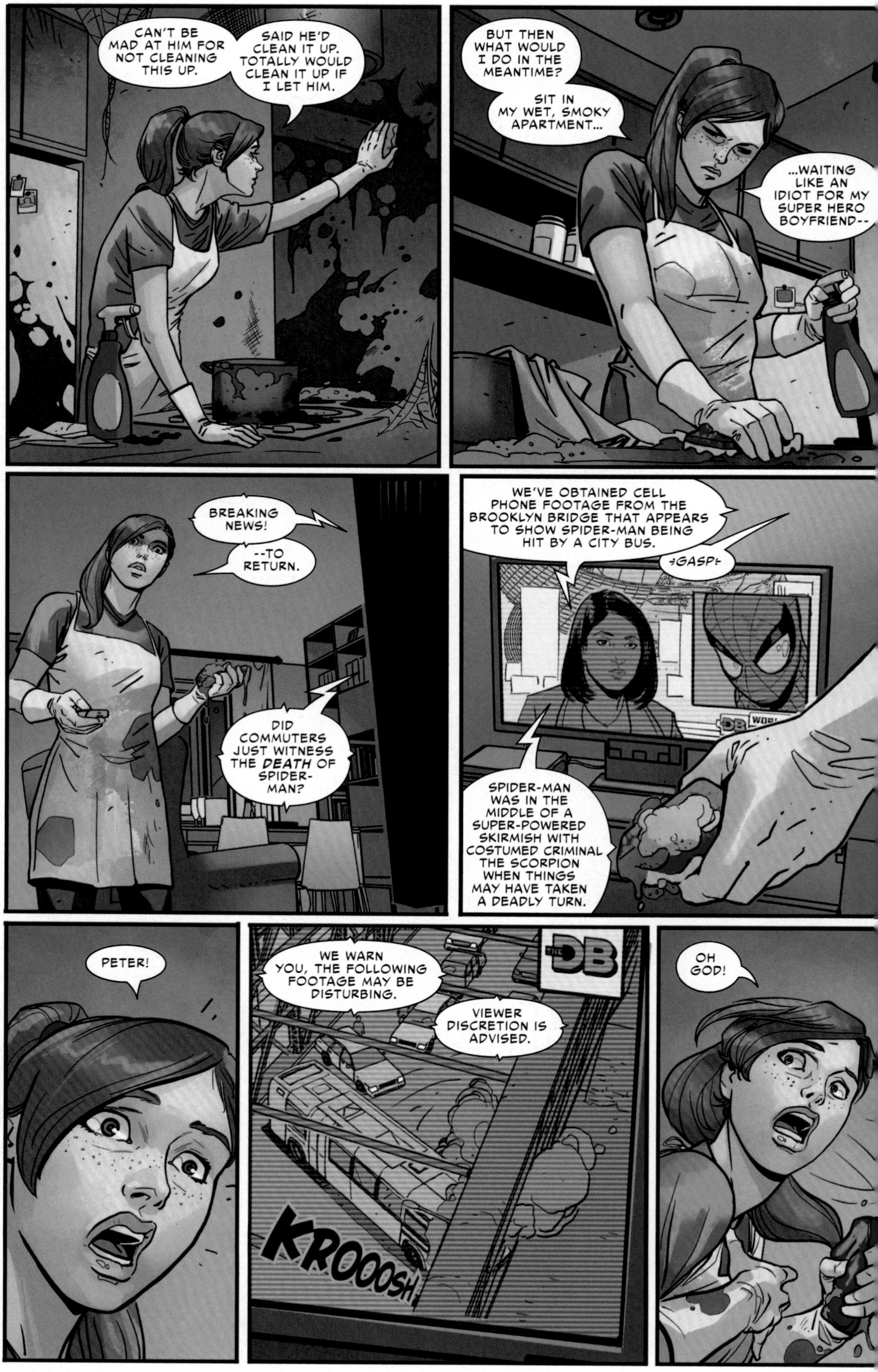
CAN'T BE MAD AT HIM FOR NOT CLEANING THIS UP.
SAID HE'D CLEAN IT UP. TOTALLY WOULD CLEAN IT UP IF I LET HIM.
BUT THEN WHAT WOULD I DO IN THE MEANTIME?
SIT IN MY WET, SMOKY APARTMENT...
...WAITING LIKE AN IDIOT FOR MY SUPER HERO BOYFRIEND--
BREAKING NEWS!
--TO RETURN.
DID COMMUTERS JUST WITNESS THE *DEATH* OF SPIDER-MAN?
WE'VE OBTAINED CELL PHONE FOOTAGE FROM THE BROOKLYN BRIDGE THAT APPEARS TO SHOW SPIDER-MAN BEING HIT BY A CITY BUS.
GASP
SPIDER-MAN WAS IN THE MIDDLE OF A SUPER-POWERED SKIRMISH WITH COSTUMED CRIMINAL THE SCORPION WHEN THINGS MAY HAVE TAKEN A DEADLY TURN.
PETER!
WE WARN YOU, THE FOLLOWING FOOTAGE MAY BE DISTURBING.
VIEWER DISCRETION IS ADVISED.
THE DB
KROOOSH
OH GOD!

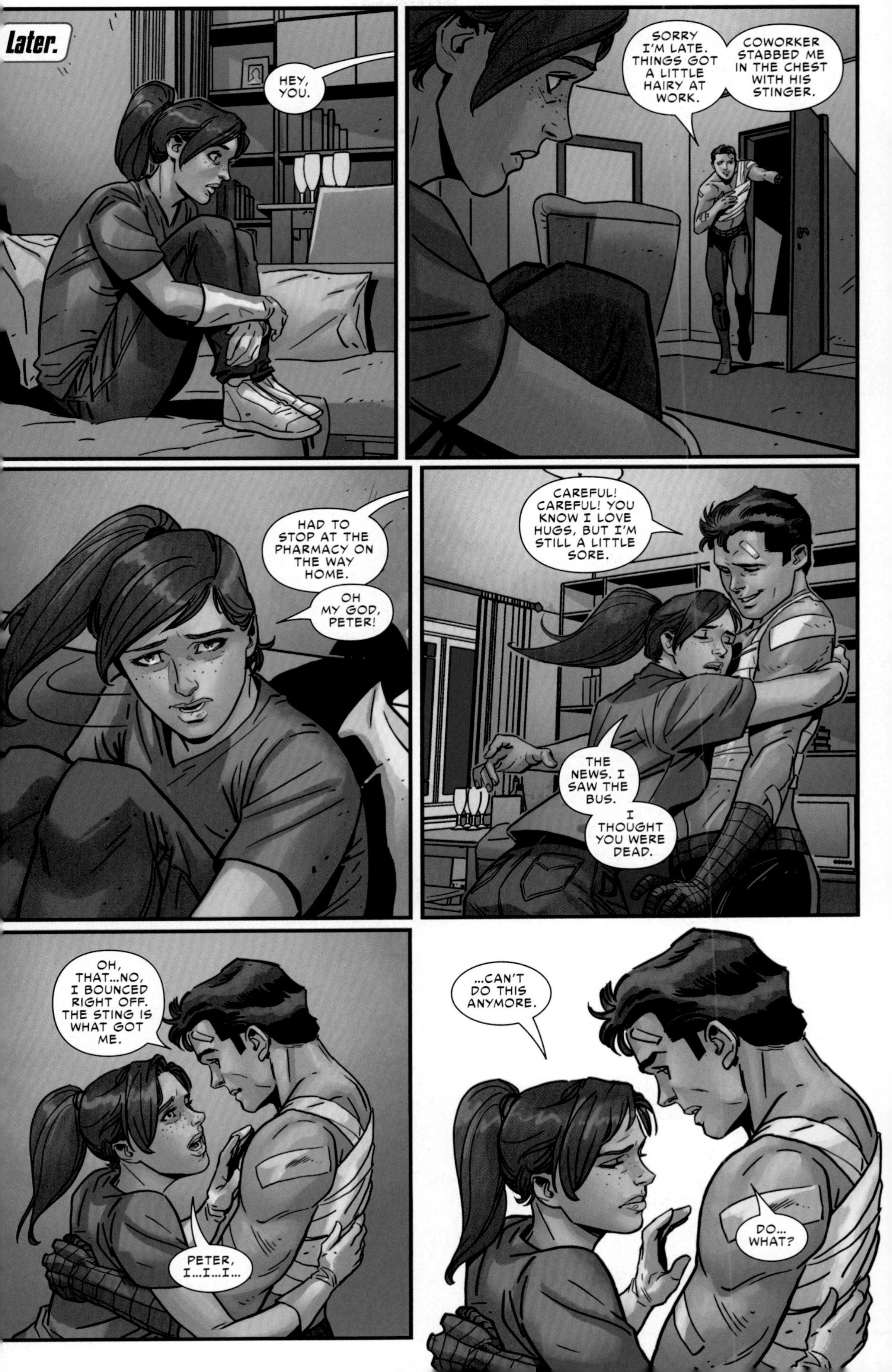
Later.
HEY, YOU.
SORRY I'M LATE. THINGS GOT A LITTLE HAIRY AT WORK.
COWORKER STABBED ME IN THE CHEST WITH HIS STINGER.
HAD TO STOP AT THE PHARMACY ON THE WAY HOME.
OH MY GOD, PETER!
CAREFUL! CAREFUL! YOU KNOW I LOVE HUGS, BUT I'M STILL A LITTLE SORE.
THE NEWS. I SAW THE BUS.
I THOUGHT YOU WERE DEAD.
OH, THAT...NO, I BOUNCED RIGHT OFF. THE STING IS WHAT GOT ME.
PETER, I...I...I...
...CAN'T DO THIS ANYMORE.
DO... WHAT?

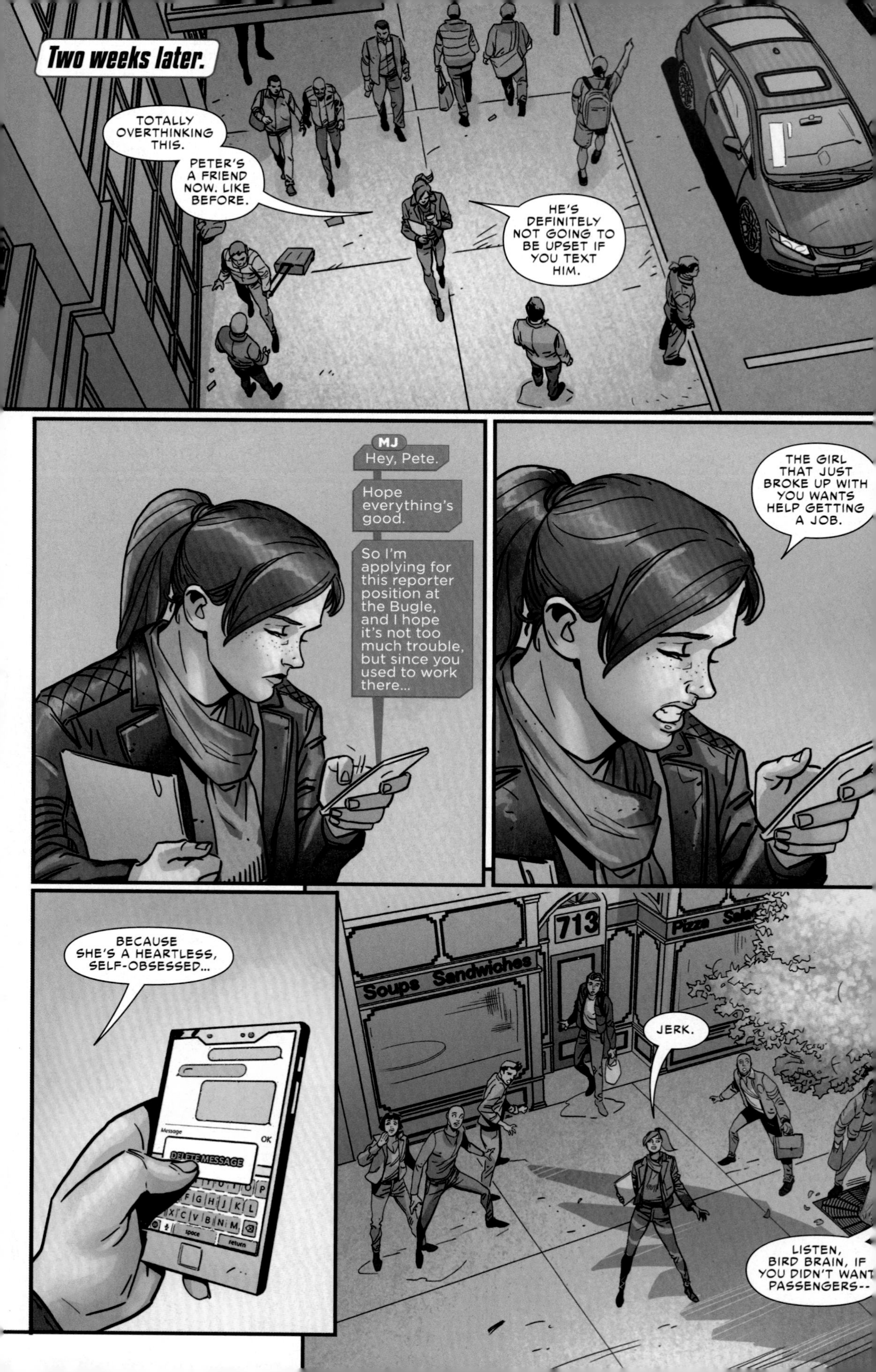
Two weeks later.
TOTALLY OVERTHINKING THIS.
PETER'S A FRIEND NOW. LIKE BEFORE.
HE'S DEFINITELY NOT GOING TO BE UPSET IF YOU TEXT HIM.
MJ
Hey, Pete.
Hope everything's good.
So I'm applying for this reporter position at the Bugle, and I hope it's not too much trouble, but since you used to work there...
THE GIRL THAT JUST BROKE UP WITH YOU WANTS HELP GETTING A JOB.
BECAUSE SHE'S A HEARTLESS, SELF-OBSESSED...
DELETE MESSAGE
713
Soups Sandwiches
JERK.
LISTEN, BIRD BRAIN, IF YOU DIDN'T WANT PASSENGERS--

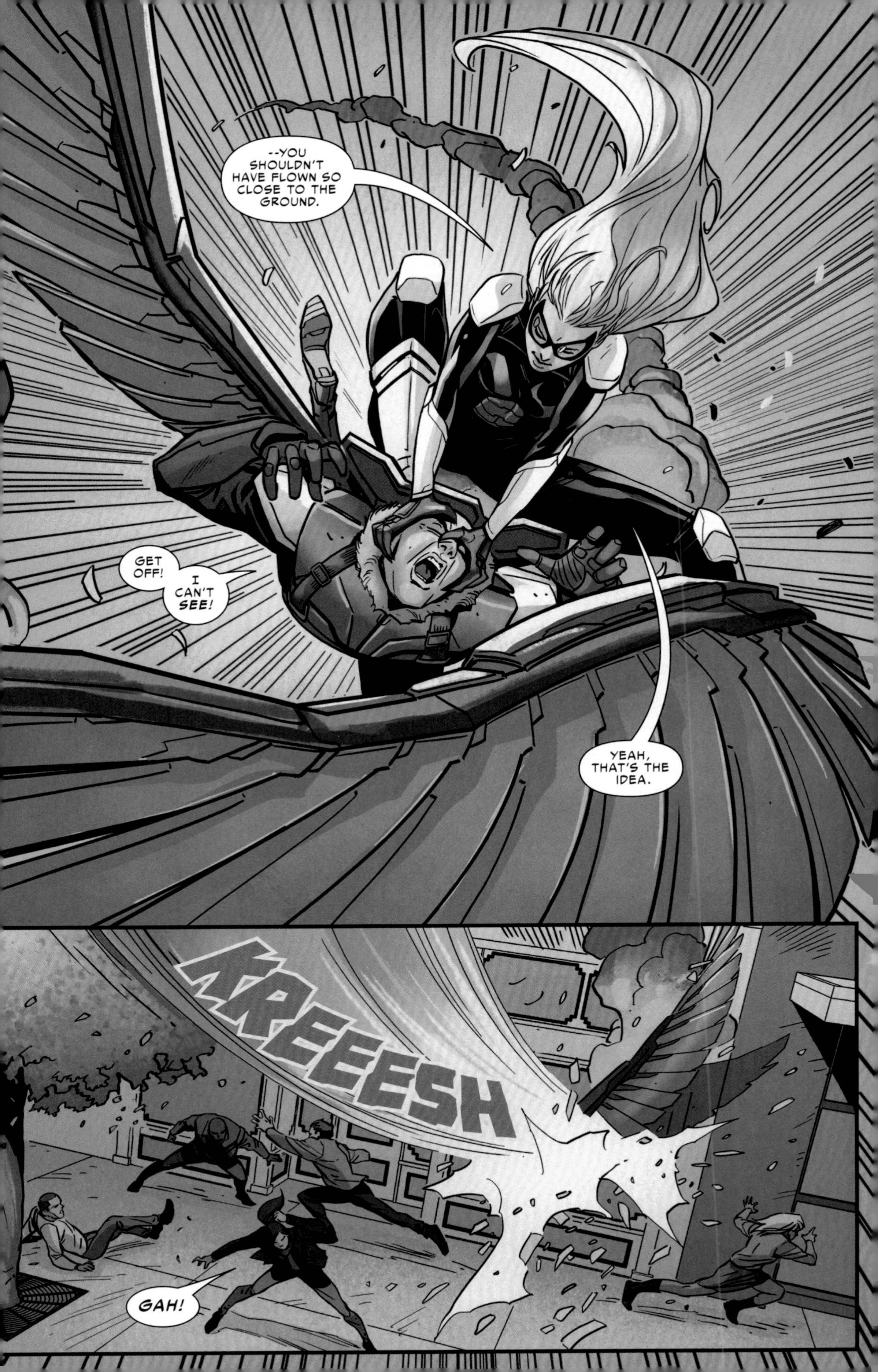
--YOU SHOULDN'T HAVE FLOWN SO CLOSE TO THE GROUND.
GET OFF!
I CAN'T SEE!
YEAH, THAT'S THE IDEA.
KREEESH
GAH!

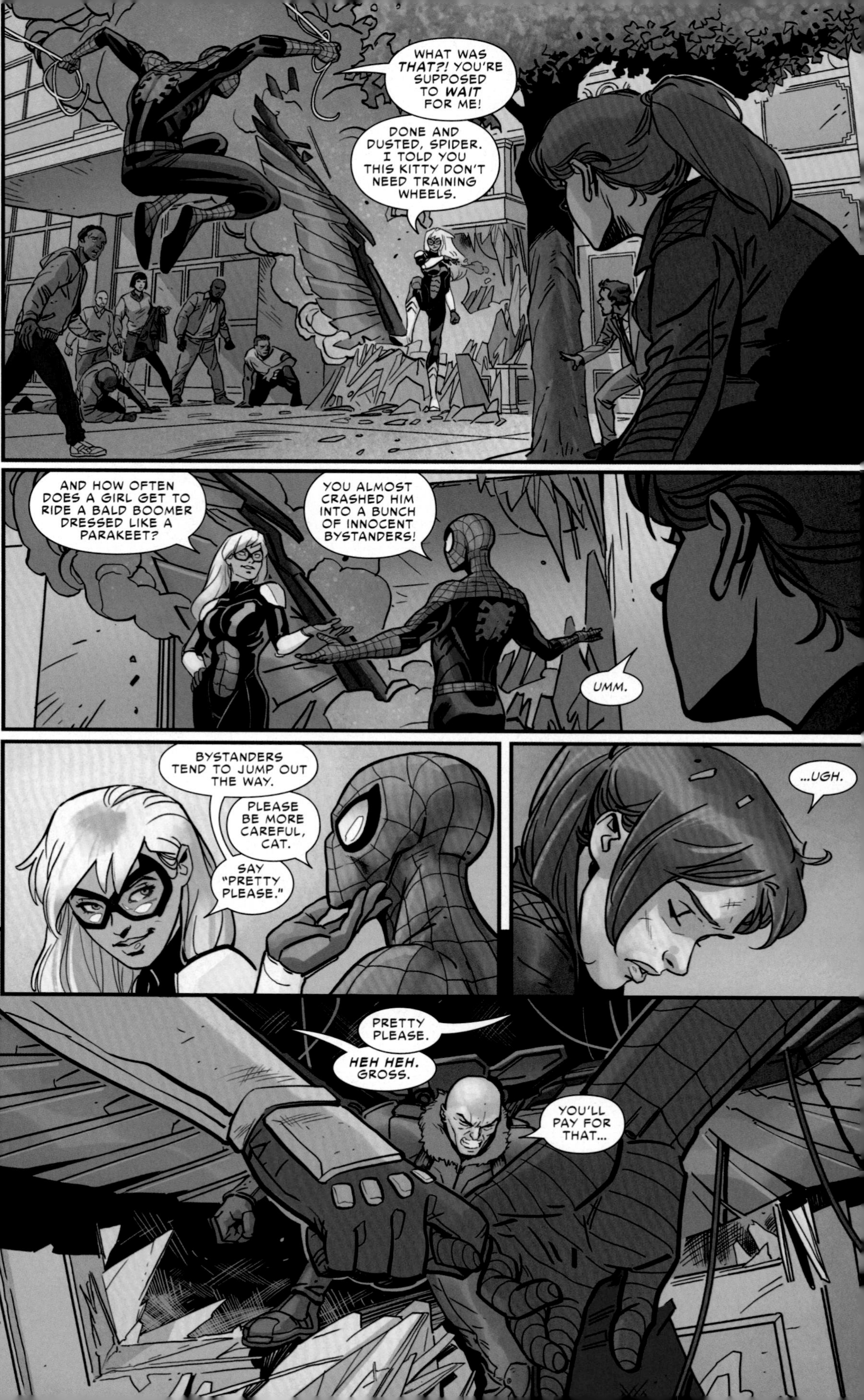
WHAT WAS *THAT?!* YOU'RE SUPPOSED TO *WAIT* FOR ME!
DONE AND DUSTED, SPIDER. I TOLD YOU THIS KITTY DON'T NEED TRAINING WHEELS.
AND HOW OFTEN DOES A GIRL GET TO RIDE A BALD BOOMER DRESSED LIKE A PARAKEET?
YOU ALMOST CRASHED HIM INTO A BUNCH OF INNOCENT BYSTANDERS!
UMM.
BYSTANDERS TEND TO JUMP OUT THE WAY.
PLEASE BE MORE CAREFUL, CAT.
SAY "PRETTY PLEASE."
...UGH.
PRETTY PLEASE.
HEH HEH. GROSS.
YOU'LL PAY FOR THAT...

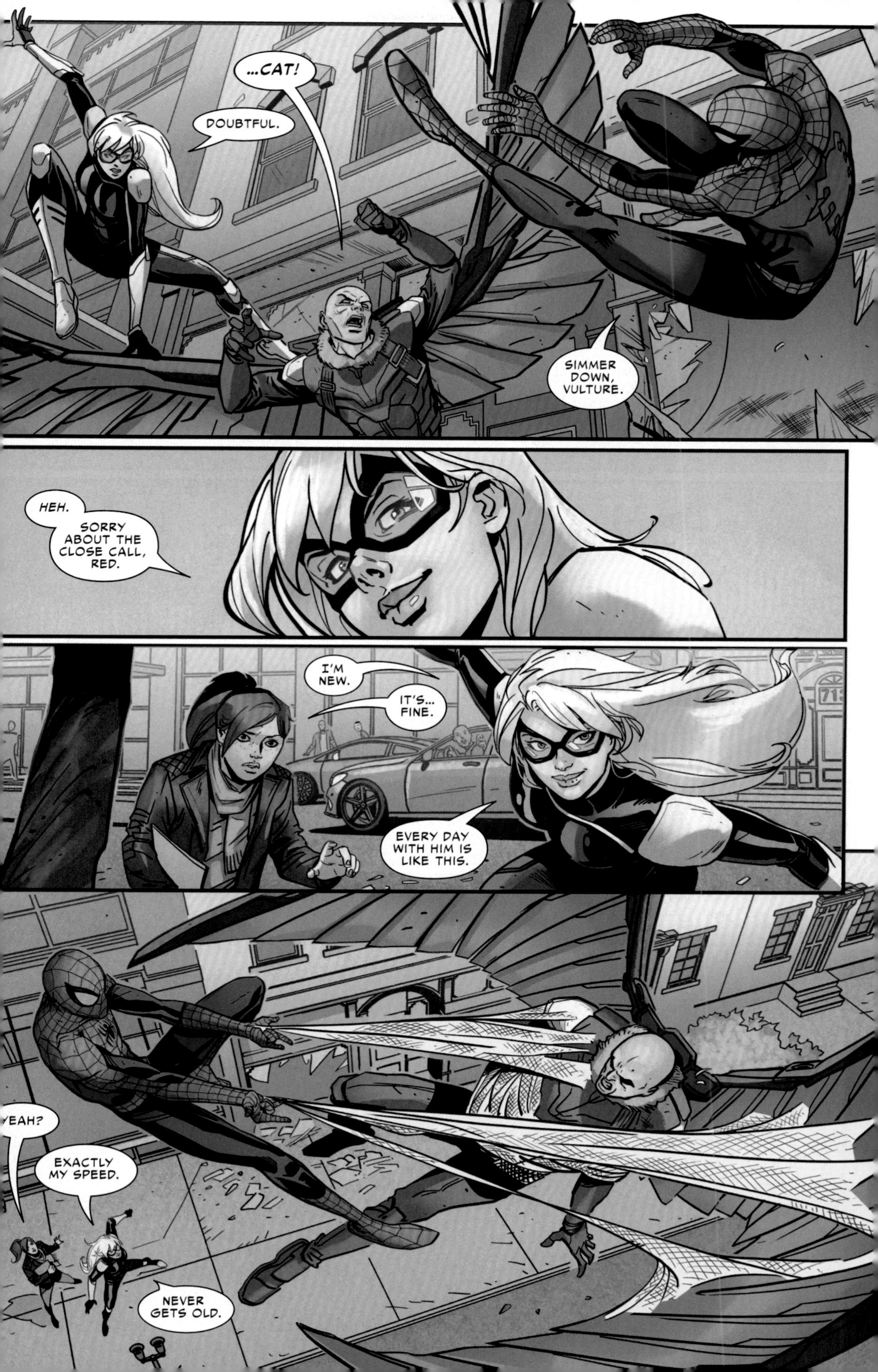
...CAT!
DOUBTFUL.
SIMMER DOWN, VULTURE.
HEH.
SORRY ABOUT THE CLOSE CALL, RED.
I'M NEW.
IT'S... FINE.
EVERY DAY WITH HIM IS LIKE THIS.
EXACTLY MY SPEED.
NEVER GETS OLD.

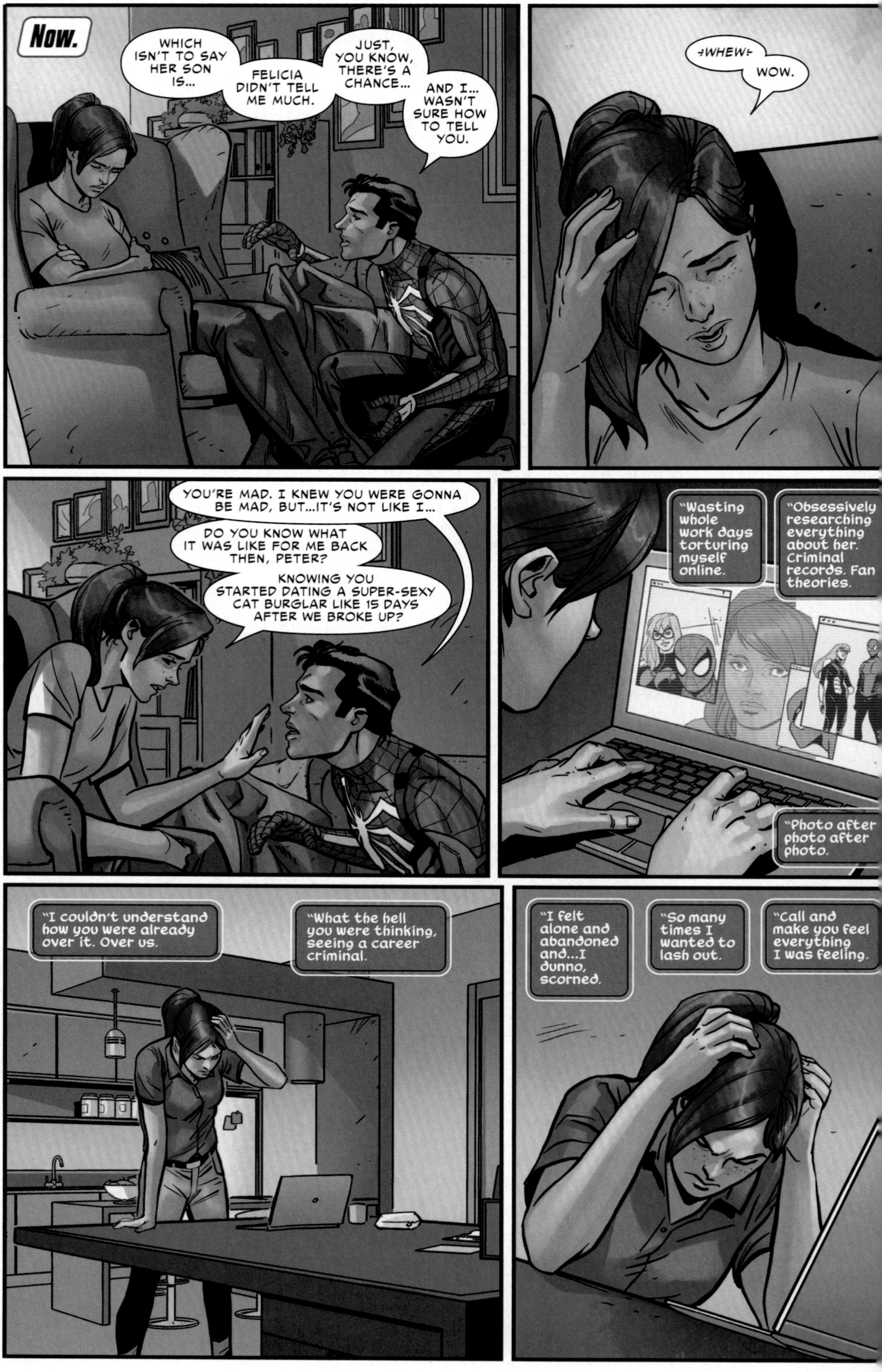

Now.
WHICH ISN'T TO SAY HER SON IS...
FELICIA DIDN'T TELL ME MUCH.
JUST, YOU KNOW, THERE'S A CHANCE...
AND I... WASN'T SURE HOW TO TELL YOU.
WHEW
WOW.
YOU'RE MAD. I KNEW YOU WERE GONNA BE MAD, BUT...IT'S NOT LIKE I...
DO YOU KNOW WHAT IT WAS LIKE FOR ME BACK THEN, PETER?
KNOWING YOU STARTED DATING A SUPER-SEXY CAT BURGLAR LIKE 15 DAYS AFTER WE BROKE UP?
"Wasting whole work days torturing myself online.
"Obsessively researching everything about her. Criminal records. Fan theories.
"Photo after photo after photo.
"I couldn't understand how you were already over it. Over us.
"What the hell you were thinking, seeing a career criminal.
"I felt alone and abandoned and...I dunno, scorned.
"So many times I wanted to lash out.
"Call and make you feel everything I was feeling.

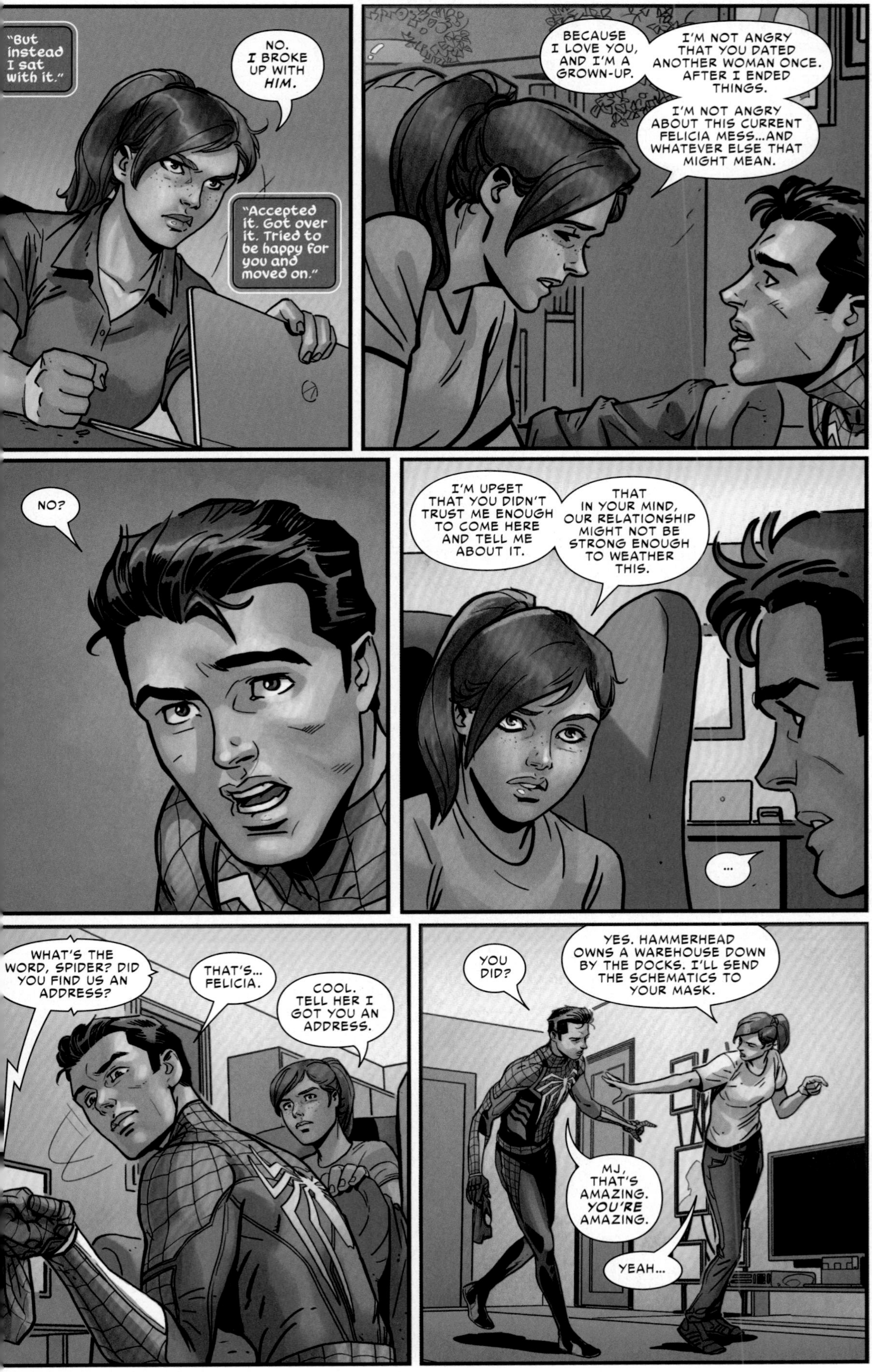
"But instead I sat with it."
NO. I BROKE UP WITH HIM.
"Accepted it. Got over it. Tried to be happy for you and moved on."
BECAUSE I LOVE YOU, AND I'M A GROWN-UP.
I'M NOT ANGRY THAT YOU DATED ANOTHER WOMAN ONCE. AFTER I ENDED THINGS.
I'M NOT ANGRY ABOUT THIS CURRENT FELICIA MESS...AND WHATEVER ELSE THAT MIGHT MEAN.
NO?
I'M UPSET THAT YOU DIDN'T TRUST ME ENOUGH TO COME HERE AND TELL ME ABOUT IT.
THAT IN YOUR MIND, OUR RELATIONSHIP MIGHT NOT BE STRONG ENOUGH TO WEATHER THIS.
...
WHAT'S THE WORD, SPIDER? DID YOU FIND US AN ADDRESS?
THAT'S... FELICIA.
COOL. TELL HER I GOT YOU AN ADDRESS.
YOU DID?
YES. HAMMERHEAD OWNS A WAREHOUSE DOWN BY THE DOCKS. I'LL SEND THE SCHEMATICS TO YOUR MASK.
MJ, THAT'S AMAZING. YOU'RE AMAZING.
YEAH...

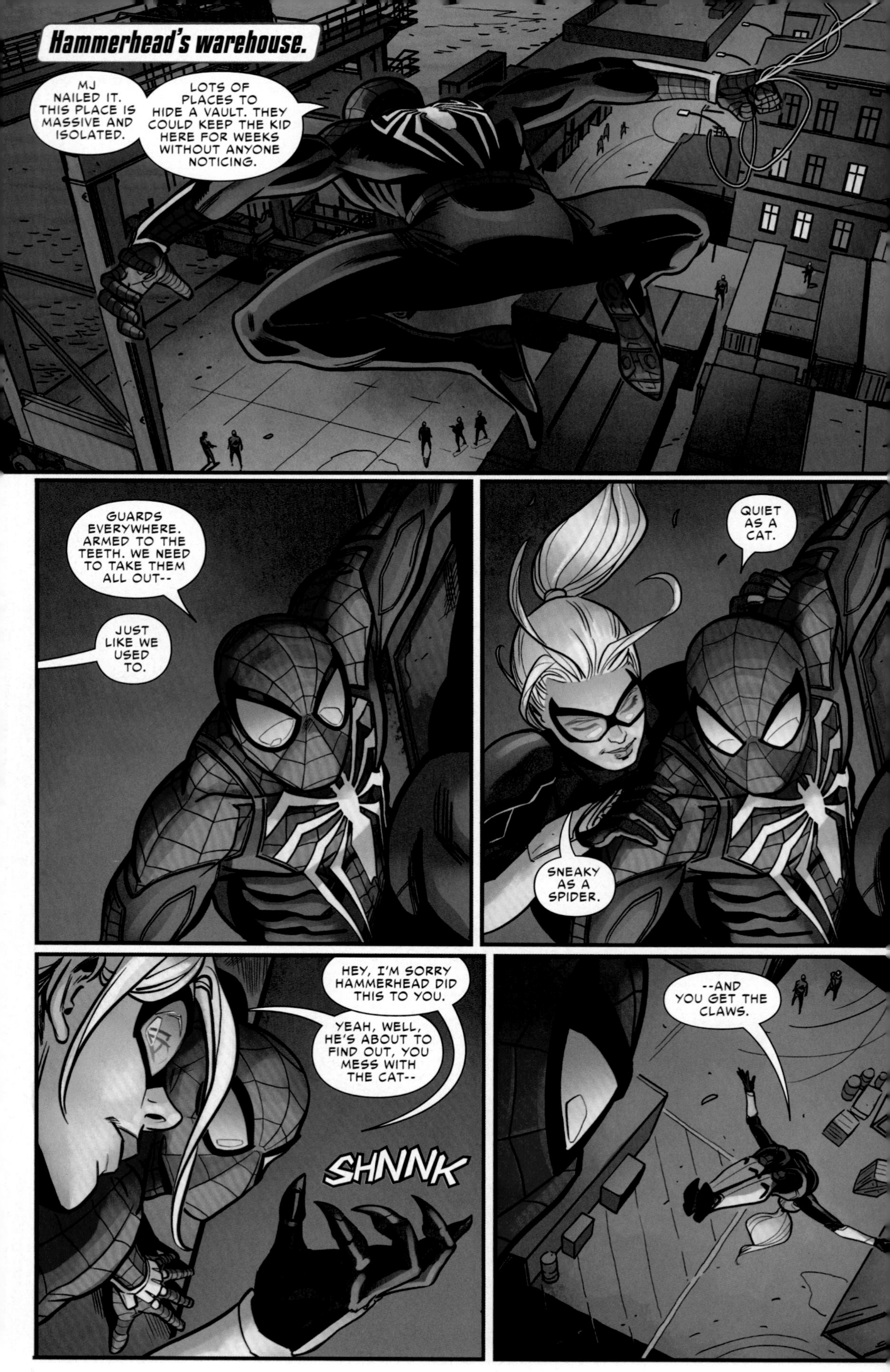

Hammerhead's warehouse.
MJ NAILED IT. THIS PLACE IS MASSIVE AND ISOLATED.
LOTS OF PLACES TO HIDE A VAULT. THEY COULD KEEP THE KID HERE FOR WEEKS WITHOUT ANYONE NOTICING.
GUARDS EVERYWHERE. ARMED TO THE TEETH. WE NEED TO TAKE THEM ALL OUT--
JUST LIKE WE USED TO.
QUIET AS A CAT.
SNEAKY AS A SPIDER.
HEY, I'M SORRY HAMMERHEAD DID THIS TO YOU.
YEAH, WELL, HE'S ABOUT TO FIND OUT, YOU MESS WITH THE CAT--
SHNNK
--AND YOU GET THE CLAWS.

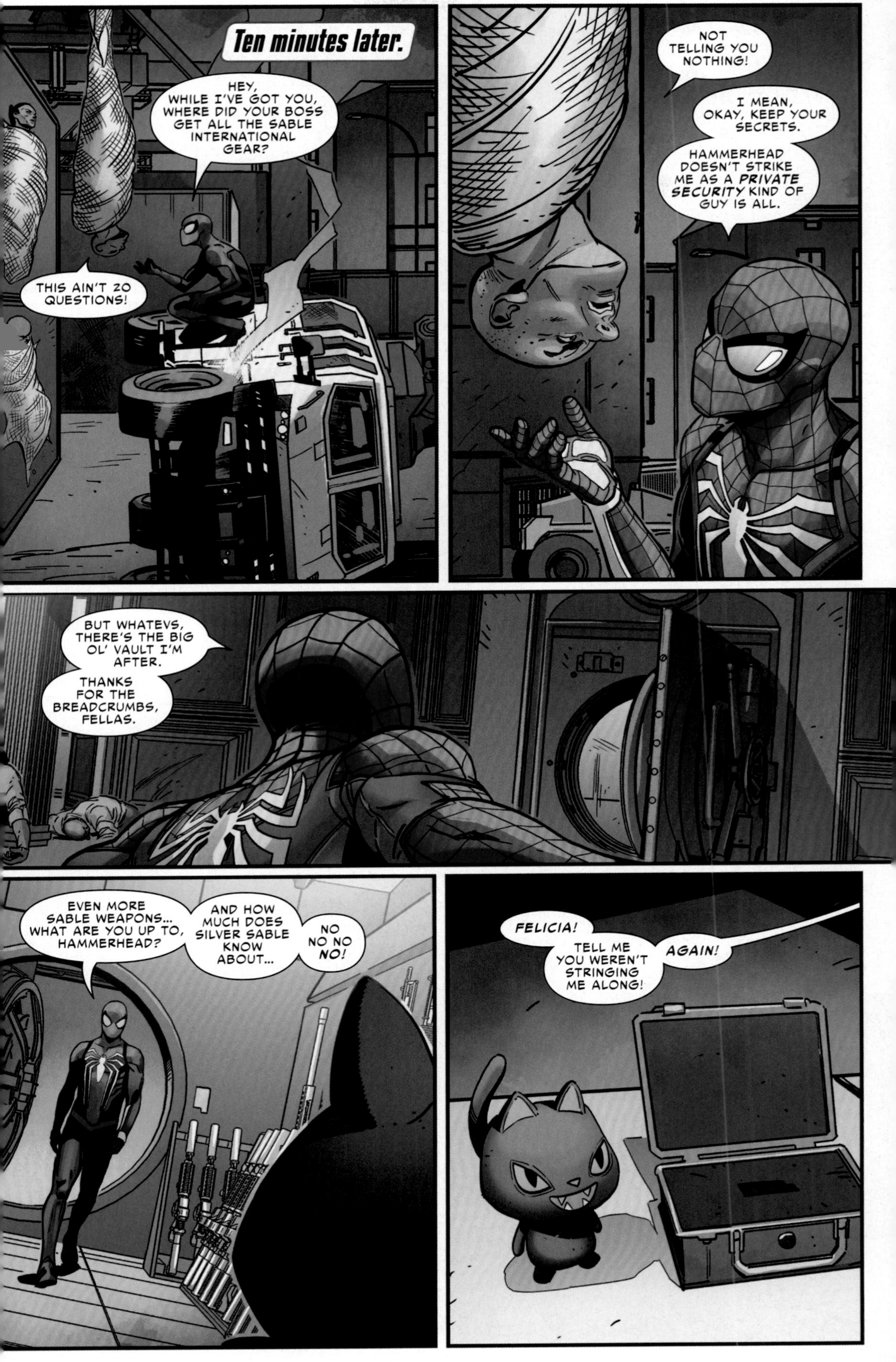

Ten minutes later.
HEY, WHILE I'VE GOT YOU, WHERE DID YOUR BOSS GET ALL THE SABLE INTERNATIONAL GEAR?
THIS AIN'T 20 QUESTIONS!
NOT TELLING YOU NOTHING!
I MEAN, OKAY, KEEP YOUR SECRETS.
HAMMERHEAD DOESN'T STRIKE ME AS A PRIVATE SECURITY KIND OF GUY IS ALL.
BUT WHATEVS, THERE'S THE BIG OL' VAULT I'M AFTER.
THANKS FOR THE BREADCRUMBS, FELLAS.
EVEN MORE SABLE WEAPONS... WHAT ARE YOU UP TO, HAMMERHEAD?
AND HOW MUCH DOES SILVER SABLE KNOW ABOUT...
NO NO NO NO!
FELICIA!
TELL ME YOU WEREN'T STRINGING ME ALONG!
AGAIN!

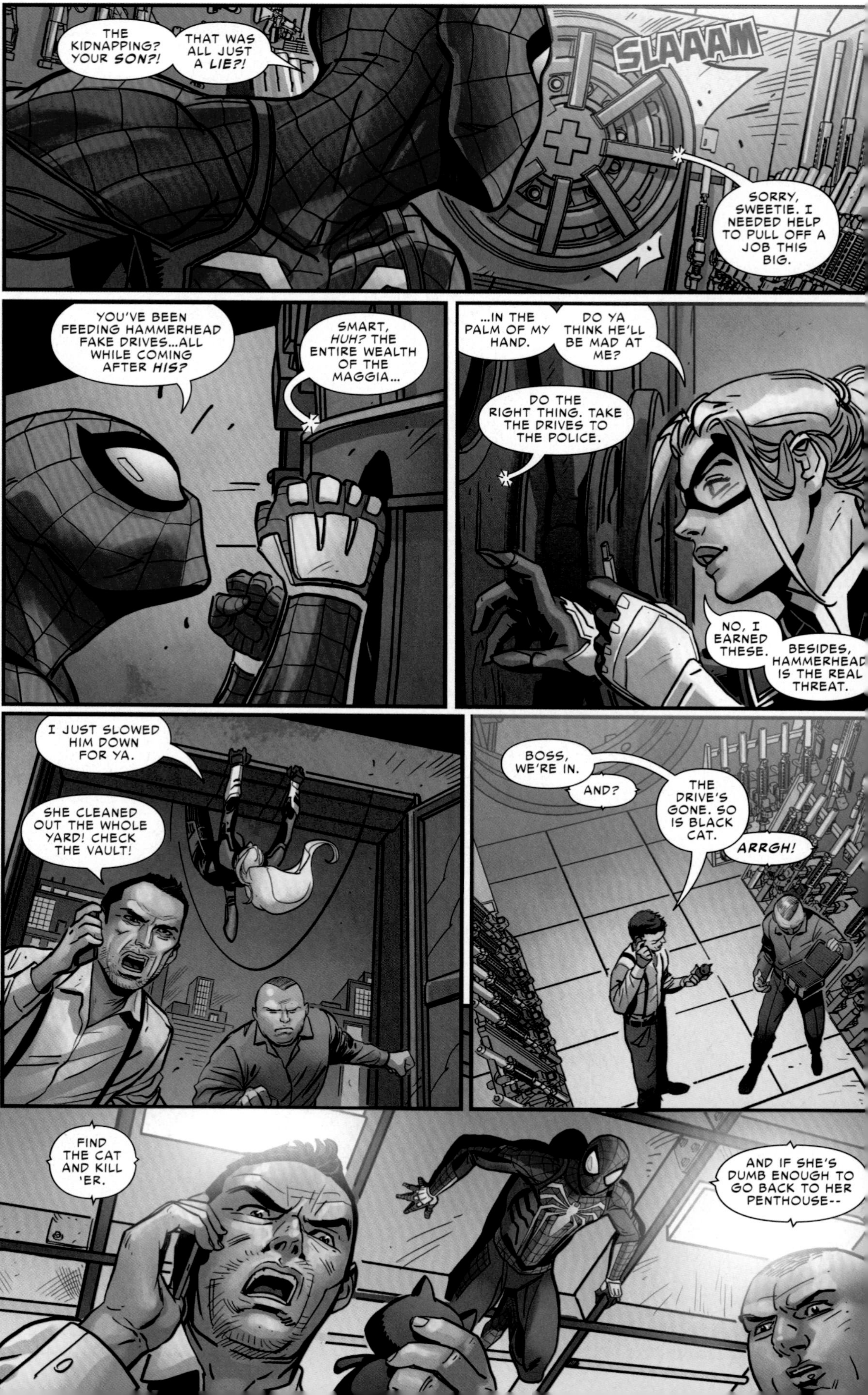
THE KIDNAPPING? YOUR SON?!
THAT WAS ALL JUST A LIE?!
SLAAAM
SORRY, SWEETIE. I NEEDED HELP TO PULL OFF A JOB THIS BIG.
YOU'VE BEEN FEEDING HAMMERHEAD FAKE DRIVES...ALL WHILE COMING AFTER HIS?
SMART, HUH? THE ENTIRE WEALTH OF THE MAGGIA...
...IN THE PALM OF MY HAND.
DO YA THINK HE'LL BE MAD AT ME?
DO THE RIGHT THING. TAKE THE DRIVES TO THE POLICE.
NO, I EARNED THESE.
BESIDES, HAMMERHEAD IS THE REAL THREAT.
I JUST SLOWED HIM DOWN FOR YA.
SHE CLEANED OUT THE WHOLE YARD! CHECK THE VAULT!
BOSS, WE'RE IN.
AND?
THE DRIVE'S GONE. SO IS BLACK CAT.
ARRGH!
FIND THE CAT AND KILL 'ER.
AND IF SHE'S DUMB ENOUGH TO GO BACK TO HER PENTHOUSE--

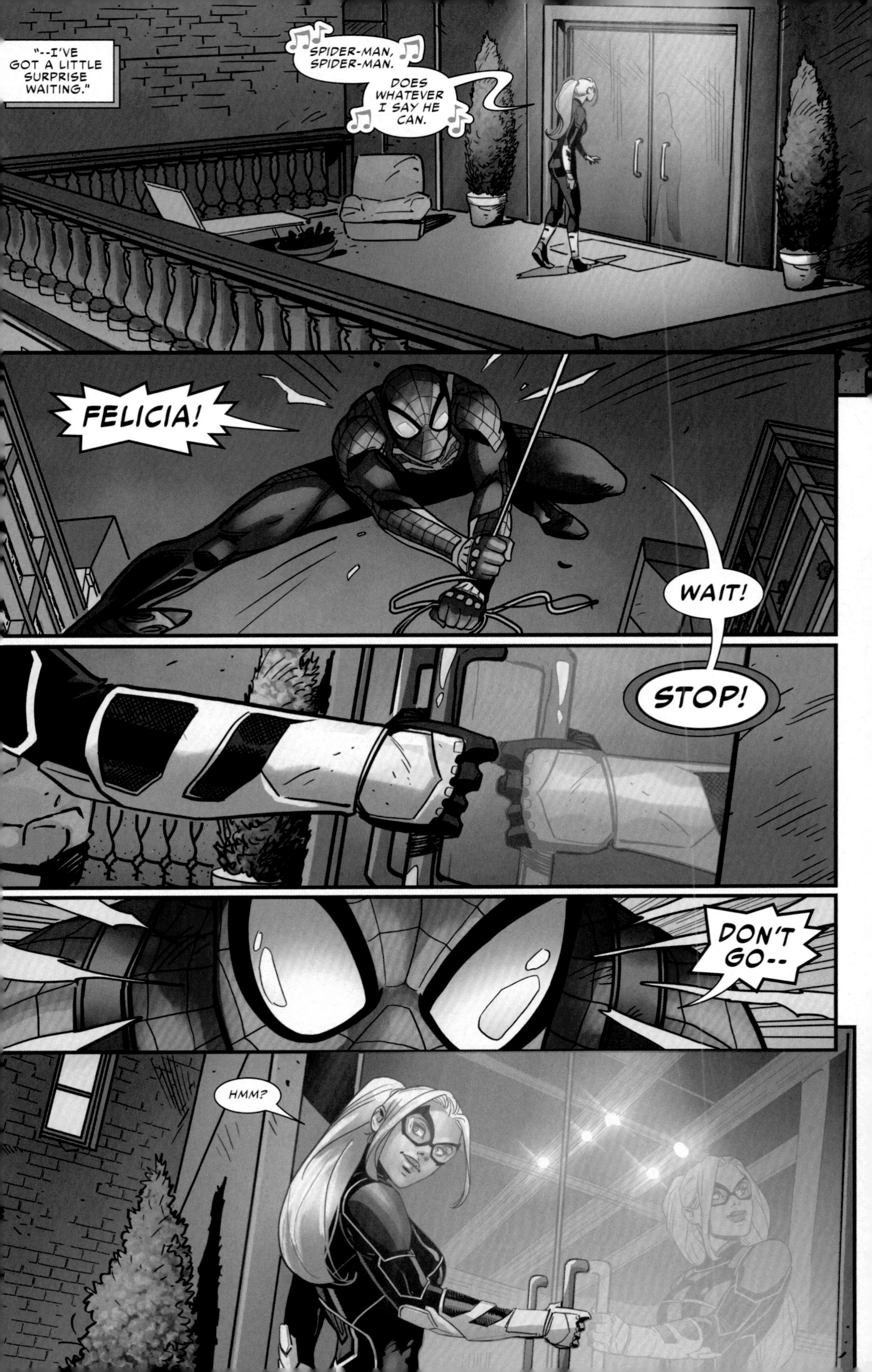
"--I'VE GOT A LITTLE SURPRISE WAITING."
SPIDER-MAN, SPIDER-MAN.
DOES WHATEVER I SAY HE CAN.
FELICIA!
WAIT!
STOP!
DON'T GO--
HMM?

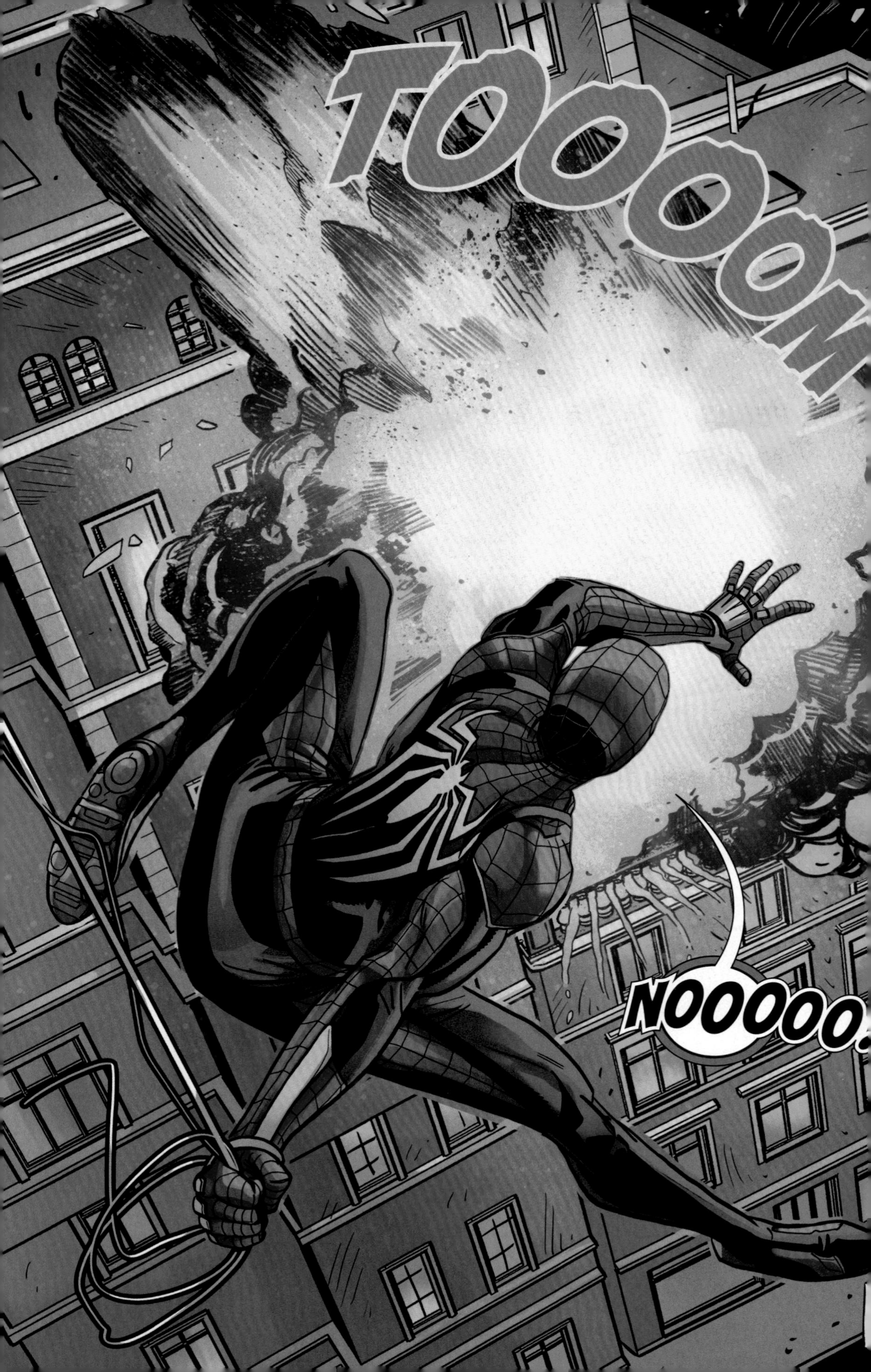
TOOOOOM
NOOOOO...

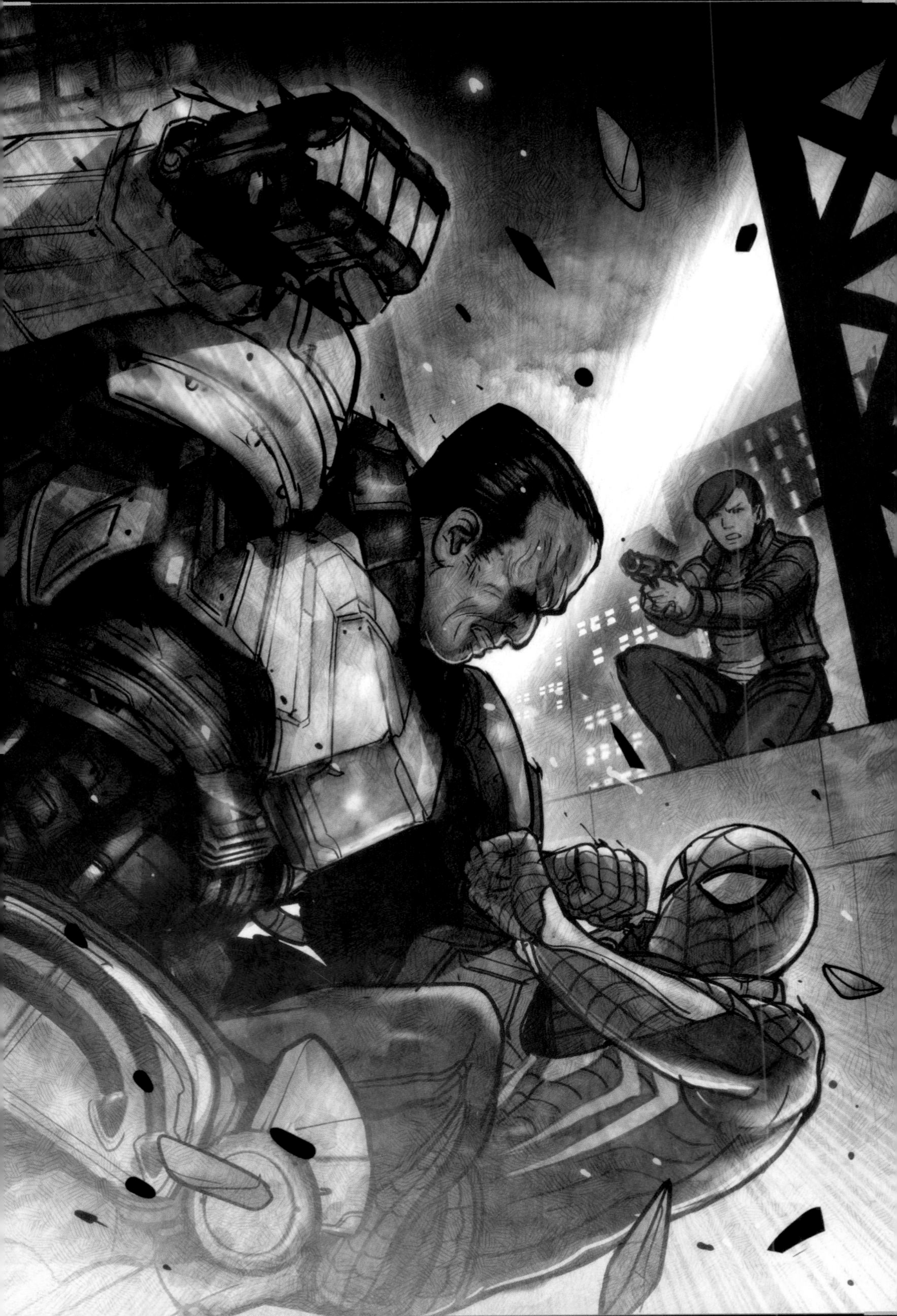

4

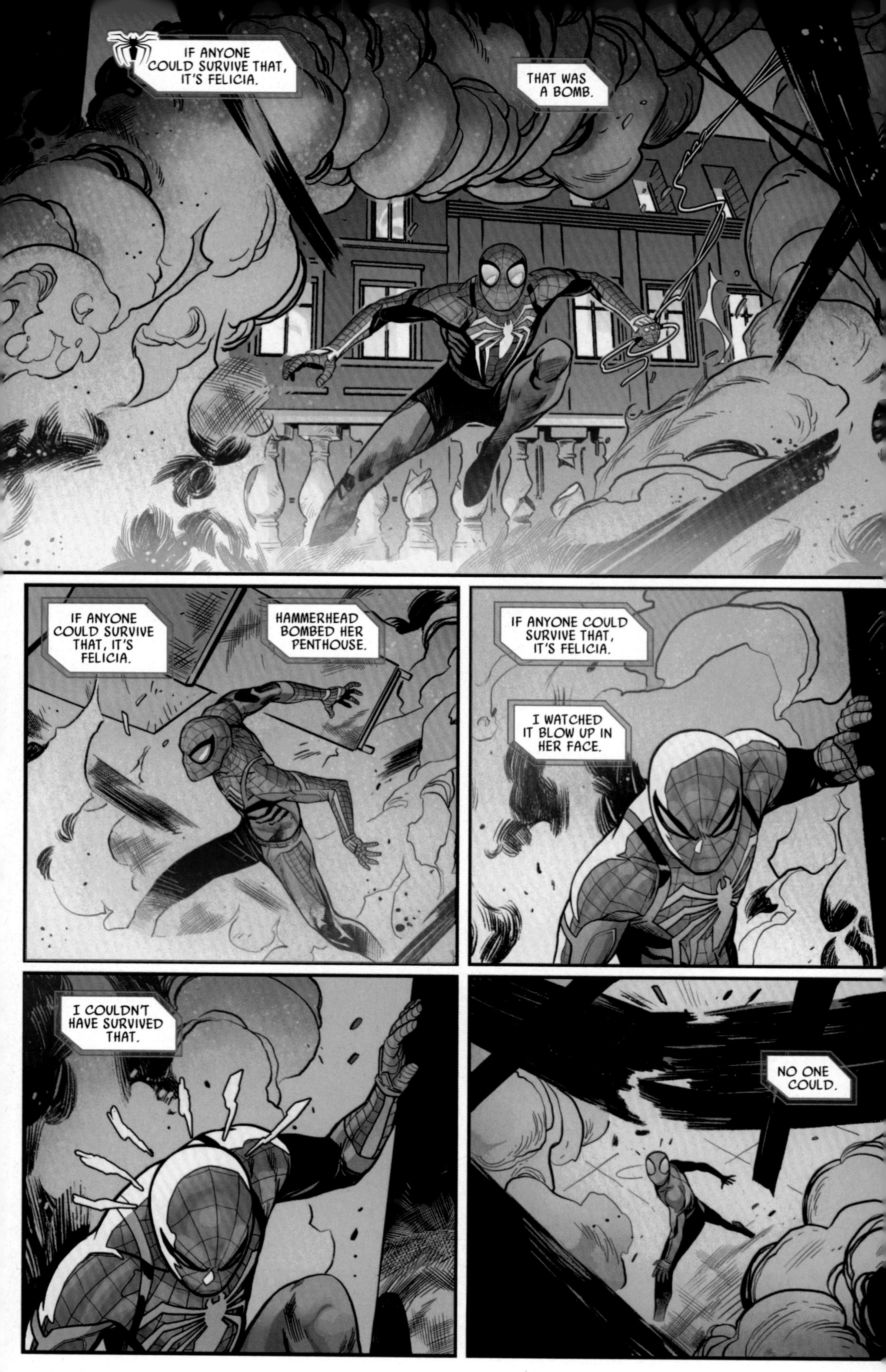
IF ANYONE COULD SURVIVE THAT, IT'S FELICIA.
THAT WAS A BOMB.
IF ANYONE COULD SURVIVE THAT, IT'S FELICIA.
HAMMERHEAD BOMBED HER PENTHOUSE.
IF ANYONE COULD SURVIVE THAT, IT'S FELICIA.
I WATCHED IT BLOW UP IN HER FACE.
I COULDN'T HAVE SURVIVED THAT.
NO ONE COULD.

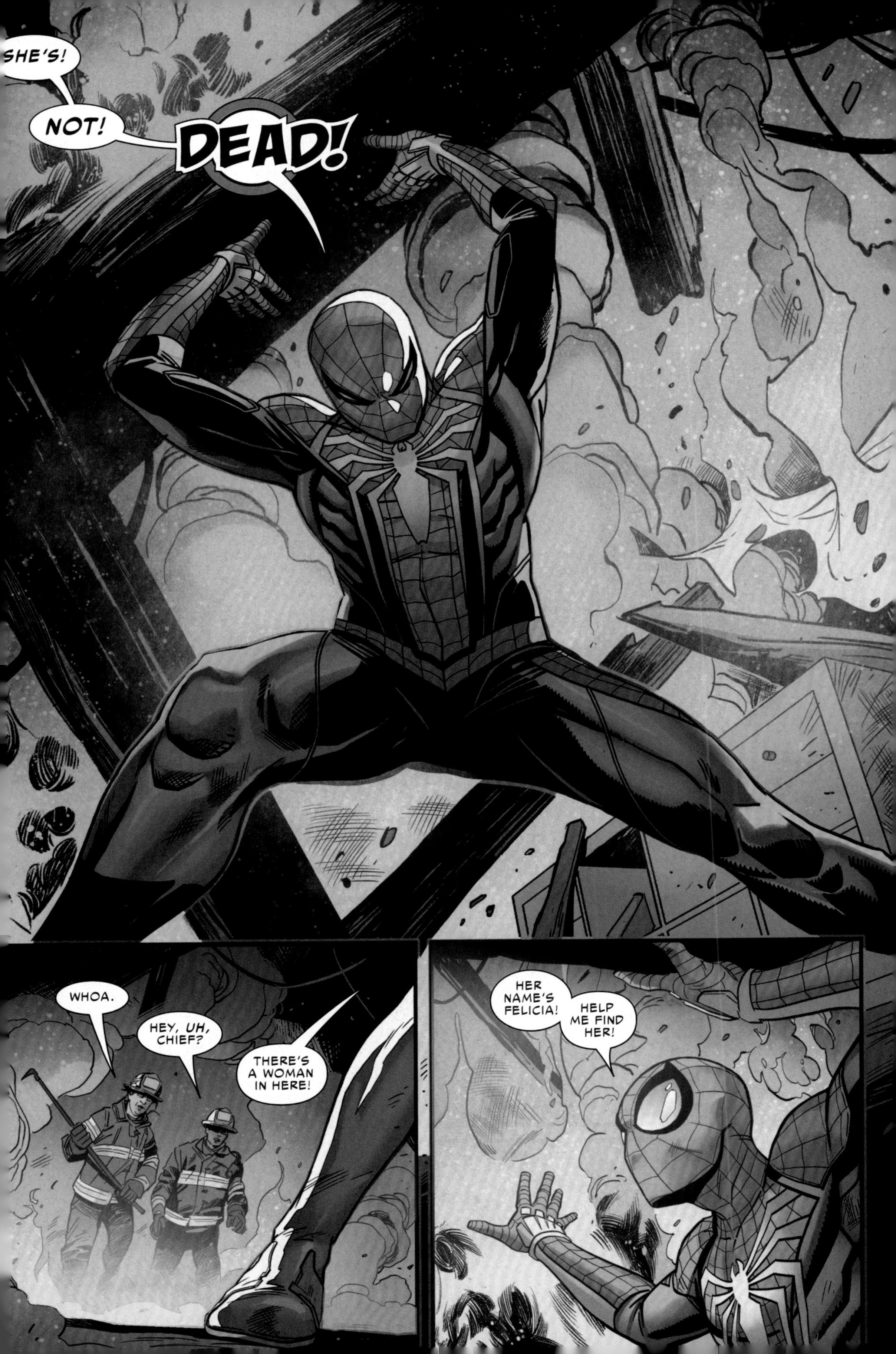
SHE'S!
NOT!
DEAD!
WHOA.
HEY, UH, CHIEF?
THERE'S A WOMAN IN HERE!
HER NAME'S FELICIA!
HELP ME FIND HER!

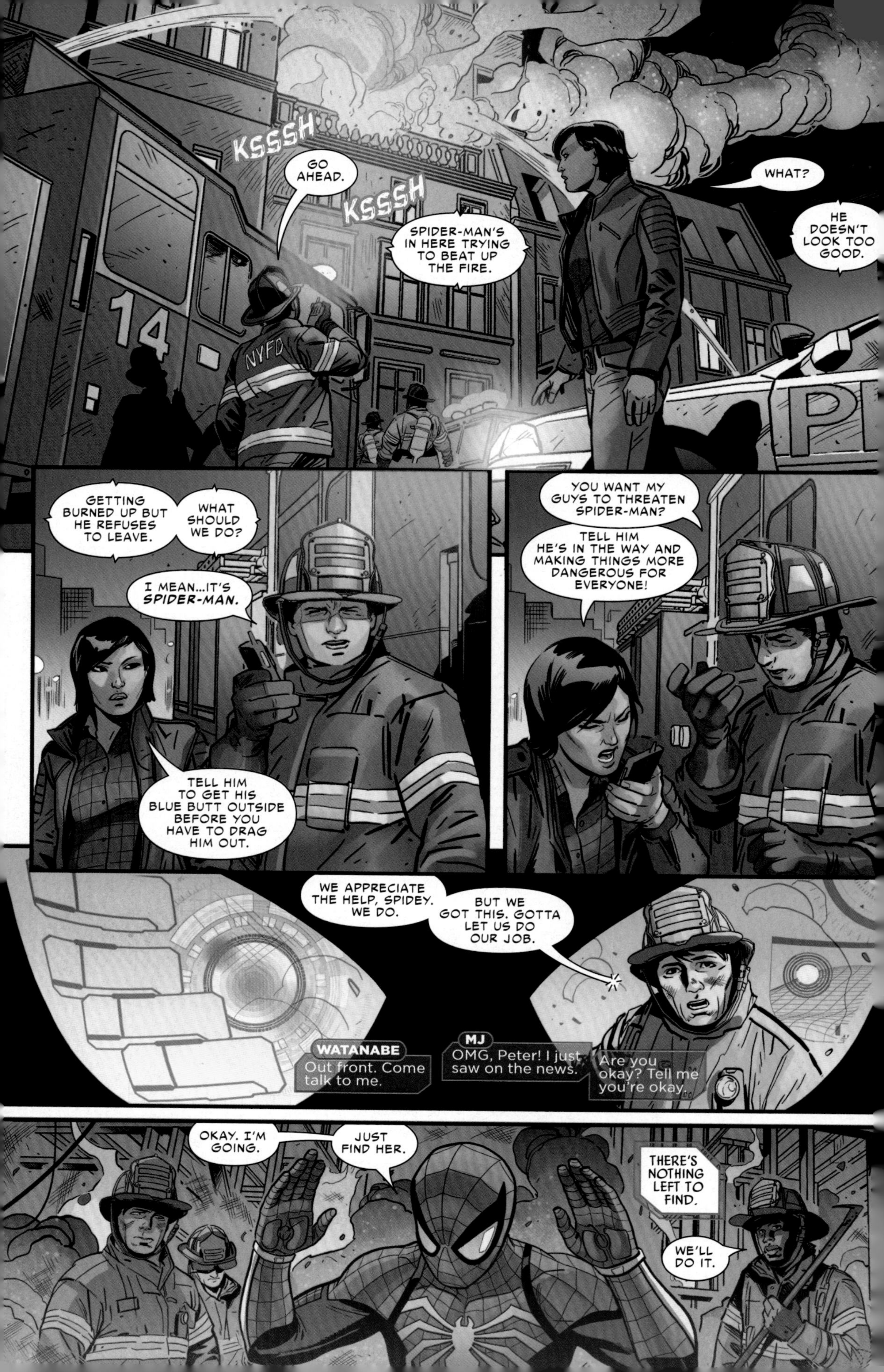
KSSSH
GO AHEAD.
KSSSH
SPIDER-MAN'S IN HERE TRYING TO BEAT UP THE FIRE.
WHAT?
HE DOESN'T LOOK TOO GOOD.
14
NYFD
GETTING BURNED UP BUT HE REFUSES TO LEAVE.
WHAT SHOULD WE DO?
I MEAN...IT'S SPIDER-MAN.
TELL HIM TO GET HIS BLUE BUTT OUTSIDE BEFORE YOU HAVE TO DRAG HIM OUT.
YOU WANT MY GUYS TO THREATEN SPIDER-MAN?
TELL HIM HE'S IN THE WAY AND MAKING THINGS MORE DANGEROUS FOR EVERYONE!
WE APPRECIATE THE HELP, SPIDEY. WE DO.
BUT WE GOT THIS. GOTTA LET US DO OUR JOB.
WATANABE
Out front. Come talk to me.
MJ
OMG, Peter! I just saw on the news.
Are you okay? Tell me you're okay.
OKAY. I'M GOING.
JUST FIND HER.
THERE'S NOTHING LEFT TO FIND.
WE'LL DO IT.

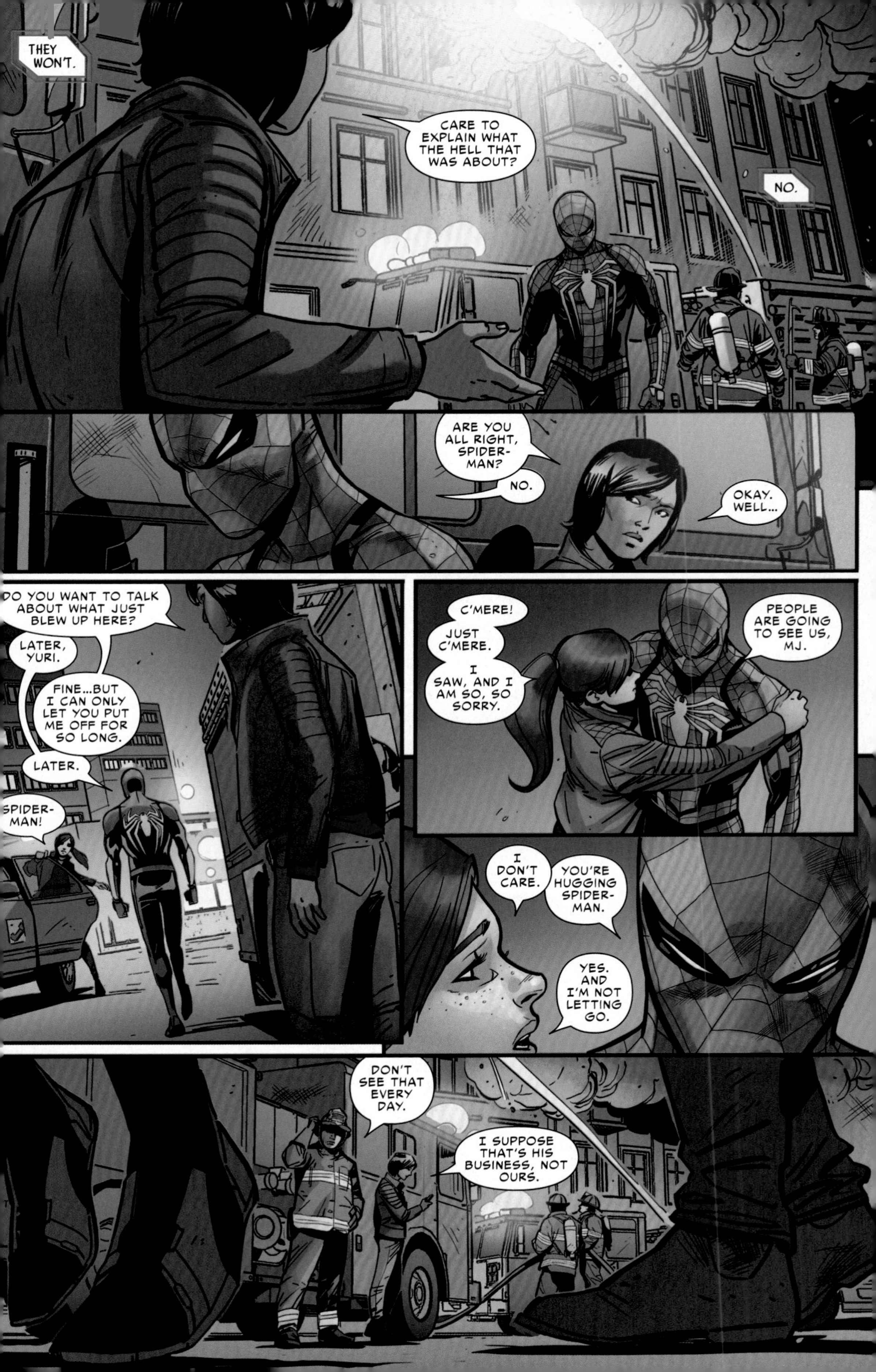
THEY WON'T.
CARE TO EXPLAIN WHAT THE HELL THAT WAS ABOUT?
NO.
ARE YOU ALL RIGHT, SPIDER-MAN?
NO.
OKAY. WELL...
DO YOU WANT TO TALK ABOUT WHAT JUST BLEW UP HERE?
LATER, YURI.
FINE...BUT I CAN ONLY LET YOU PUT ME OFF FOR SO LONG.
LATER.
SPIDER-MAN!
C'MERE!
JUST C'MERE.
I SAW, AND I AM SO, SO SORRY.
PEOPLE ARE GOING TO SEE US, MJ.
I DON'T CARE.
YOU'RE HUGGING SPIDER-MAN.
YES. AND I'M NOT LETTING GO.
DON'T SEE THAT EVERY DAY.
I SUPPOSE THAT'S HIS BUSINESS, NOT OURS.

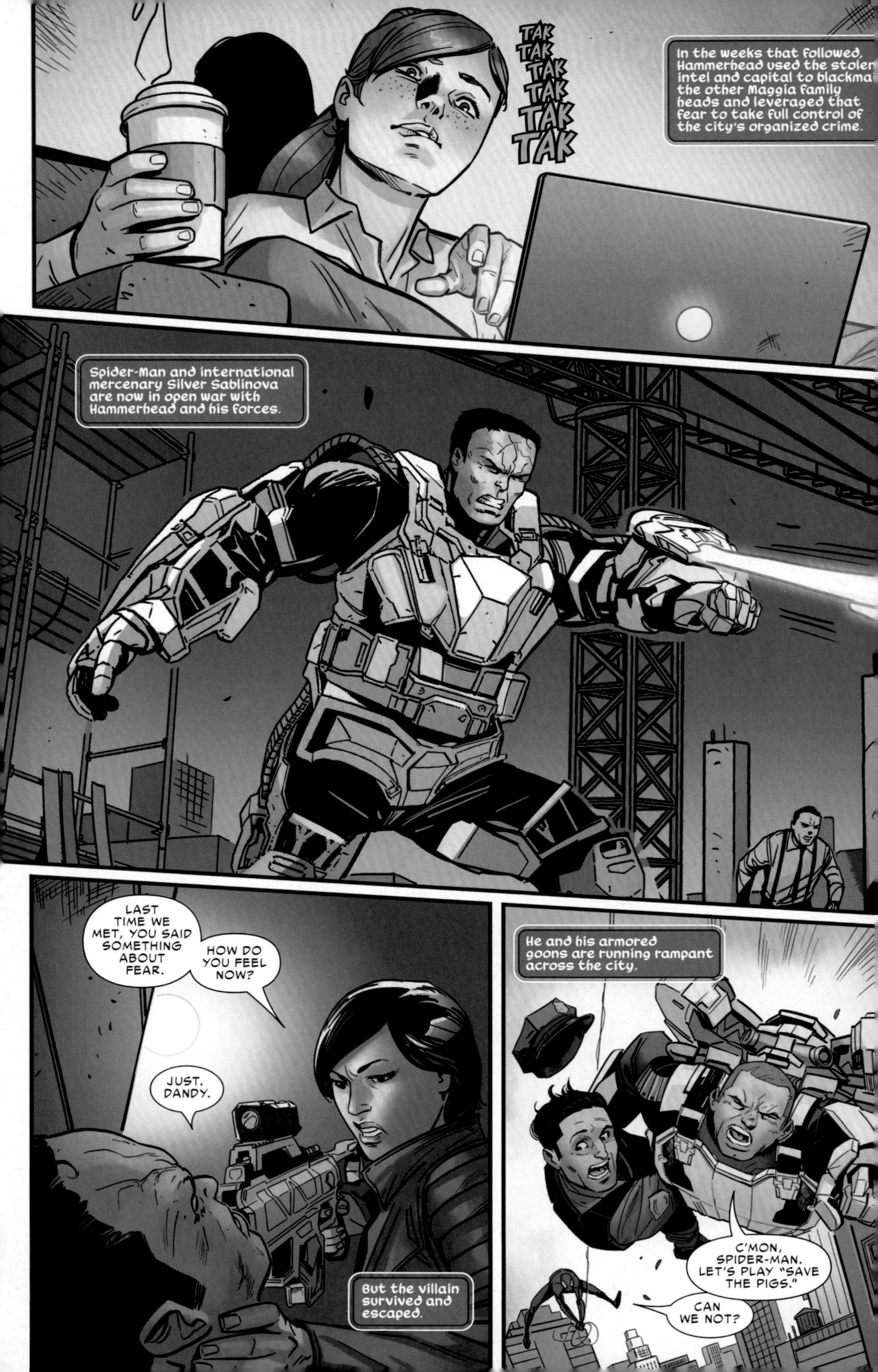
TAK TAK TAK TAK TAK TAK TAK
In the weeks that followed, Hammerhead used the stolen intel and capital to blackmail the other Maggia family heads and leveraged that fear to take full control of the city's organized crime.
Spider-Man and international mercenary Silver Sablinova are now in open war with Hammerhead and his forces.
LAST TIME WE MET, YOU SAID SOMETHING ABOUT FEAR.
HOW DO YOU FEEL NOW?
JUST. DANDY.
But the villain survived and escaped.
He and his armored goons are running rampant across the city.
C'MON, SPIDER-MAN. LET'S PLAY "SAVE THE PIGS."
CAN WE NOT?

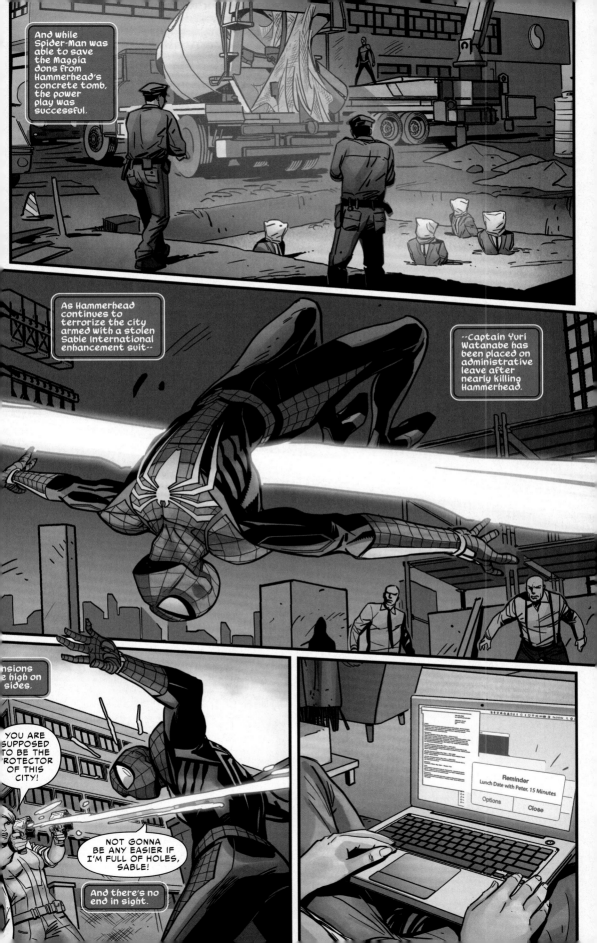

And while Spider-Man was able to save the Maggia dons from Hammerhead's concrete tomb, the power play was successful.

As Hammerhead continues to terrorize the city armed with a stolen Sable International enhancement suit--

--Captain Yuri Watanabe has been placed on administrative leave after nearly killing Hammerhead.

...nsions ...e high on ...sides.

YOU ARE SUPPOSED TO BE THE PROTECTOR OF THIS CITY!

NOT GONNA BE ANY EASIER IF I'M FULL OF HOLES, SABLE!

And there's no end in sight.

Reminder
Lunch Date with Peter. 15 Minutes
Options   Close

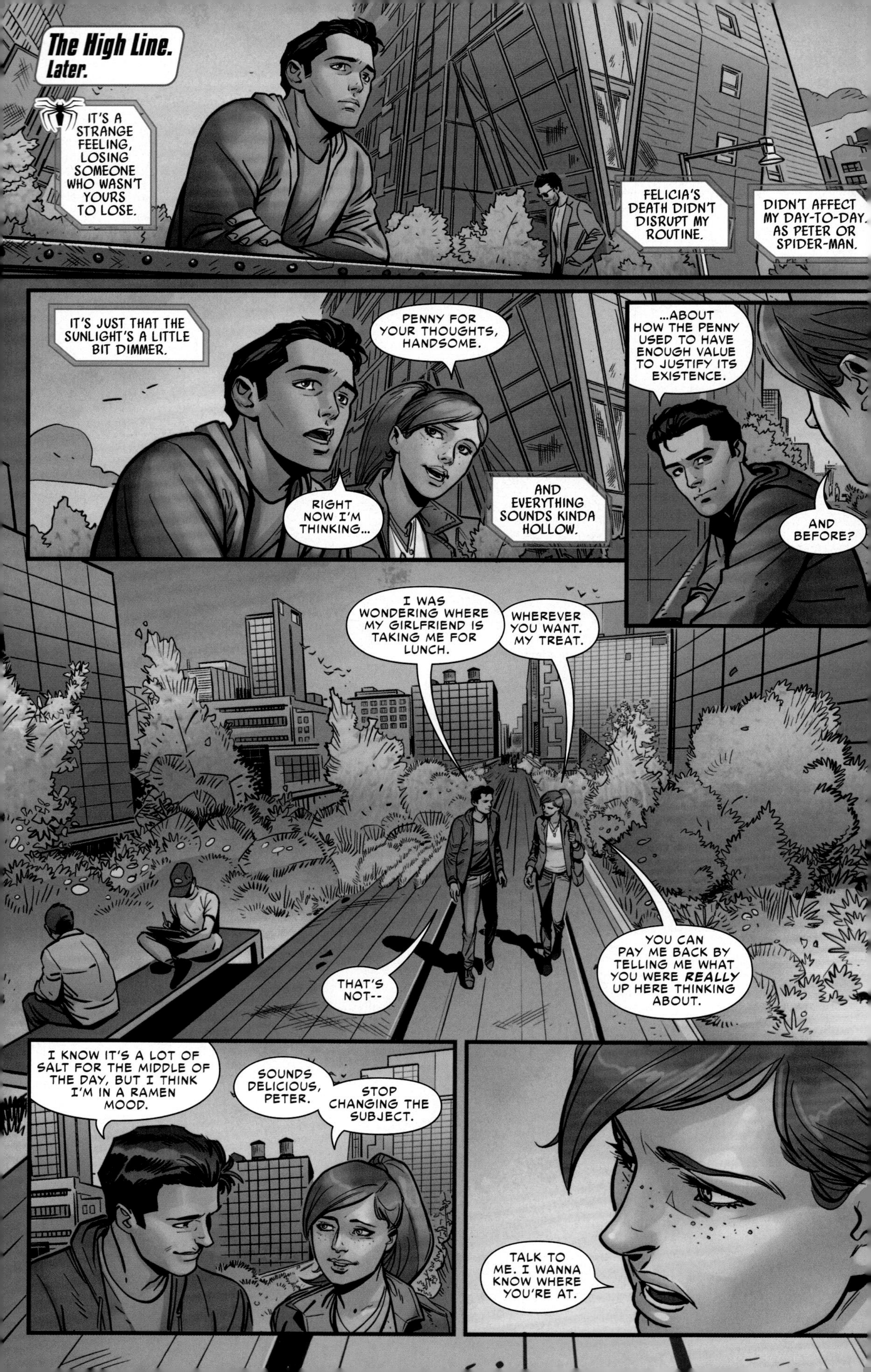
The High Line.
Later.
IT'S A STRANGE FEELING, LOSING SOMEONE WHO WASN'T YOURS TO LOSE.
FELICIA'S DEATH DIDN'T DISRUPT MY ROUTINE.
DIDN'T AFFECT MY DAY-TO-DAY. AS PETER OR SPIDER-MAN.
IT'S JUST THAT THE SUNLIGHT'S A LITTLE BIT DIMMER.
PENNY FOR YOUR THOUGHTS, HANDSOME.
RIGHT NOW I'M THINKING...
AND EVERYTHING SOUNDS KINDA HOLLOW.
...ABOUT HOW THE PENNY USED TO HAVE ENOUGH VALUE TO JUSTIFY ITS EXISTENCE.
AND BEFORE?
I WAS WONDERING WHERE MY GIRLFRIEND IS TAKING ME FOR LUNCH.
WHEREVER YOU WANT. MY TREAT.
THAT'S NOT--
YOU CAN PAY ME BACK BY TELLING ME WHAT YOU WERE REALLY UP HERE THINKING ABOUT.
I KNOW IT'S A LOT OF SALT FOR THE MIDDLE OF THE DAY, BUT I THINK I'M IN A RAMEN MOOD.
SOUNDS DELICIOUS, PETER.
STOP CHANGING THE SUBJECT.
TALK TO ME. I WANNA KNOW WHERE YOU'RE AT.

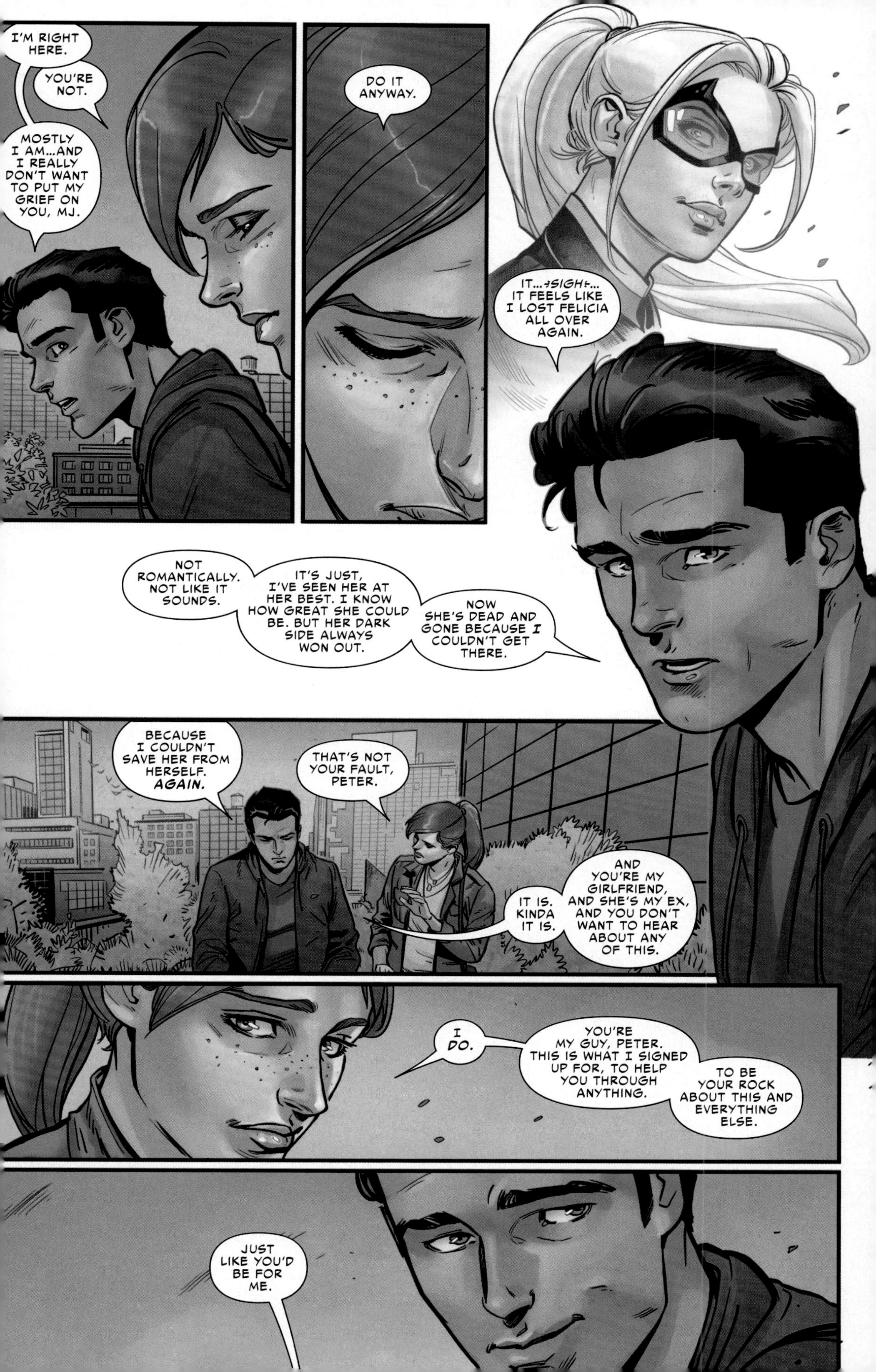
I'M RIGHT HERE.
YOU'RE NOT.
MOSTLY I AM...AND I REALLY DON'T WANT TO PUT MY GRIEF ON YOU, MJ.
DO IT ANYWAY.
IT... ⸗SIGH⸗... IT FEELS LIKE I LOST FELICIA ALL OVER AGAIN.
NOT ROMANTICALLY. NOT LIKE IT SOUNDS.
IT'S JUST, I'VE SEEN HER AT HER BEST. I KNOW HOW GREAT SHE COULD BE. BUT HER DARK SIDE ALWAYS WON OUT.
NOW SHE'S DEAD AND GONE BECAUSE I COULDN'T GET THERE.
BECAUSE I COULDN'T SAVE HER FROM HERSELF. AGAIN.
THAT'S NOT YOUR FAULT, PETER.
IT IS. KINDA IT IS.
AND YOU'RE MY GIRLFRIEND, AND SHE'S MY EX, AND YOU DON'T WANT TO HEAR ABOUT ANY OF THIS.
I DO.
YOU'RE MY GUY, PETER. THIS IS WHAT I SIGNED UP FOR, TO HELP YOU THROUGH ANYTHING.
TO BE YOUR ROCK ABOUT THIS AND EVERYTHING ELSE.
JUST LIKE YOU'D BE FOR ME.

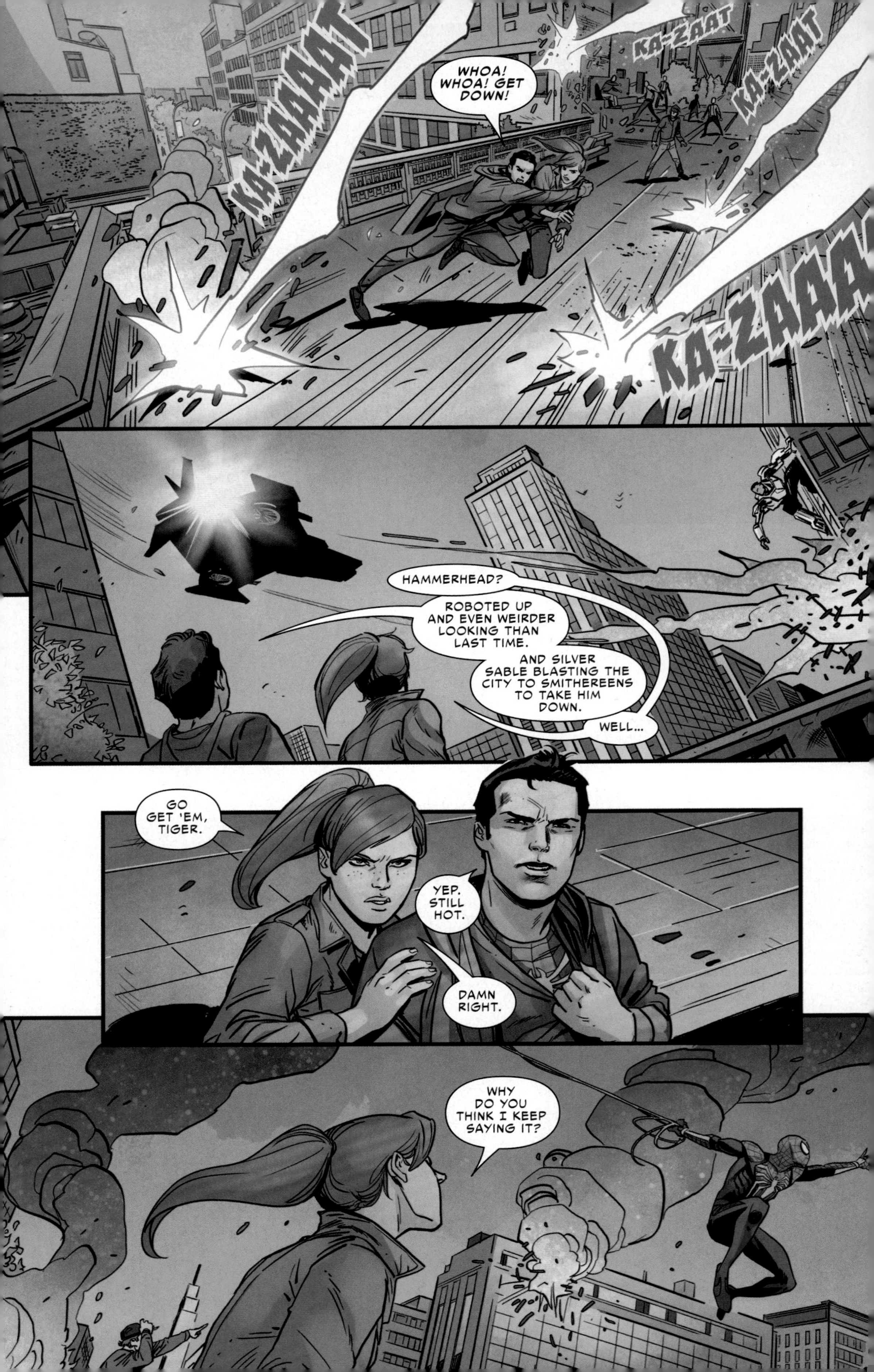
KA-ZAAAAT
WHOA! WHOA! GET DOWN!
KA-ZAAT
KA-ZAAT
KA-ZAAAA
HAMMERHEAD?
ROBOTED UP AND EVEN WEIRDER LOOKING THAN LAST TIME.
AND SILVER SABLE BLASTING THE CITY TO SMITHEREENS TO TAKE HIM DOWN.
WELL...
GO GET 'EM, TIGER.
YEP. STILL HOT.
DAMN RIGHT.
WHY DO YOU THINK I KEEP SAYING IT?

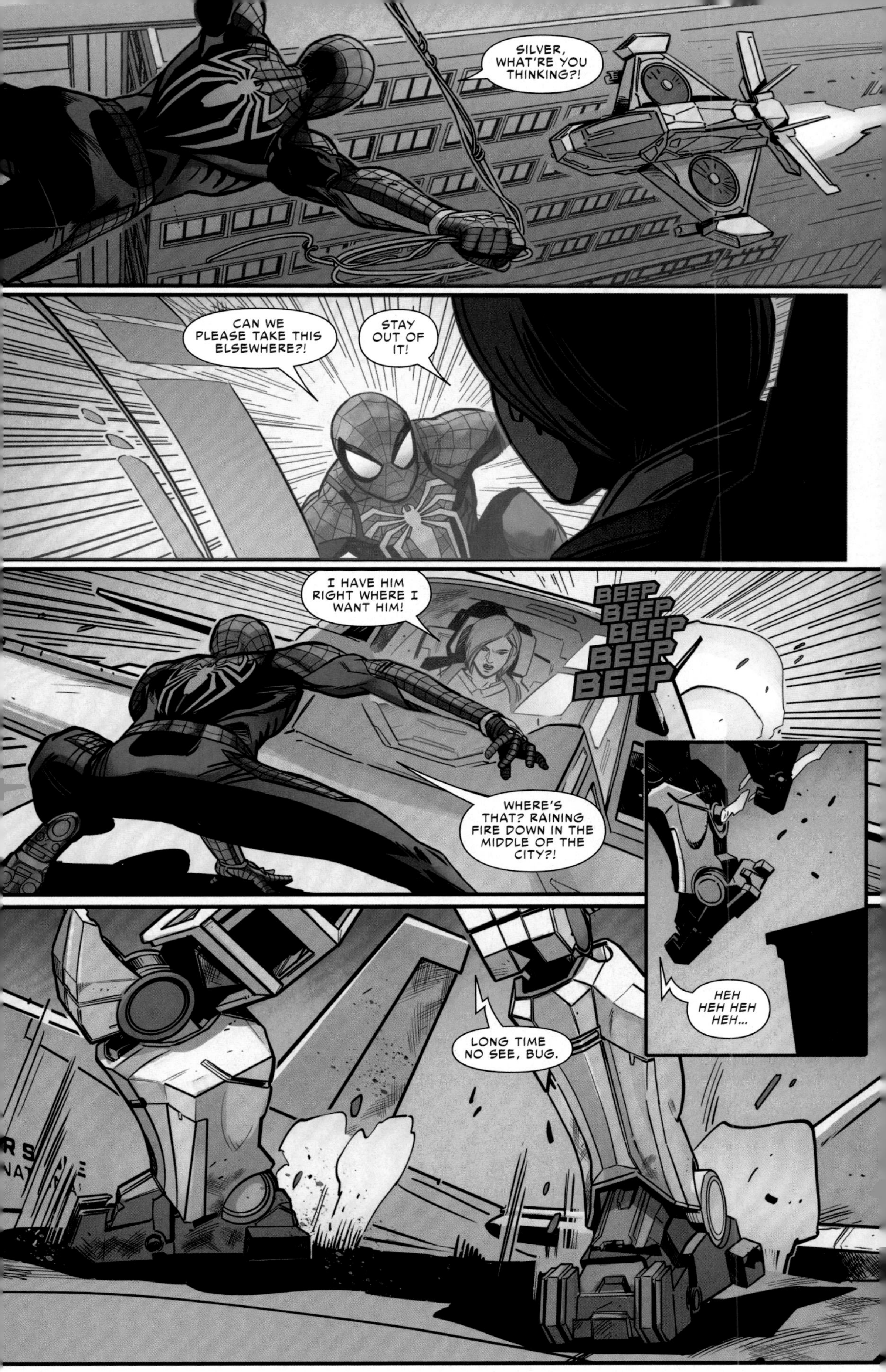
SILVER, WHAT'RE YOU THINKING?!
CAN WE PLEASE TAKE THIS ELSEWHERE?!
STAY OUT OF IT!
I HAVE HIM RIGHT WHERE I WANT HIM!
BEEP BEEP BEEP BEEP BEEP
WHERE'S THAT? RAINING FIRE DOWN IN THE MIDDLE OF THE CITY?!
HEH HEH HEH HEH...
LONG TIME NO SEE, BUG.

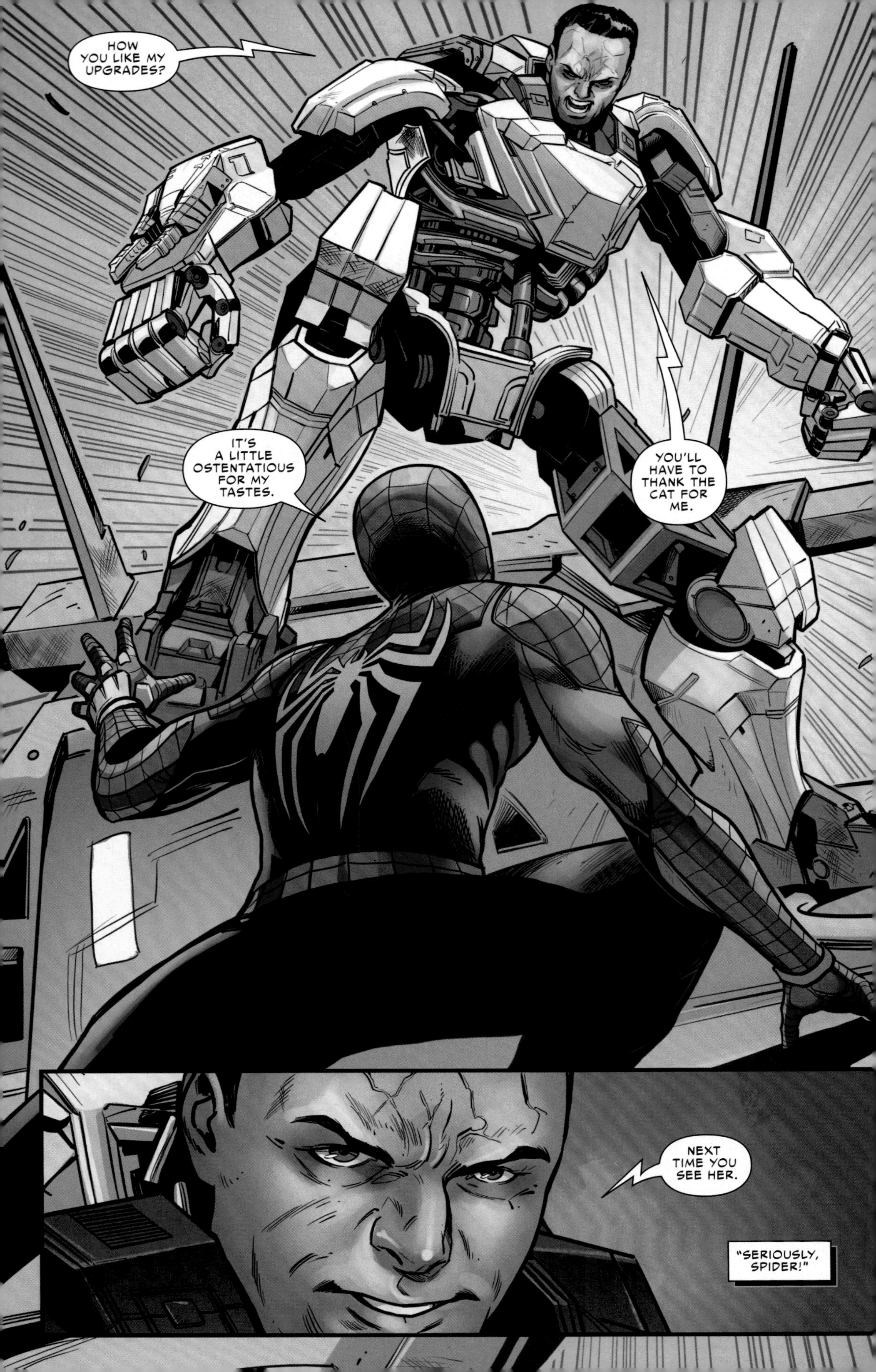
HOW YOU LIKE MY UPGRADES?
IT'S A LITTLE OSTENTATIOUS FOR MY TASTES.
YOU'LL HAVE TO THANK THE CAT FOR ME.
NEXT TIME YOU SEE HER.
"SERIOUSLY, SPIDER!"

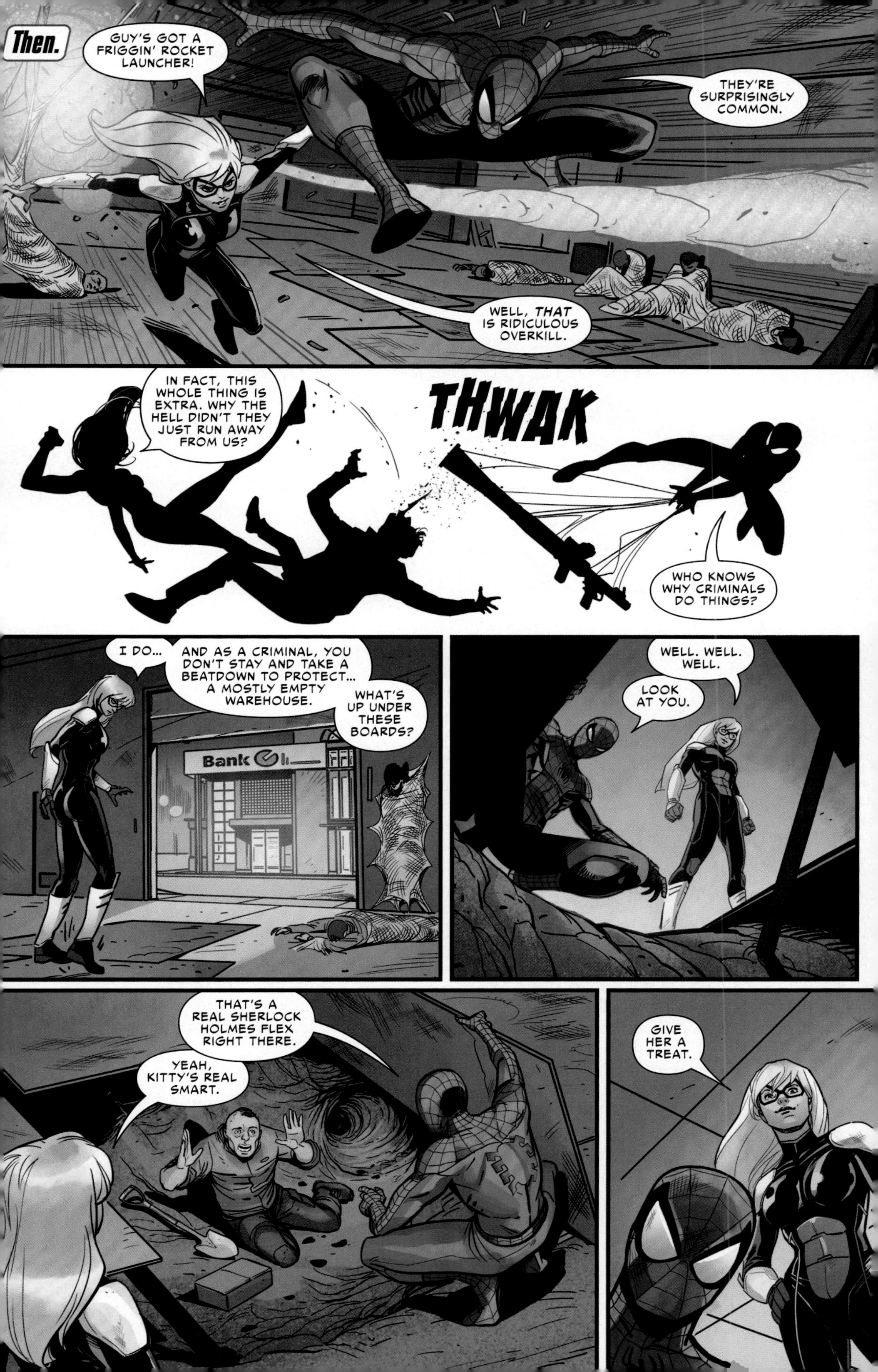
Then.
GUY'S GOT A FRIGGIN' ROCKET LAUNCHER!
THEY'RE SURPRISINGLY COMMON.
WELL, *THAT* IS RIDICULOUS OVERKILL.
IN FACT, THIS WHOLE THING IS EXTRA. WHY THE HELL DIDN'T THEY JUST RUN AWAY FROM US?
THWAK
WHO KNOWS WHY CRIMINALS DO THINGS?
I DO...
AND AS A CRIMINAL, YOU DON'T STAY AND TAKE A BEATDOWN TO PROTECT... A MOSTLY EMPTY WAREHOUSE.
WHAT'S UP UNDER THESE BOARDS?
Bank
WELL. WELL. WELL.
LOOK AT YOU.
THAT'S A REAL SHERLOCK HOLMES FLEX RIGHT THERE.
YEAH, KITTY'S REAL SMART.
GIVE HER A TREAT.

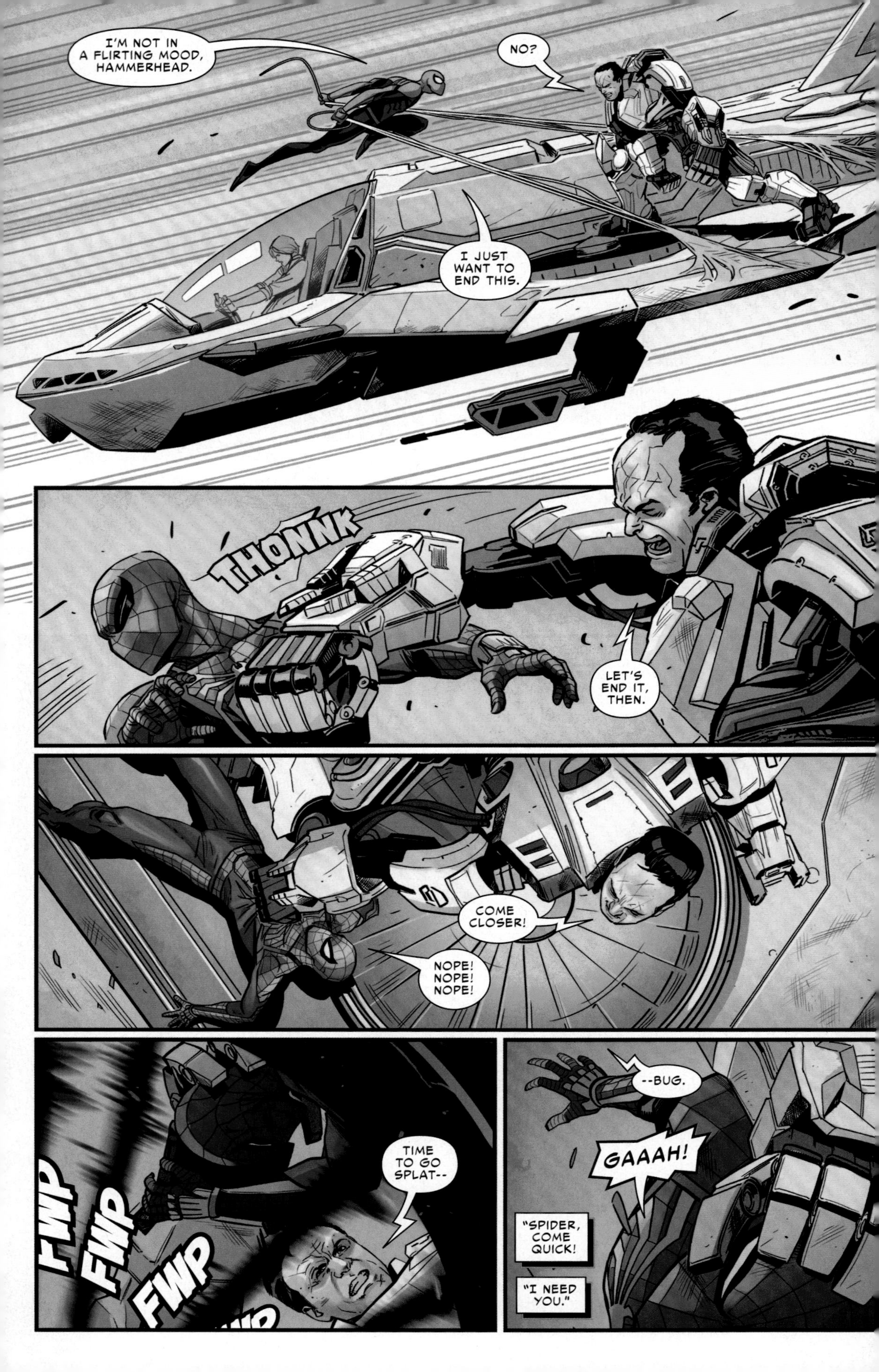
I'M NOT IN A FLIRTING MOOD, HAMMERHEAD.
NO?
I JUST WANT TO END THIS.
THONNK
LET'S END IT, THEN.
COME CLOSER!
NOPE! NOPE! NOPE!
FWP
FWP
FWP
TIME TO GO SPLAT--
--BUG.
GAAAH!
"SPIDER, COME QUICK!
"I NEED YOU."

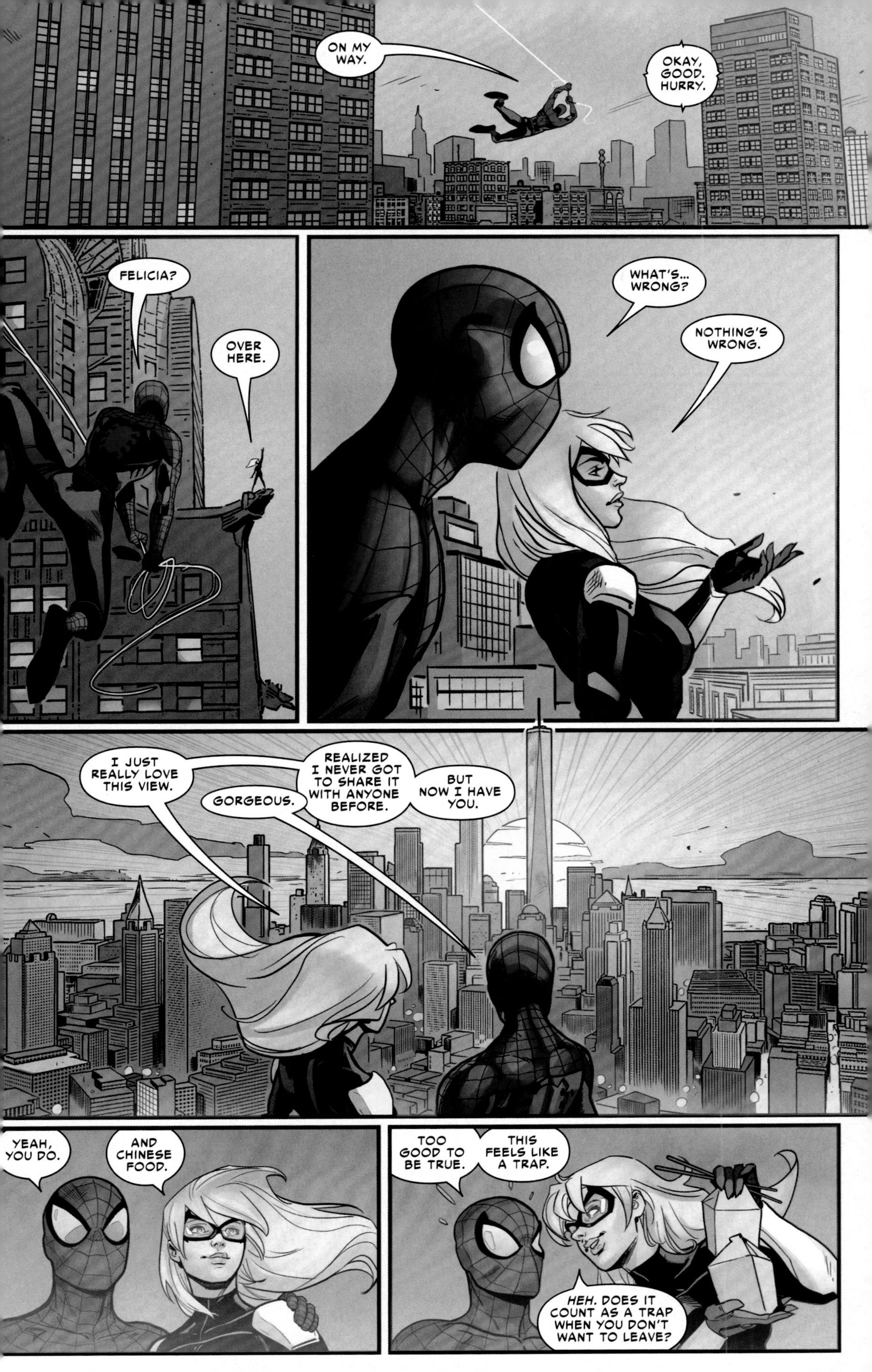
ON MY WAY.
OKAY, GOOD. HURRY.
FELICIA?
OVER HERE.
WHAT'S... WRONG?
NOTHING'S WRONG.
I JUST REALLY LOVE THIS VIEW.
GORGEOUS.
REALIZED I NEVER GOT TO SHARE IT WITH ANYONE BEFORE.
BUT NOW I HAVE YOU.
YEAH, YOU DO.
AND CHINESE FOOD.
TOO GOOD TO BE TRUE.
THIS FEELS LIKE A TRAP.
HEH. DOES IT COUNT AS A TRAP WHEN YOU DON'T WANT TO LEAVE?

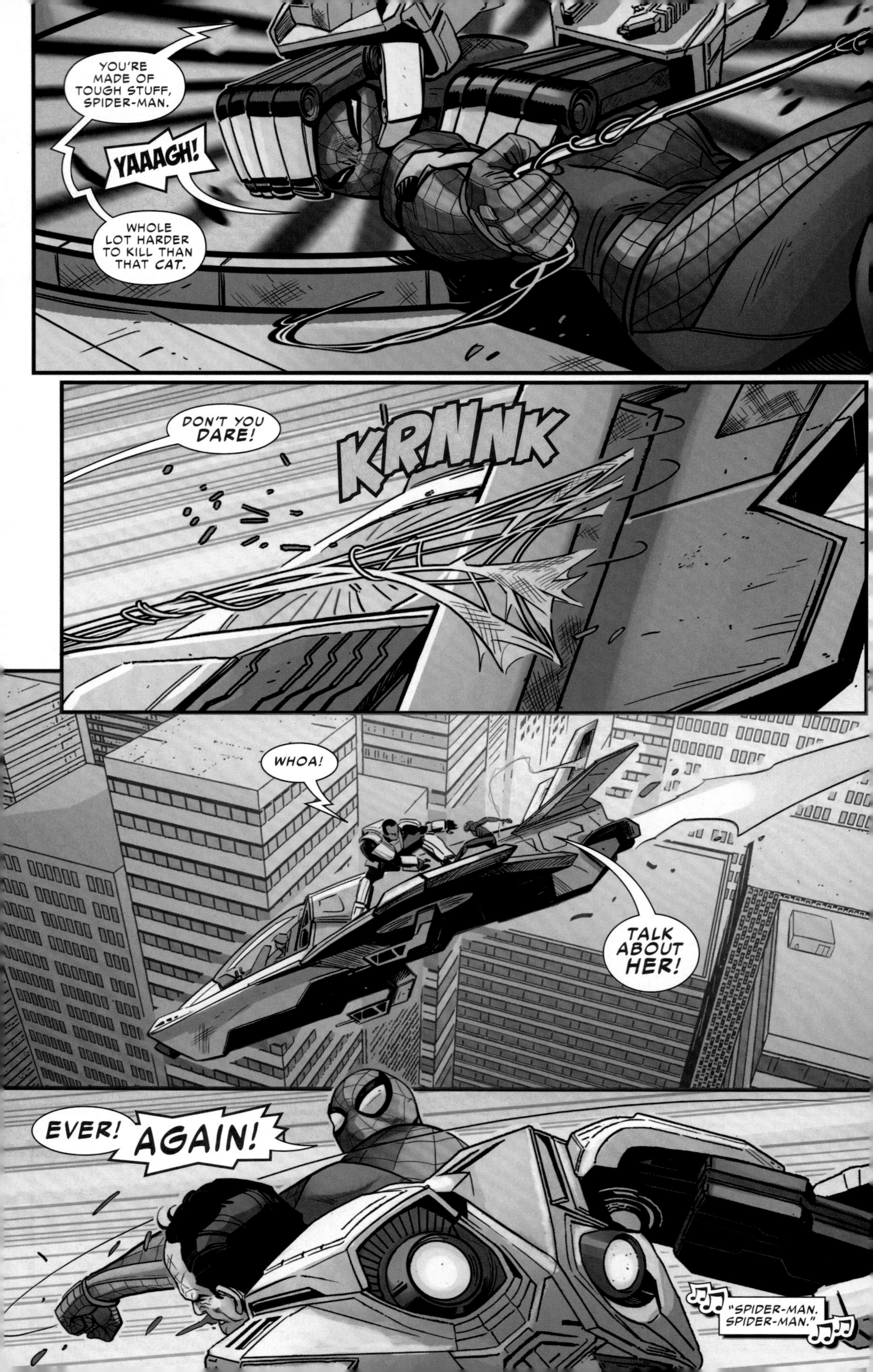
YOU'RE MADE OF TOUGH STUFF, SPIDER-MAN.
YAAAGH!
WHOLE LOT HARDER TO KILL THAN THAT CAT.
DON'T YOU DARE!
KRNNK
WHOA!
TALK ABOUT HER!
EVER! AGAIN!
"SPIDER-MAN. SPIDER-MAN."

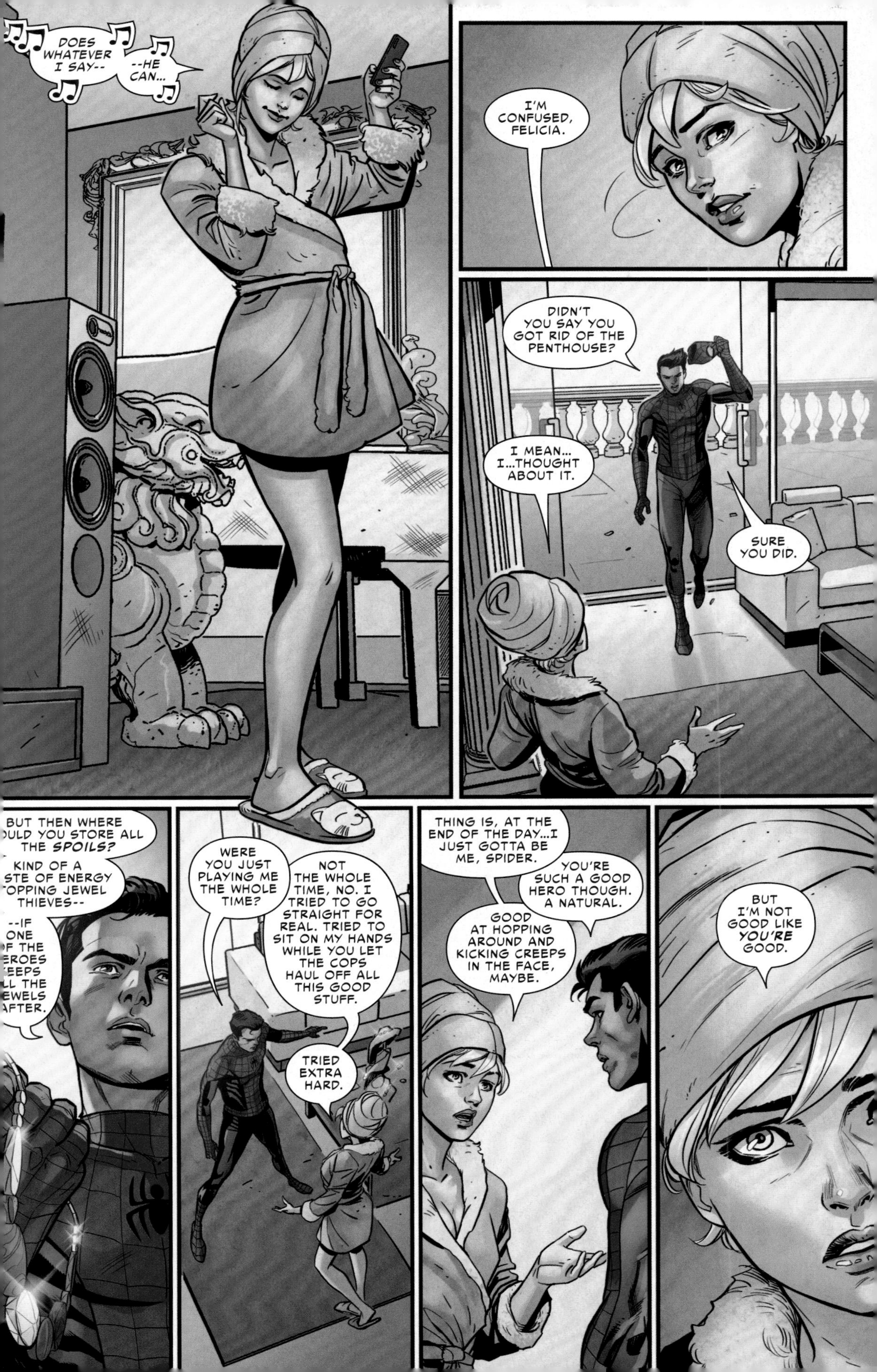
DOES WHATEVER I SAY--
--HE CAN...
I'M CONFUSED, FELICIA.
DIDN'T YOU SAY YOU GOT RID OF THE PENTHOUSE?
I MEAN... I...THOUGHT ABOUT IT.
SURE YOU DID.
BUT THEN WHERE OULD YOU STORE ALL THE *SPOILS?*
KIND OF A STE OF ENERGY TOPPING JEWEL THIEVES--
--IF ONE F THE EROES EEPS LL THE EWELS AFTER.
WERE YOU JUST PLAYING ME THE WHOLE TIME?
NOT THE WHOLE TIME, NO. I TRIED TO GO STRAIGHT FOR REAL. TRIED TO SIT ON MY HANDS WHILE YOU LET THE COPS HAUL OFF ALL THIS GOOD STUFF.
TRIED EXTRA HARD.
THING IS, AT THE END OF THE DAY...I JUST GOTTA BE ME, SPIDER.
YOU'RE SUCH A GOOD HERO THOUGH. A NATURAL.
GOOD AT HOPPING AROUND AND KICKING CREEPS IN THE FACE, MAYBE.
BUT I'M NOT GOOD LIKE *YOU'RE* GOOD.

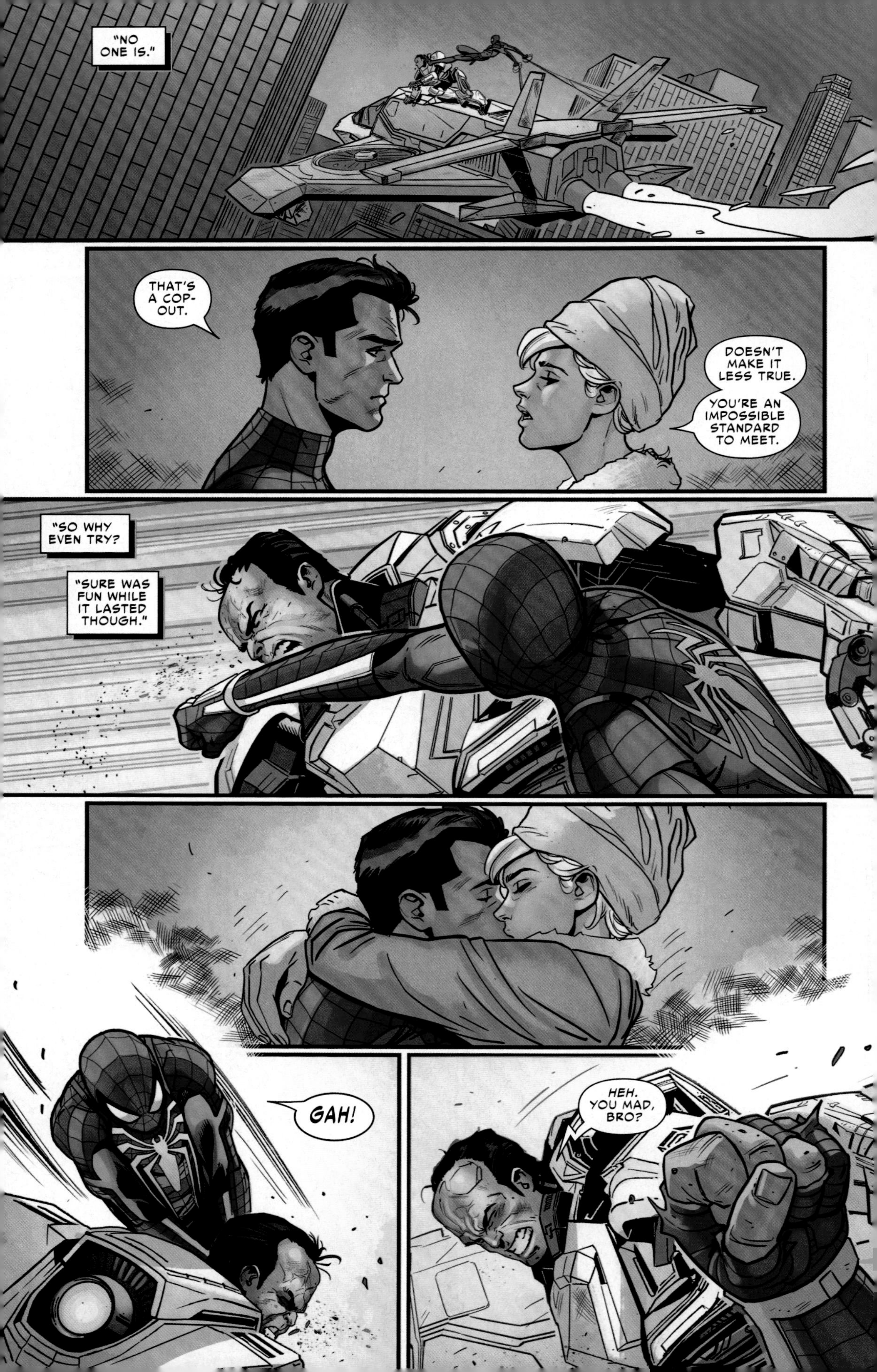
"NO ONE IS."
THAT'S A COP-OUT.
DOESN'T MAKE IT LESS TRUE.
YOU'RE AN IMPOSSIBLE STANDARD TO MEET.
"SO WHY EVEN TRY?
"SURE WAS FUN WHILE IT LASTED THOUGH."
GAH!
HEH. YOU MAD, BRO?

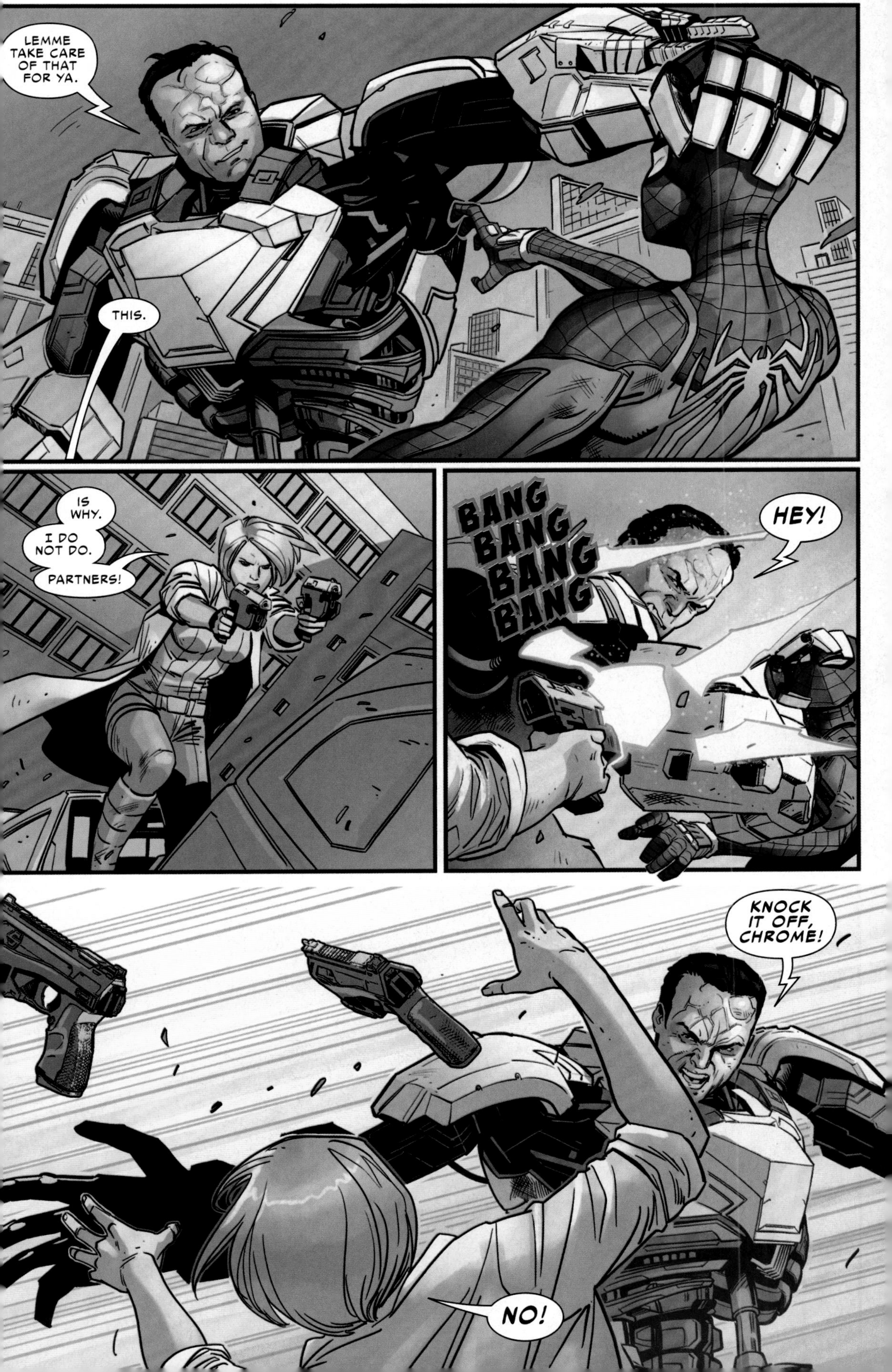
LEMME TAKE CARE OF THAT FOR YA.
THIS.
IS WHY.
I DO NOT DO.
PARTNERS!
BANG BANG BANG BANG
HEY!
KNOCK IT OFF, CHROME!
NO!

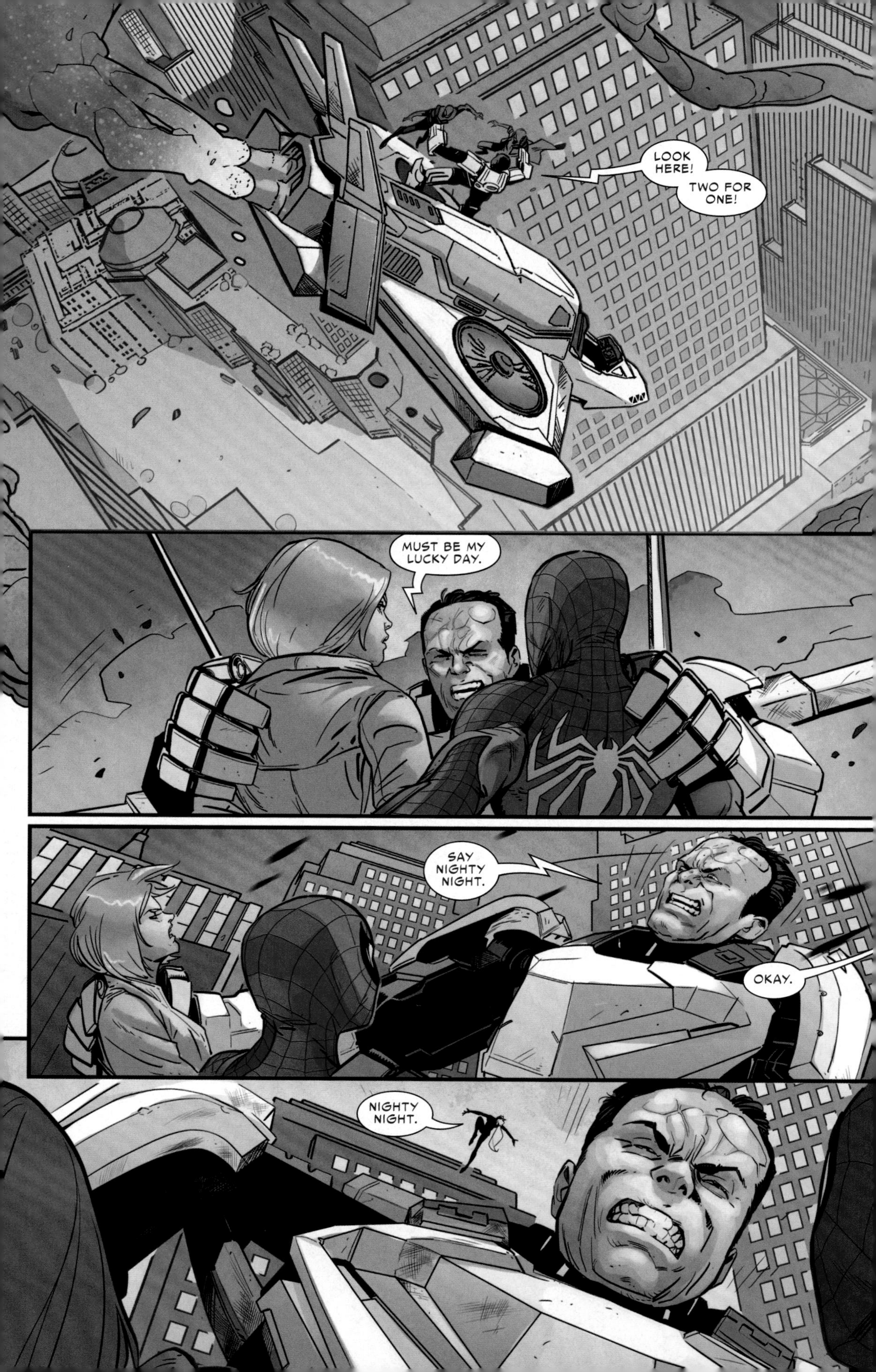
LOOK HERE!
TWO FOR ONE!
MUST BE MY LUCKY DAY.
SAY NIGHTY NIGHT.
OKAY.
NIGHTY NIGHT.

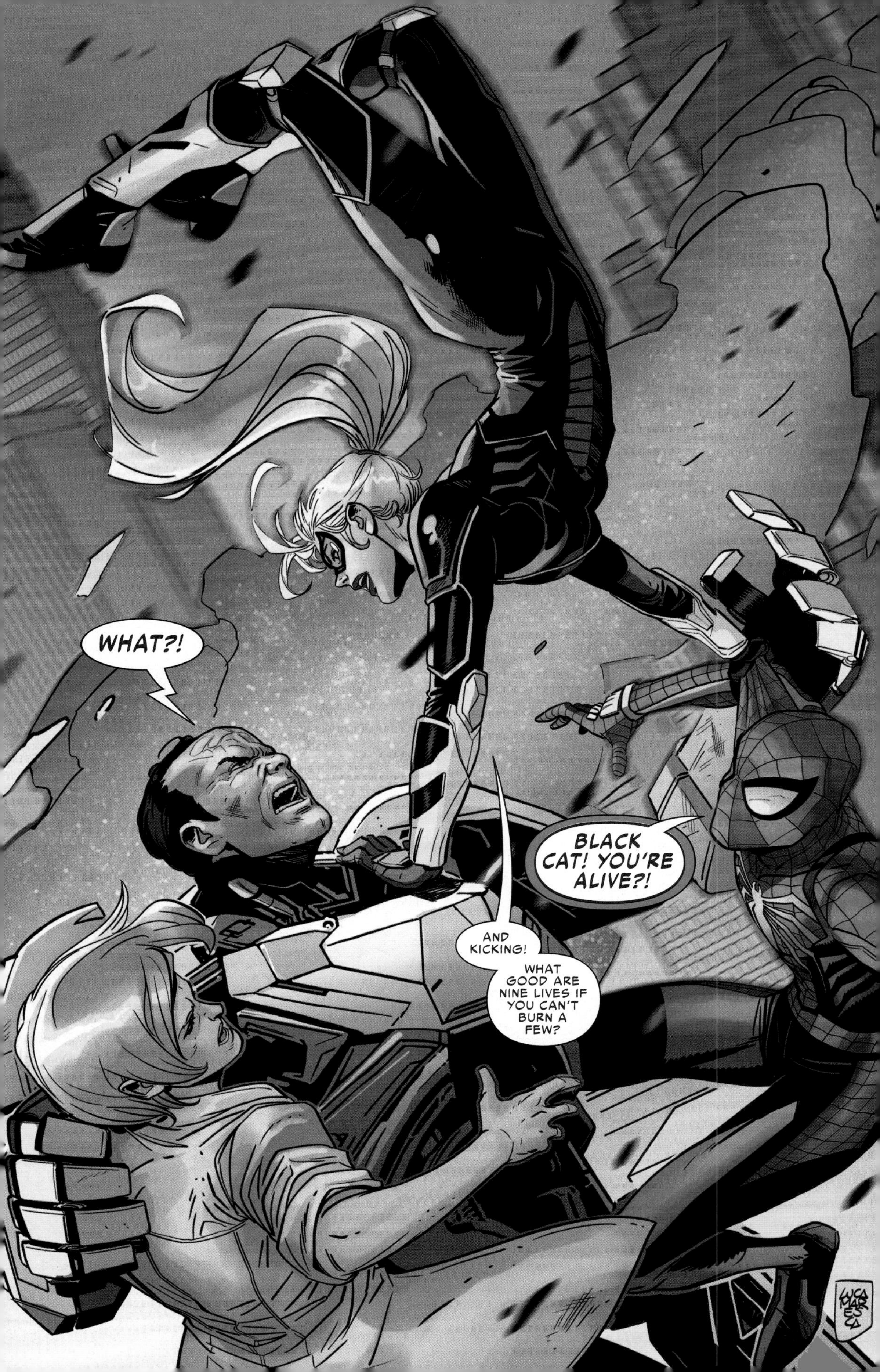
WHAT?!
BLACK CAT! YOU'RE ALIVE?!
AND KICKING!
WHAT GOOD ARE NINE LIVES IF YOU CAN'T BURN A FEW?
LUCA MARESCA

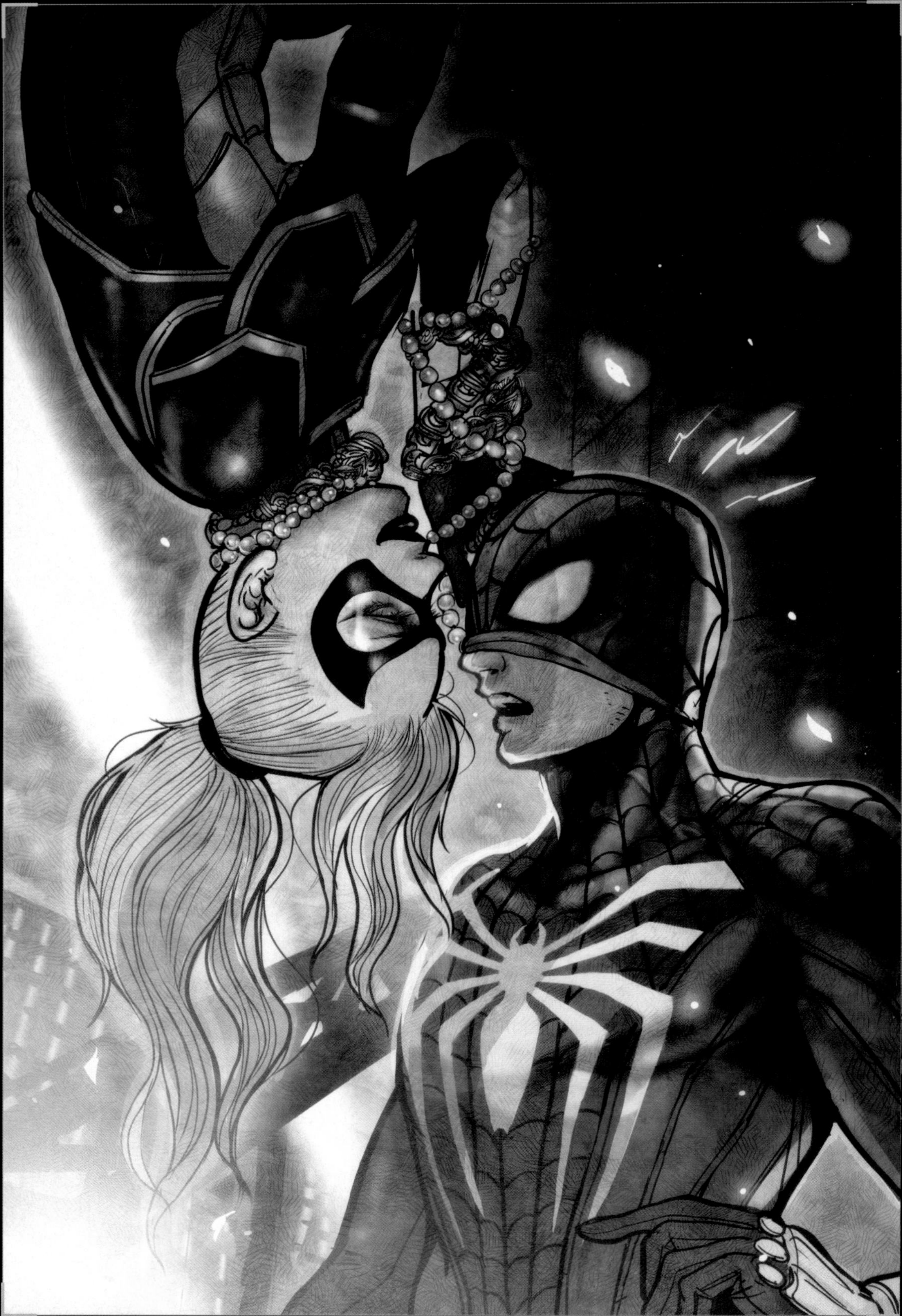

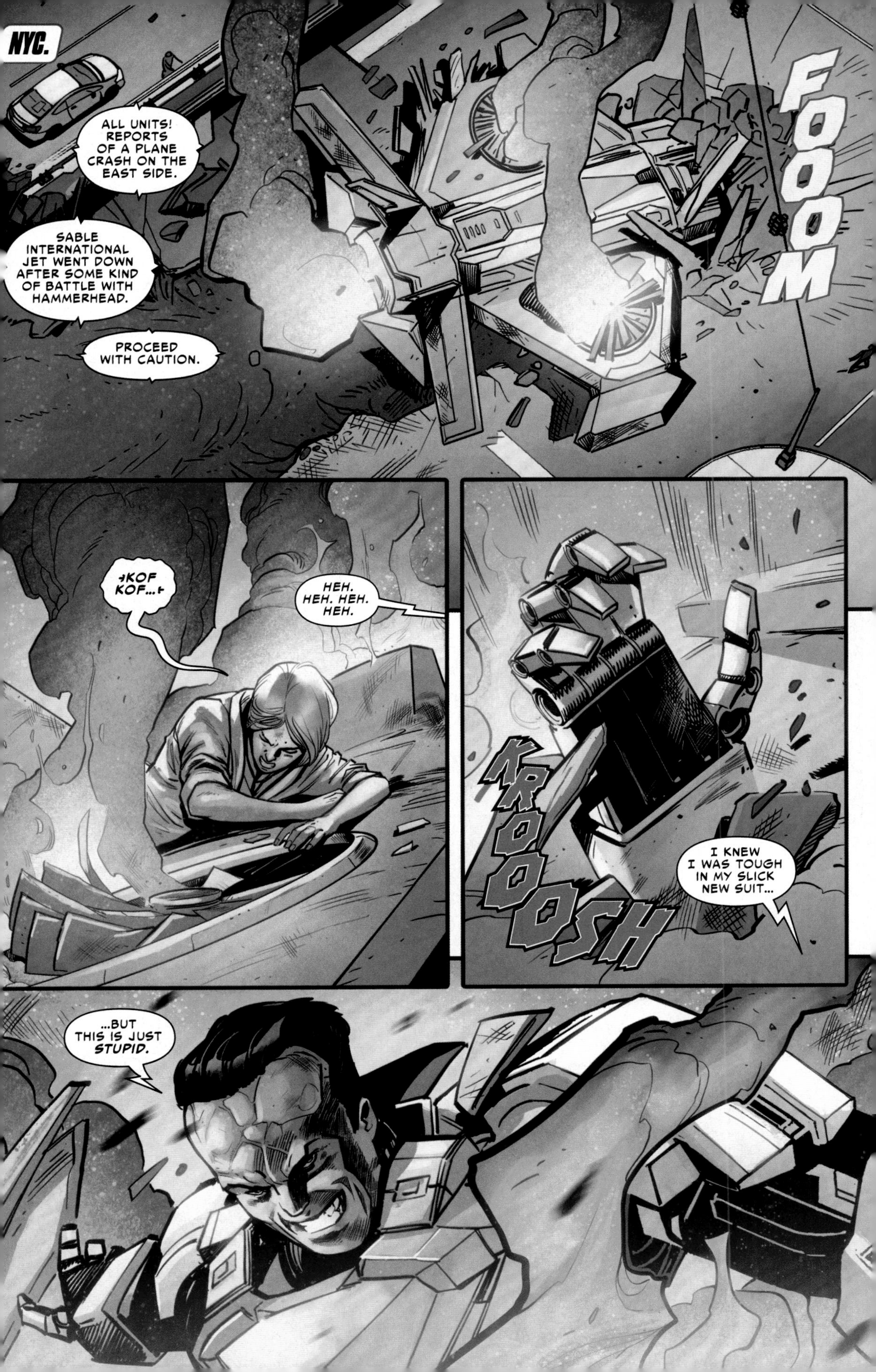
NYC.
ALL UNITS! REPORTS OF A PLANE CRASH ON THE EAST SIDE.
SABLE INTERNATIONAL JET WENT DOWN AFTER SOME KIND OF BATTLE WITH HAMMERHEAD.
PROCEED WITH CAUTION.
FOOOOM
KOF KOF...
HEH. HEH. HEH. HEH.
KROOOSH
I KNEW I WAS TOUGH IN MY SLICK NEW SUIT...
...BUT THIS IS JUST STUPID.

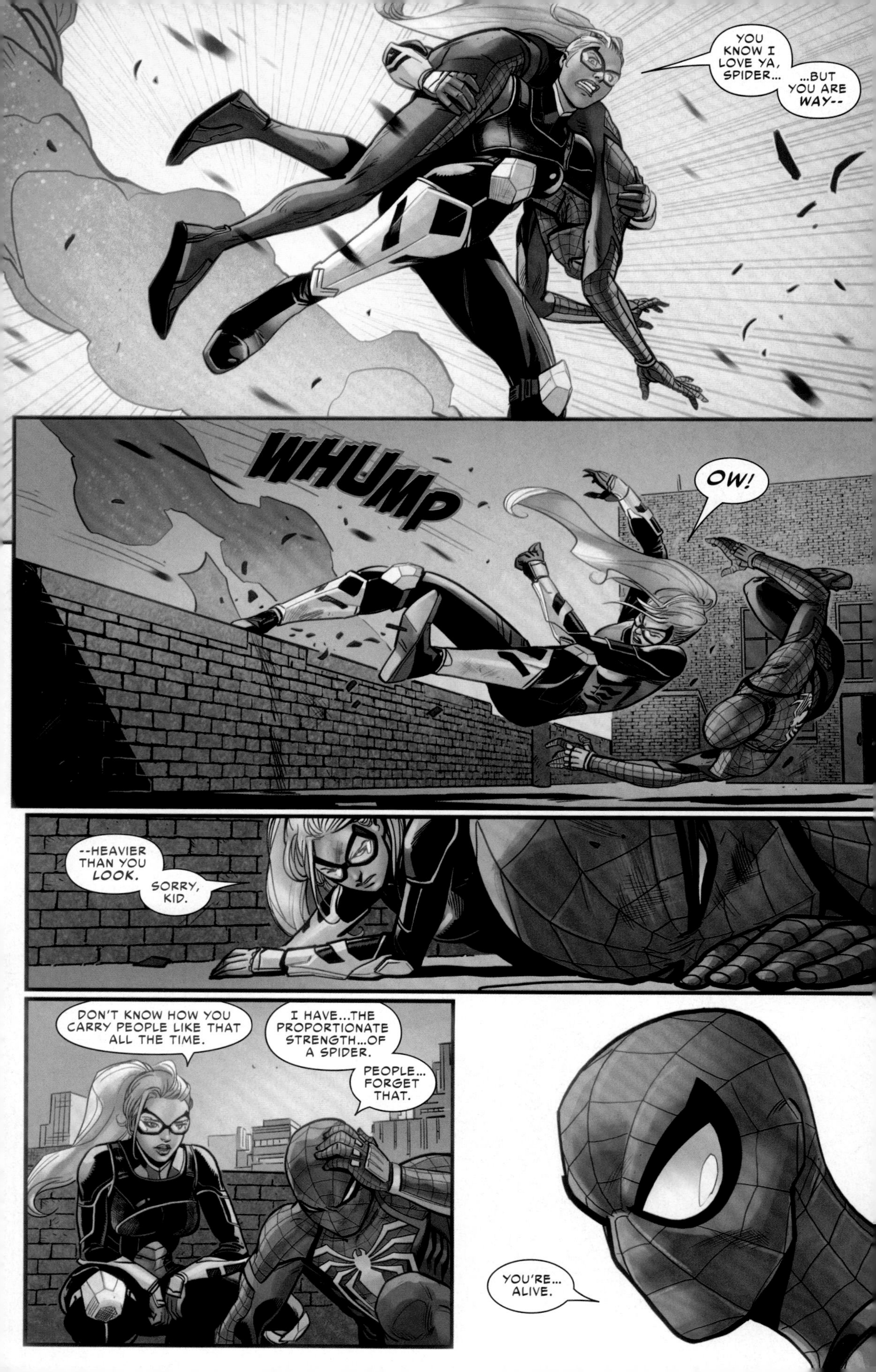
YOU KNOW I LOVE YA, SPIDER...
...BUT YOU ARE WAY--
WHUMP
OW!
--HEAVIER THAN YOU LOOK.
SORRY, KID.
DON'T KNOW HOW YOU CARRY PEOPLE LIKE THAT ALL THE TIME.
I HAVE...THE PROPORTIONATE STRENGTH...OF A SPIDER.
PEOPLE... FORGET THAT.
YOU'RE... ALIVE.

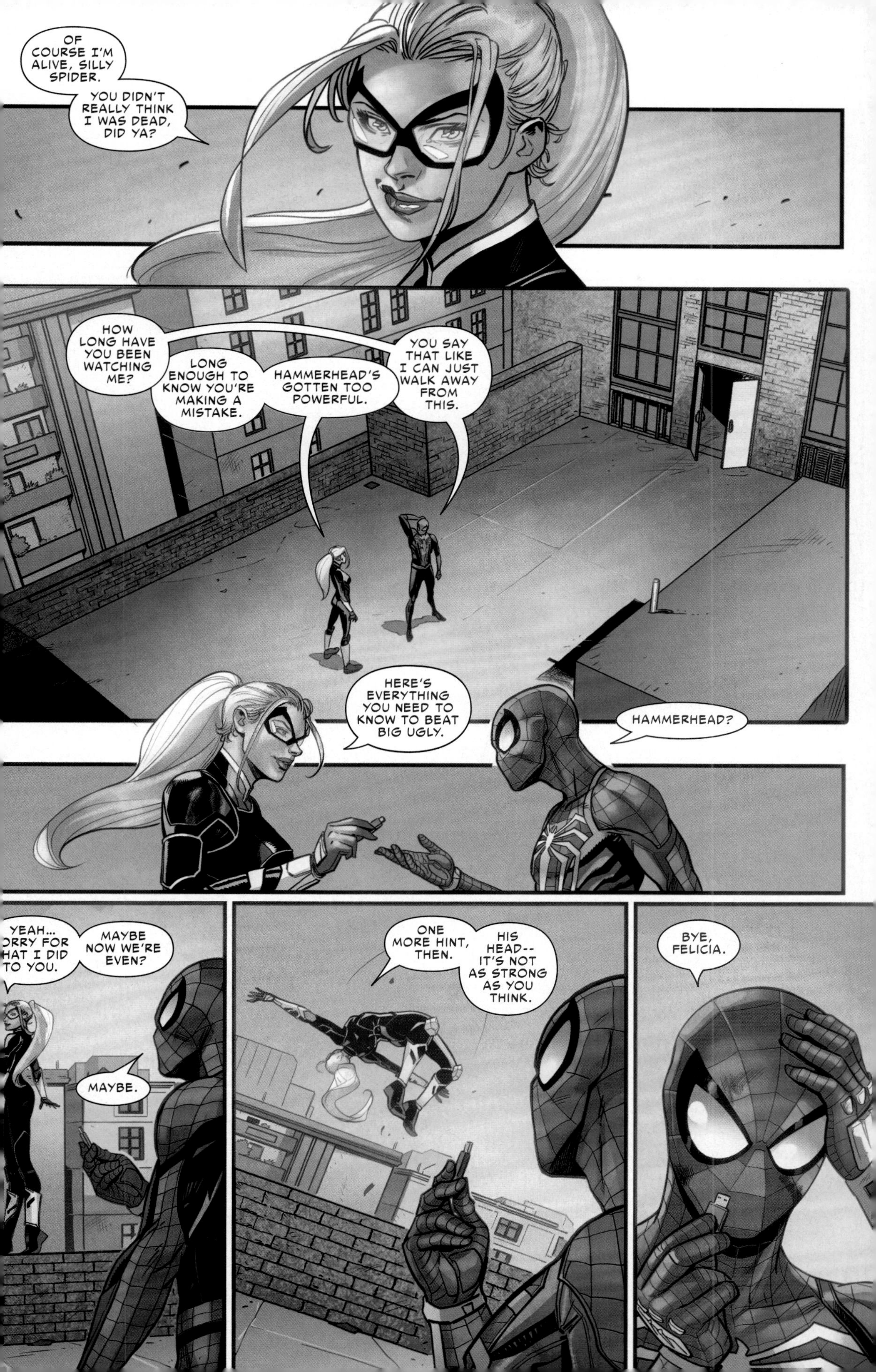
OF COURSE I'M ALIVE, SILLY SPIDER.
YOU DIDN'T REALLY THINK I WAS DEAD, DID YA?
HOW LONG HAVE YOU BEEN WATCHING ME?
LONG ENOUGH TO KNOW YOU'RE MAKING A MISTAKE.
HAMMERHEAD'S GOTTEN TOO POWERFUL.
YOU SAY THAT LIKE I CAN JUST WALK AWAY FROM THIS.
HERE'S EVERYTHING YOU NEED TO KNOW TO BEAT BIG UGLY.
HAMMERHEAD?
YEAH... ORRY FOR HAT I DID TO YOU.
MAYBE NOW WE'RE EVEN?
MAYBE.
ONE MORE HINT, THEN.
HIS HEAD-- IT'S NOT AS STRONG AS YOU THINK.
BYE, FELICIA.

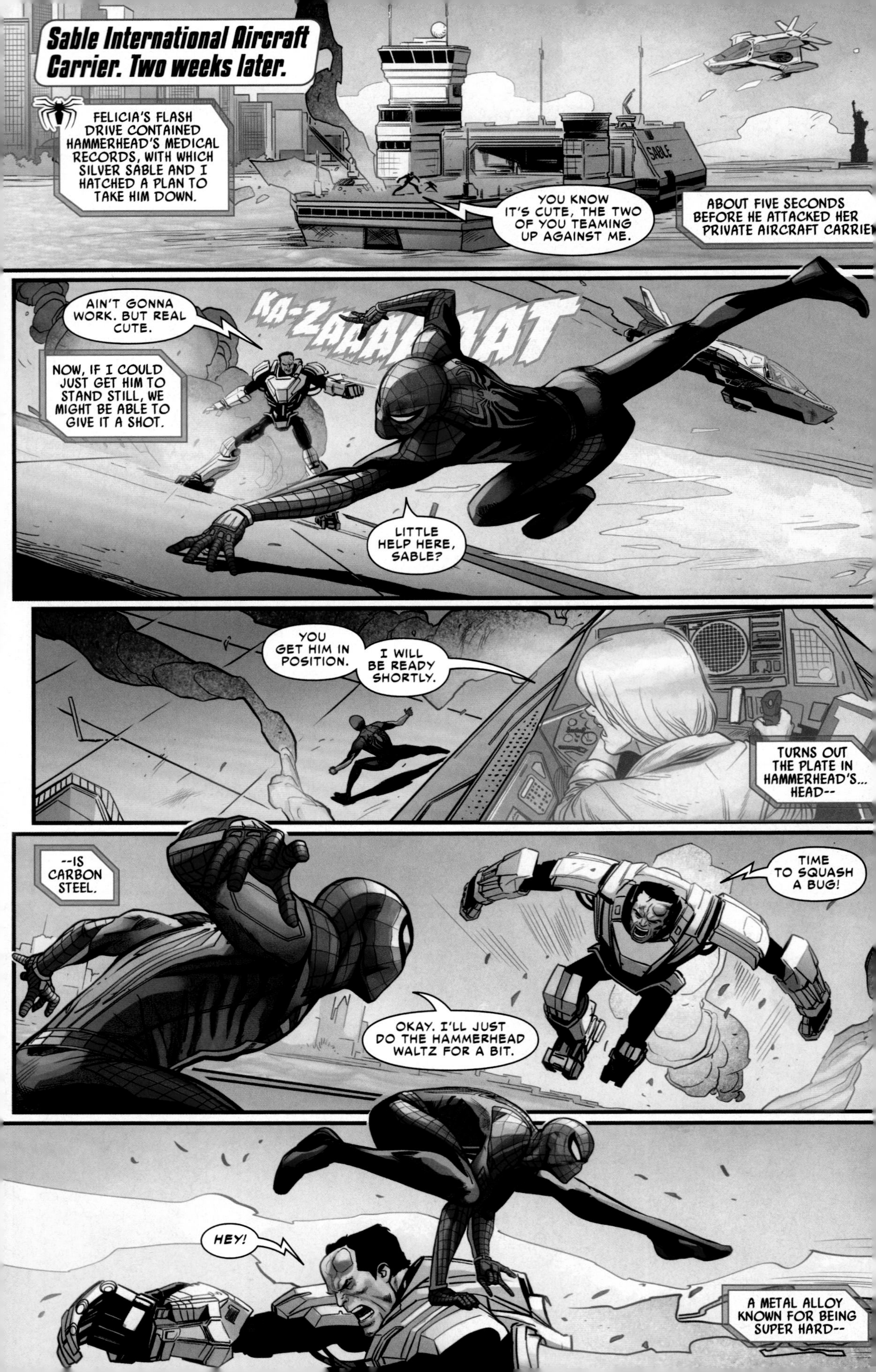
Sable International Aircraft Carrier. Two weeks later.
FELICIA'S FLASH DRIVE CONTAINED HAMMERHEAD'S MEDICAL RECORDS, WITH WHICH SILVER SABLE AND I HATCHED A PLAN TO TAKE HIM DOWN.
SABLE
YOU KNOW IT'S CUTE, THE TWO OF YOU TEAMING UP AGAINST ME.
ABOUT FIVE SECONDS BEFORE HE ATTACKED HER PRIVATE AIRCRAFT CARRIE
AIN'T GONNA WORK. BUT REAL CUTE.
KA-ZAAAK
NOW, IF I COULD JUST GET HIM TO STAND STILL, WE MIGHT BE ABLE TO GIVE IT A SHOT.
LITTLE HELP HERE, SABLE?
YOU GET HIM IN POSITION.
I WILL BE READY SHORTLY.
TURNS OUT THE PLATE IN HAMMERHEAD'S... HEAD--
--IS CARBON STEEL.
TIME TO SQUASH A BUG!
OKAY. I'LL JUST DO THE HAMMERHEAD WALTZ FOR A BIT.
HEY!
A METAL ALLOY KNOWN FOR BEING SUPER HARD--

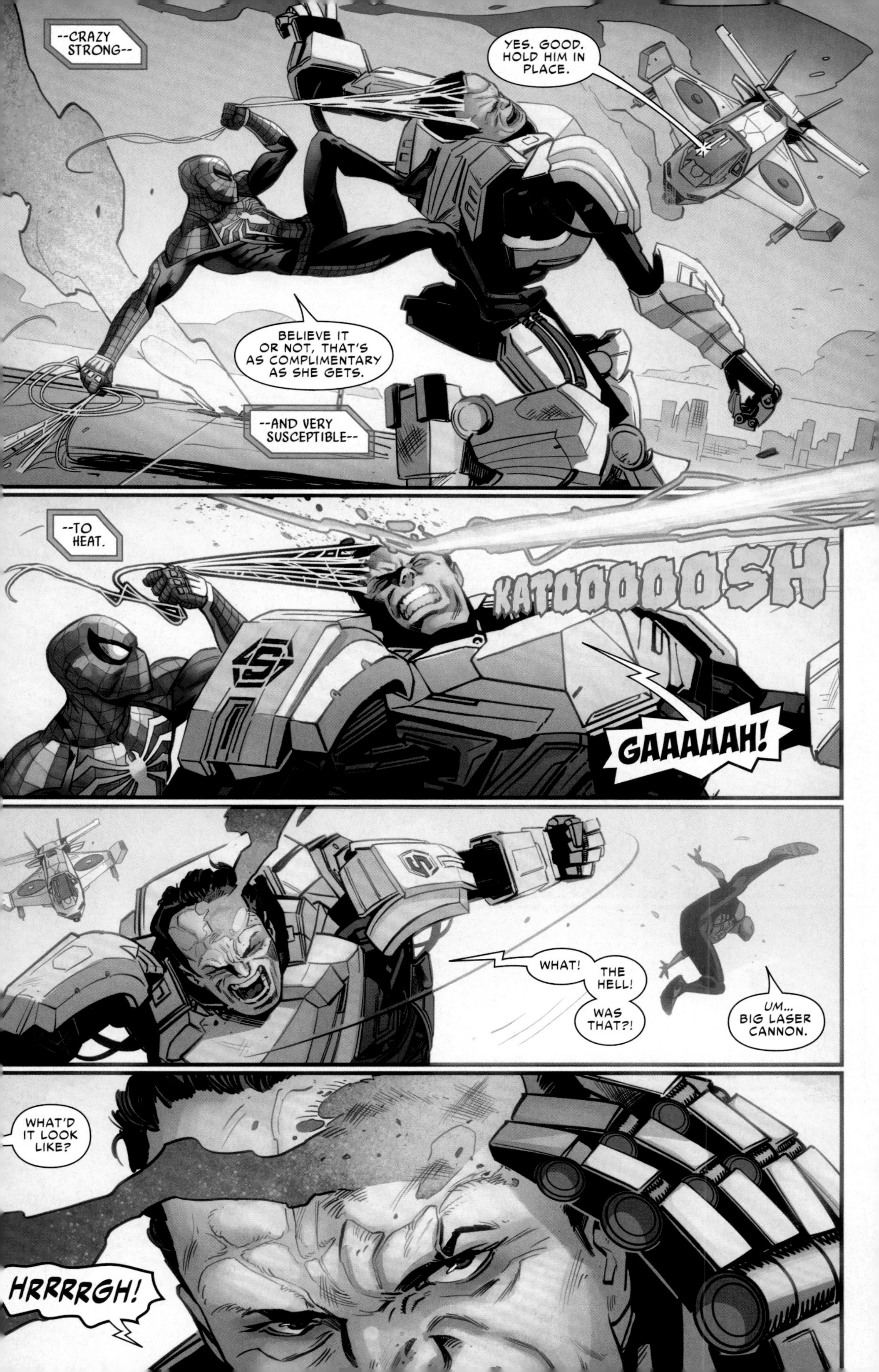
--CRAZY STRONG--
YES. GOOD. HOLD HIM IN PLACE.
BELIEVE IT OR NOT, THAT'S AS COMPLIMENTARY AS SHE GETS.
--AND VERY SUSCEPTIBLE--
--TO HEAT.
KATOOOOOOSH
GAAAAAH!
WHAT!
THE HELL!
WAS THAT?!
UM... BIG LASER CANNON.
WHAT'D IT LOOK LIKE?
HRRRRGH!

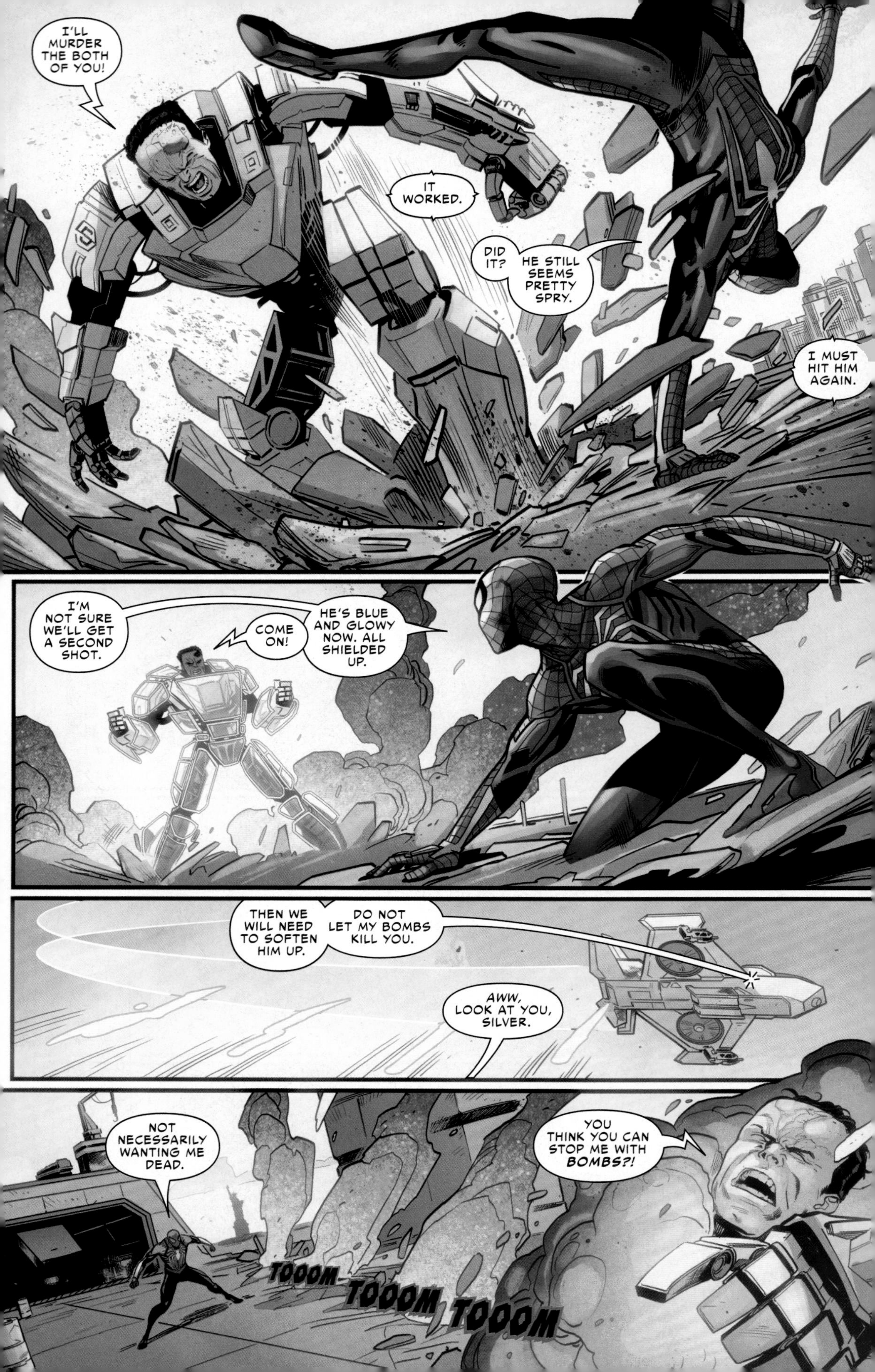
I'LL MURDER THE BOTH OF YOU!
IT WORKED.
DID IT?
HE STILL SEEMS PRETTY SPRY.
I MUST HIT HIM AGAIN.
I'M NOT SURE WE'LL GET A SECOND SHOT.
HE'S BLUE AND GLOWY NOW. ALL SHIELDED UP.
COME ON!
THEN WE WILL NEED TO SOFTEN HIM UP.
DO NOT LET MY BOMBS KILL YOU.
AWW, LOOK AT YOU, SILVER.
NOT NECESSARILY WANTING ME DEAD.
YOU THINK YOU CAN STOP ME WITH BOMBS?!
TOOOM TOOOM TOOOM

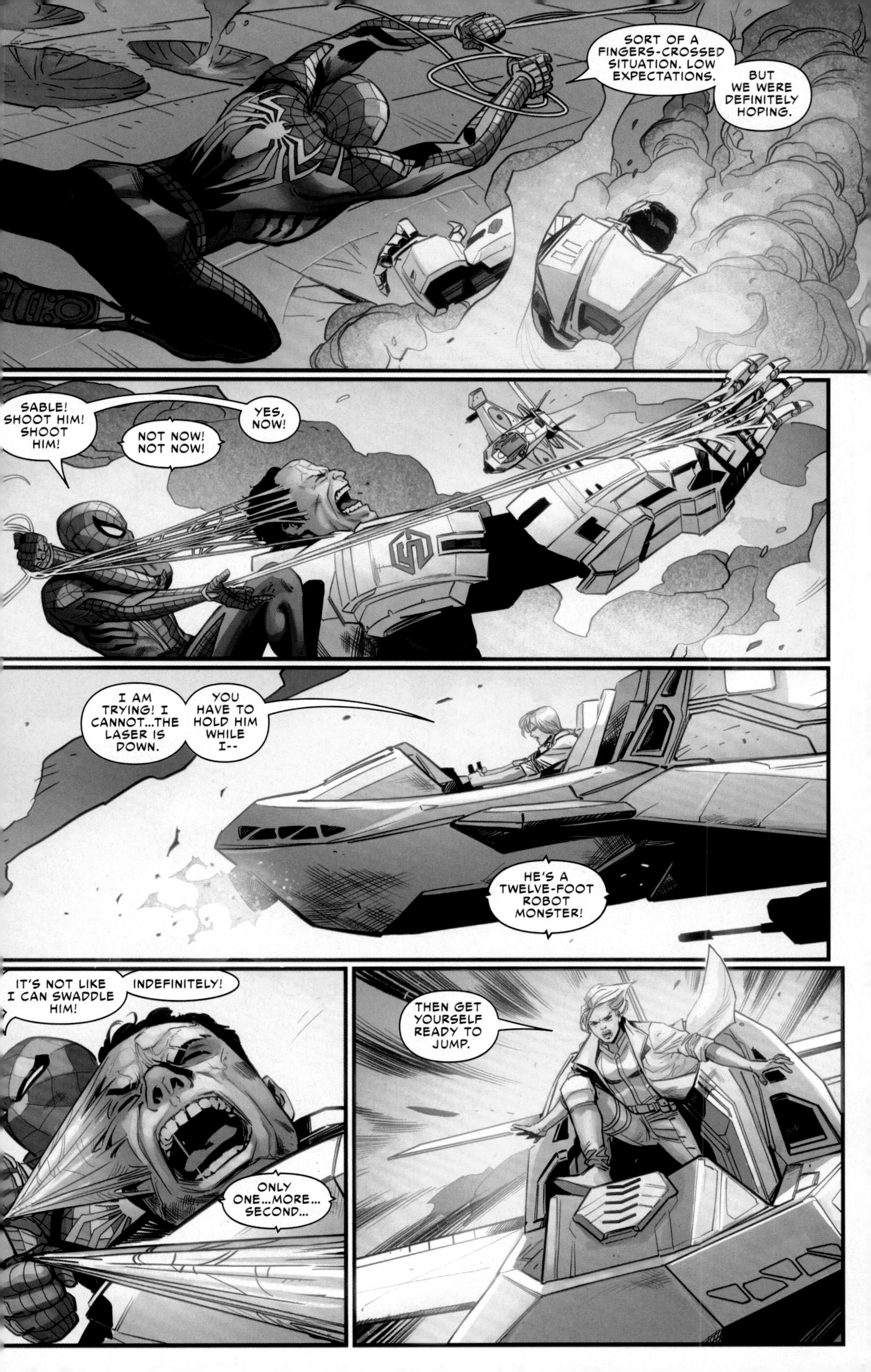

SORT OF A FINGERS-CROSSED SITUATION. LOW EXPECTATIONS.
BUT WE WERE DEFINITELY HOPING.
SABLE! SHOOT HIM! SHOOT HIM!
NOT NOW! NOT NOW!
YES, NOW!
I AM TRYING! I CANNOT...THE LASER IS DOWN.
YOU HAVE TO HOLD HIM WHILE I--
HE'S A TWELVE-FOOT ROBOT MONSTER!
IT'S NOT LIKE I CAN SWADDLE HIM!
INDEFINITELY!
ONLY ONE...MORE... SECOND...
THEN GET YOURSELF READY TO JUMP.

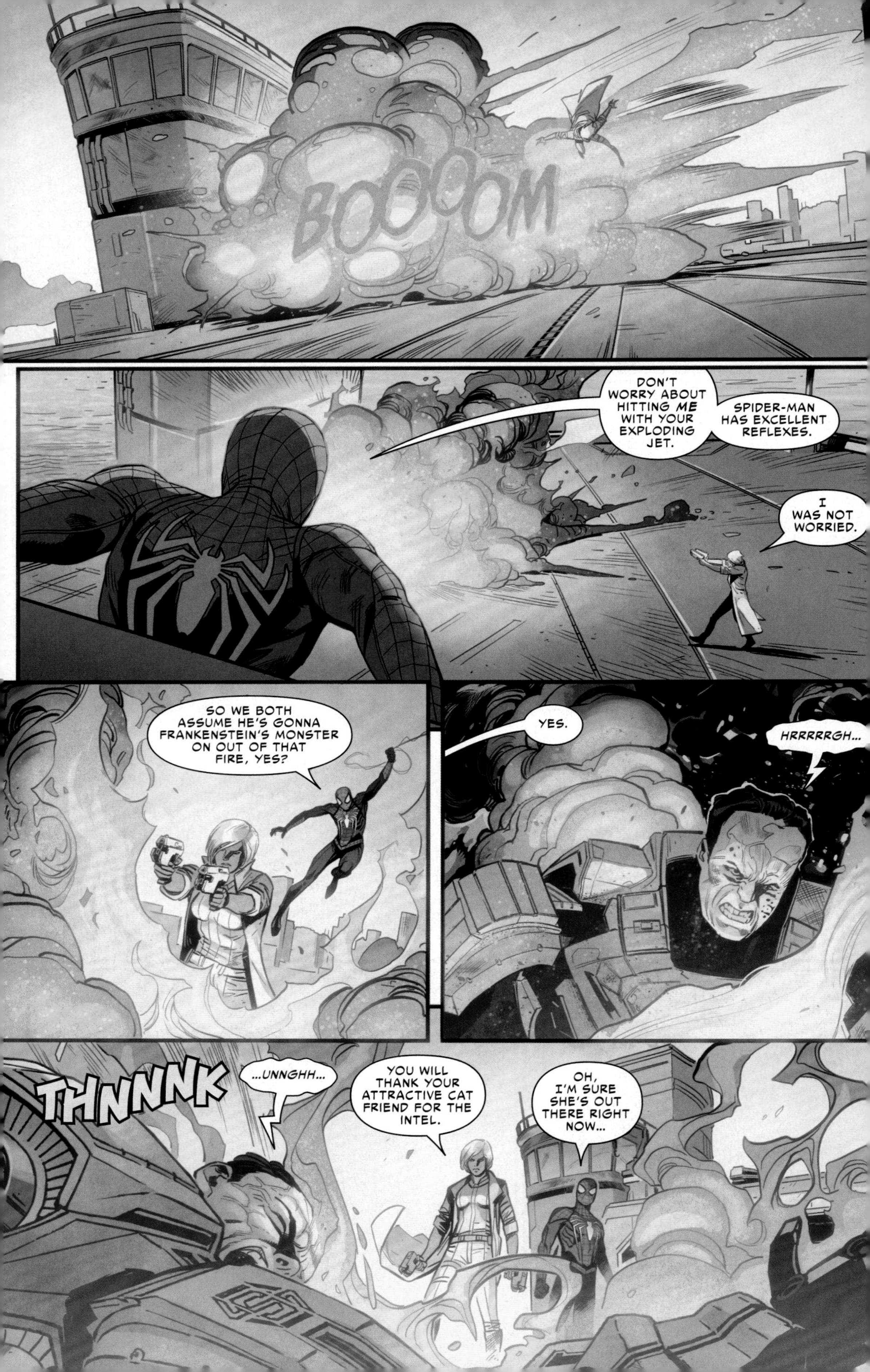
BOOOOOM
DON'T WORRY ABOUT HITTING *ME* WITH YOUR EXPLODING JET.
SPIDER-MAN HAS EXCELLENT REFLEXES.
I WAS NOT WORRIED.
SO WE BOTH ASSUME HE'S GONNA FRANKENSTEIN'S MONSTER ON OUT OF THAT FIRE, YES?
YES.
HRRRRRGH...
THNNNK
...UNNGHH...
YOU WILL THANK YOUR ATTRACTIVE CAT FRIEND FOR THE INTEL.
OH, I'M SURE SHE'S OUT THERE RIGHT NOW...

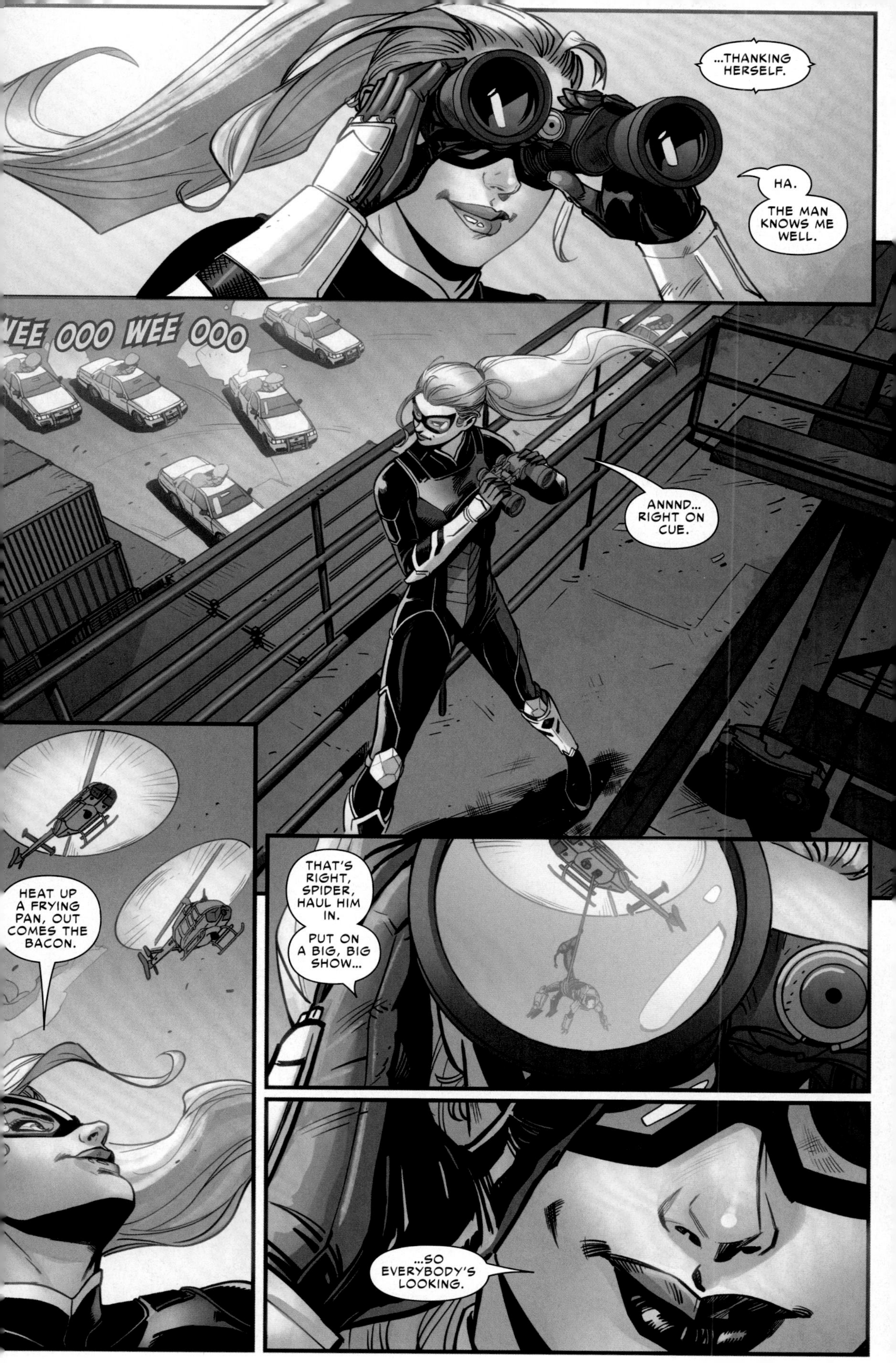
...THANKING HERSELF.
HA.
THE MAN KNOWS ME WELL.
WEE OOO WEE OOO
ANNND... RIGHT ON CUE.
HEAT UP A FRYING PAN, OUT COMES THE BACON.
THAT'S RIGHT, SPIDER, HAUL HIM IN.
PUT ON A BIG, BIG SHOW...
...SO EVERYBODY'S LOOKING.

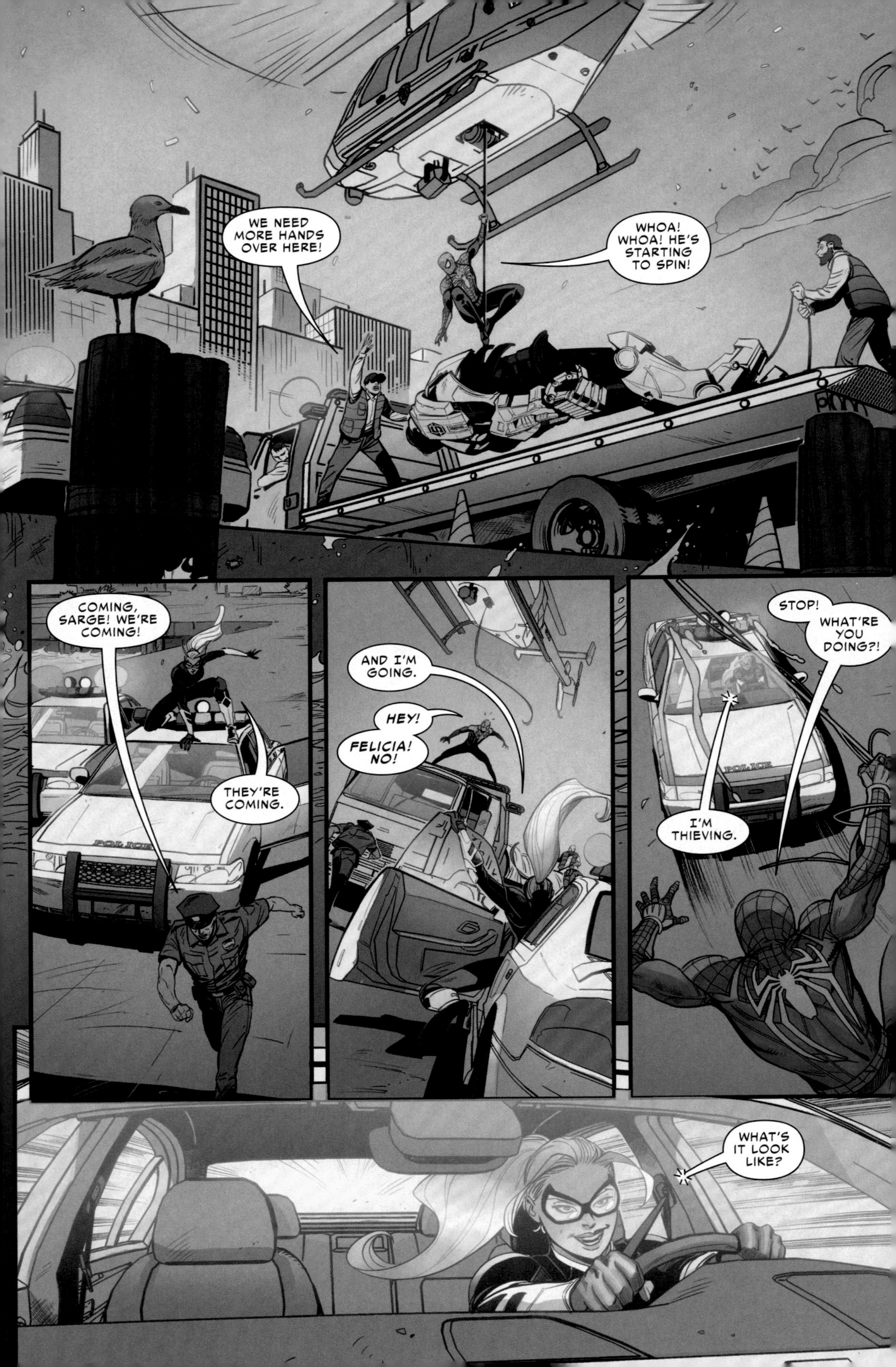
WE NEED MORE HANDS OVER HERE!
WHOA! WHOA! HE'S STARTING TO SPIN!
COMING, SARGE! WE'RE COMING!
THEY'RE COMING.
AND I'M GOING.
HEY!
FELICIA! NO!
STOP!
WHAT'RE YOU DOING?!
I'M THIEVING.
WHAT'S IT LOOK LIKE?

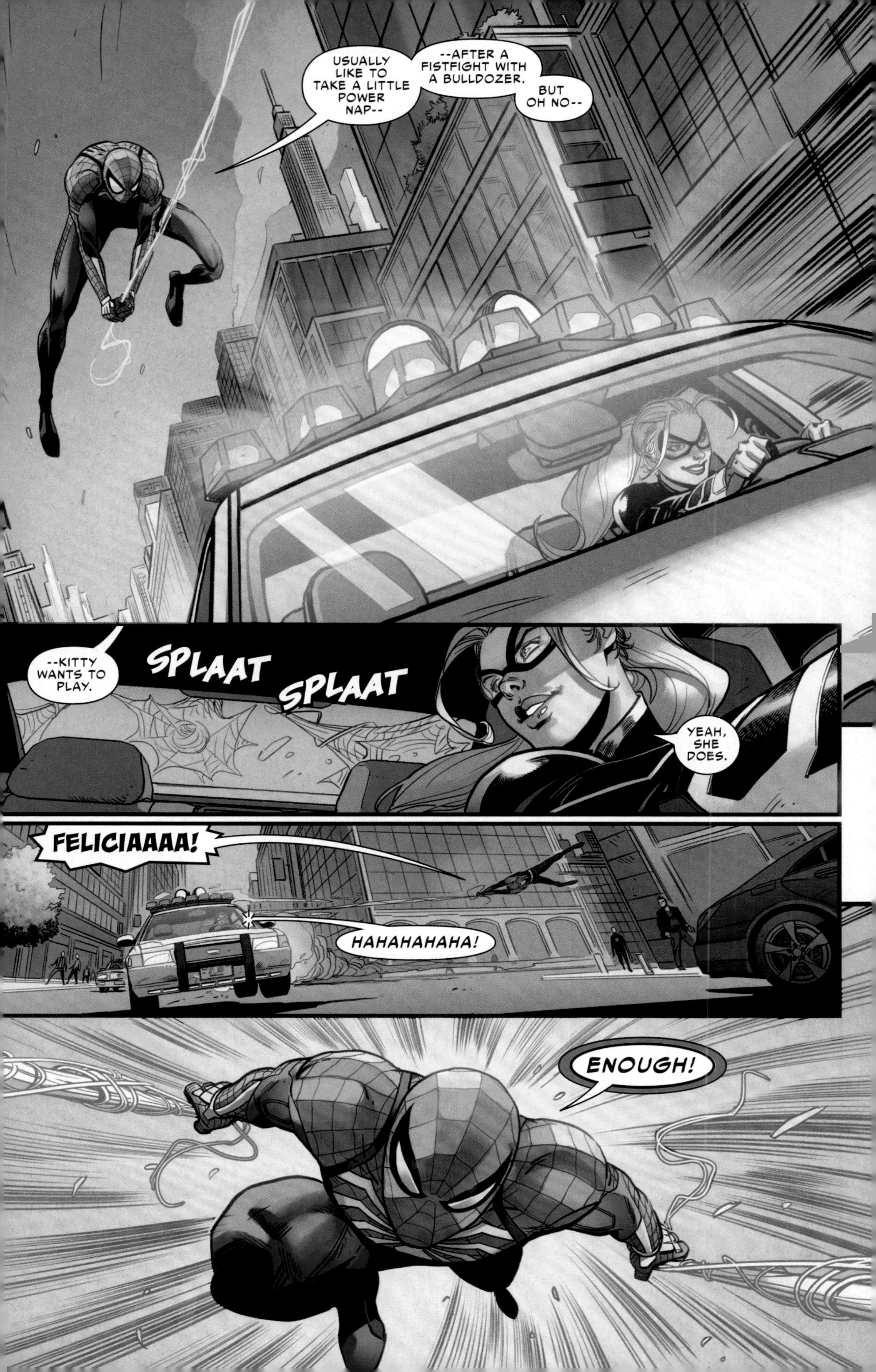
USUALLY LIKE TO TAKE A LITTLE POWER NAP--
--AFTER A FISTFIGHT WITH A BULLDOZER.
BUT OH NO--
--KITTY WANTS TO PLAY.
SPLAAT
SPLAAT
YEAH, SHE DOES.
FELICIAAAA!
HAHAHAHAHA!
ENOUGH!

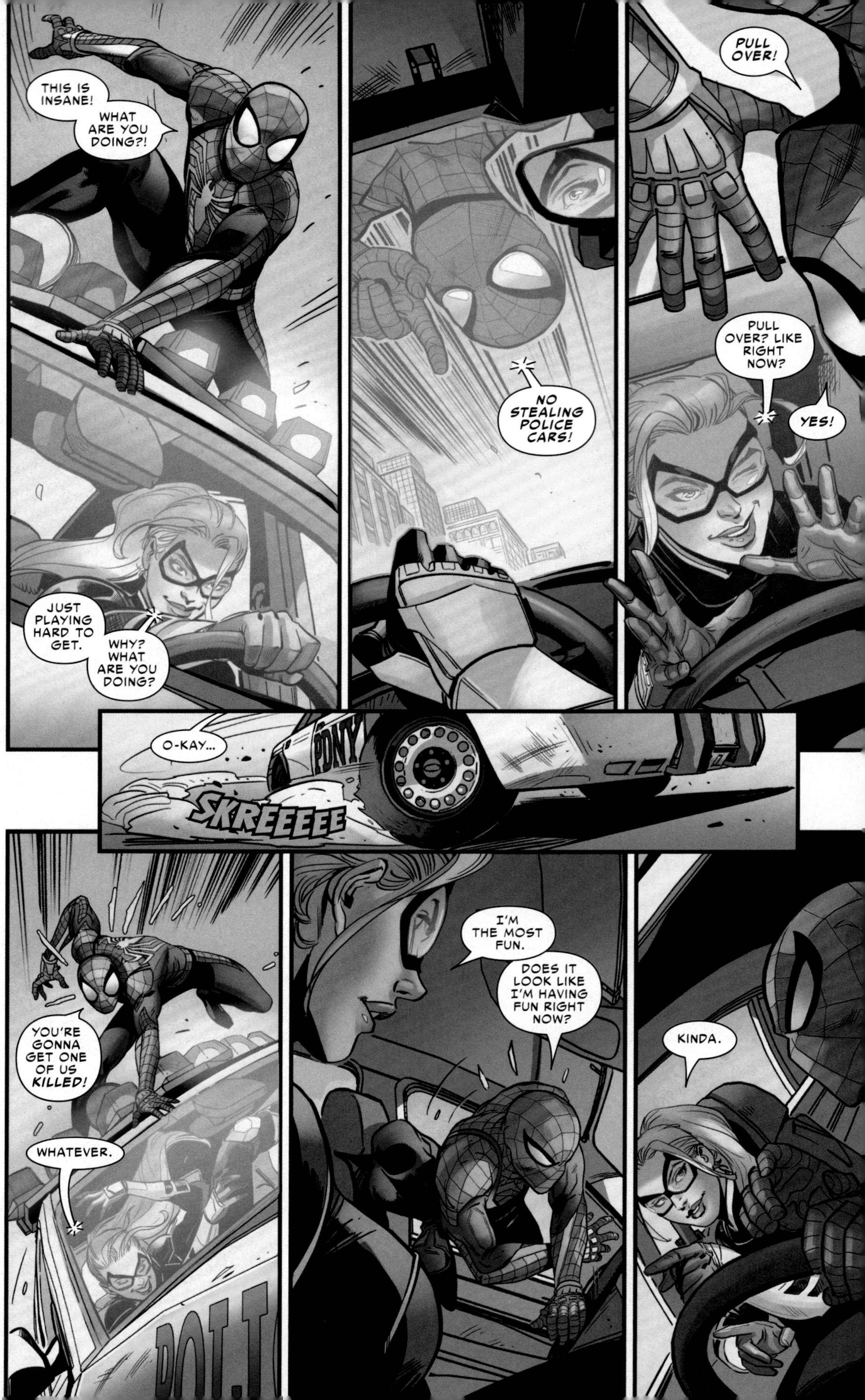
THIS IS INSANE!
WHAT ARE YOU DOING?!
JUST PLAYING HARD TO GET.
WHY? WHAT ARE YOU DOING?
NO STEALING POLICE CARS!
PULL OVER!
PULL OVER? LIKE RIGHT NOW?
YES!
O-KAY...
PDNY
SKREEEEE
YOU'RE GONNA GET ONE OF US *KILLED*!
WHATEVER.
I'M THE MOST FUN.
DOES IT LOOK LIKE I'M HAVING FUN RIGHT NOW?
KINDA.

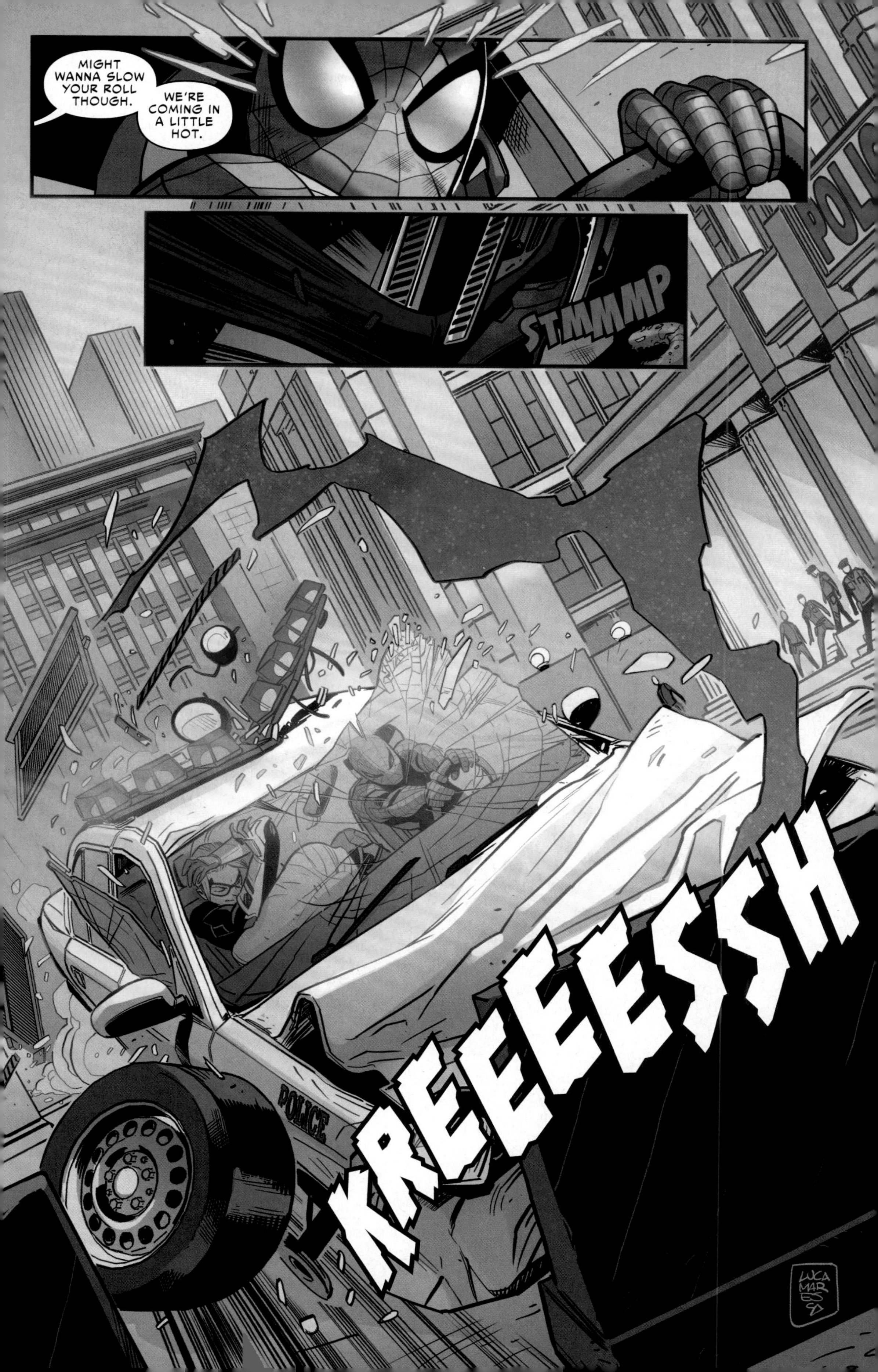
MIGHT WANNA SLOW YOUR ROLL THOUGH.
WE'RE COMING IN A LITTLE HOT.
STMMMP
POLICE
KREEEESSH

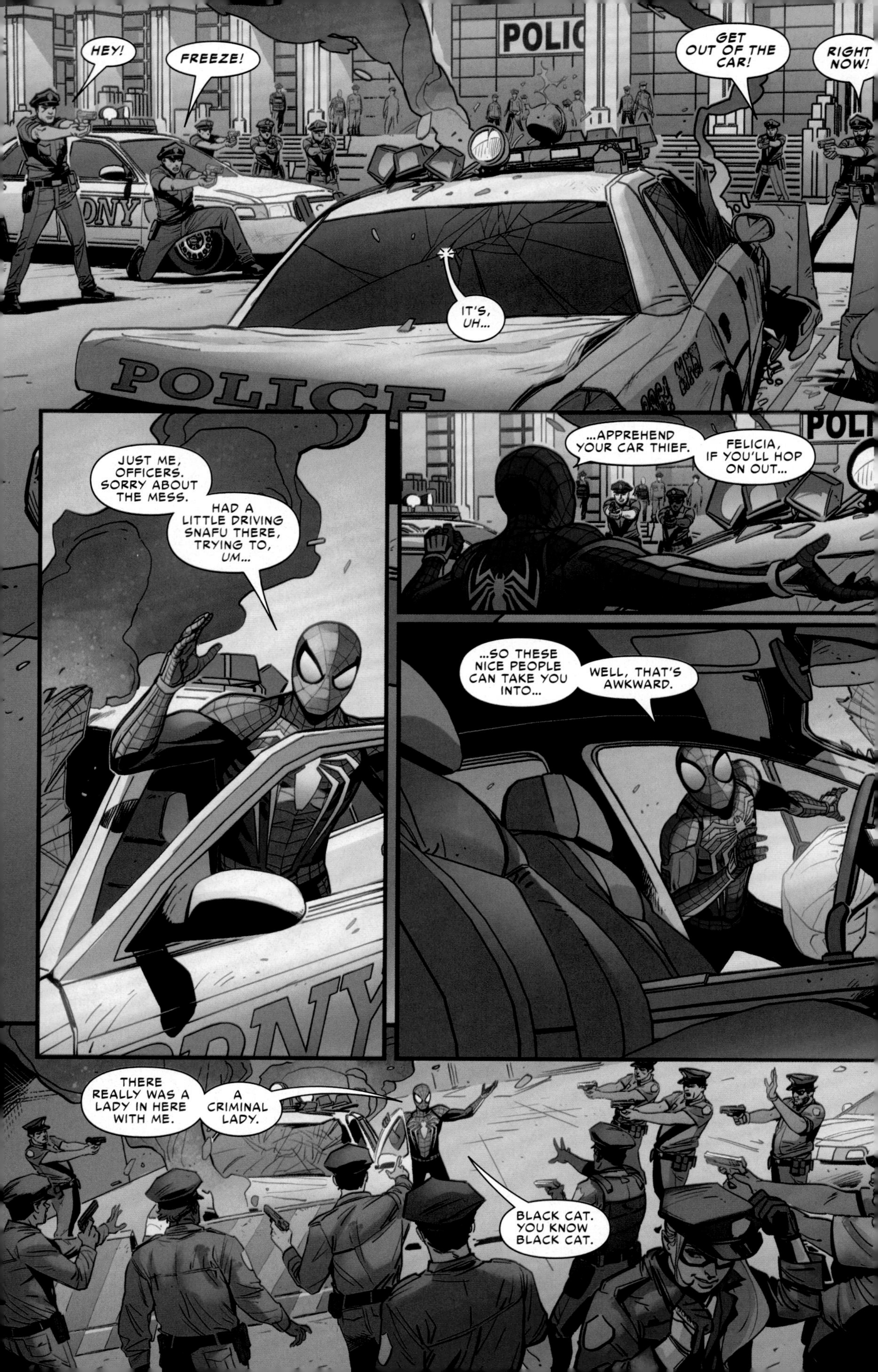

POLIC
HEY!
FREEZE!
GET OUT OF THE CAR!
RIGHT NOW!
DNY
IT'S, UH...
POLICE
JUST ME, OFFICERS. SORRY ABOUT THE MESS.
HAD A LITTLE DRIVING SNAFU THERE, TRYING TO, UM...
DNY
...APPREHEND YOUR CAR THIEF.
FELICIA, IF YOU'LL HOP ON OUT...
POLI
...SO THESE NICE PEOPLE CAN TAKE YOU INTO...
WELL, THAT'S AWKWARD.
THERE REALLY WAS A LADY IN HERE WITH ME.
A CRIMINAL LADY.
BLACK CAT. YOU KNOW BLACK CAT.

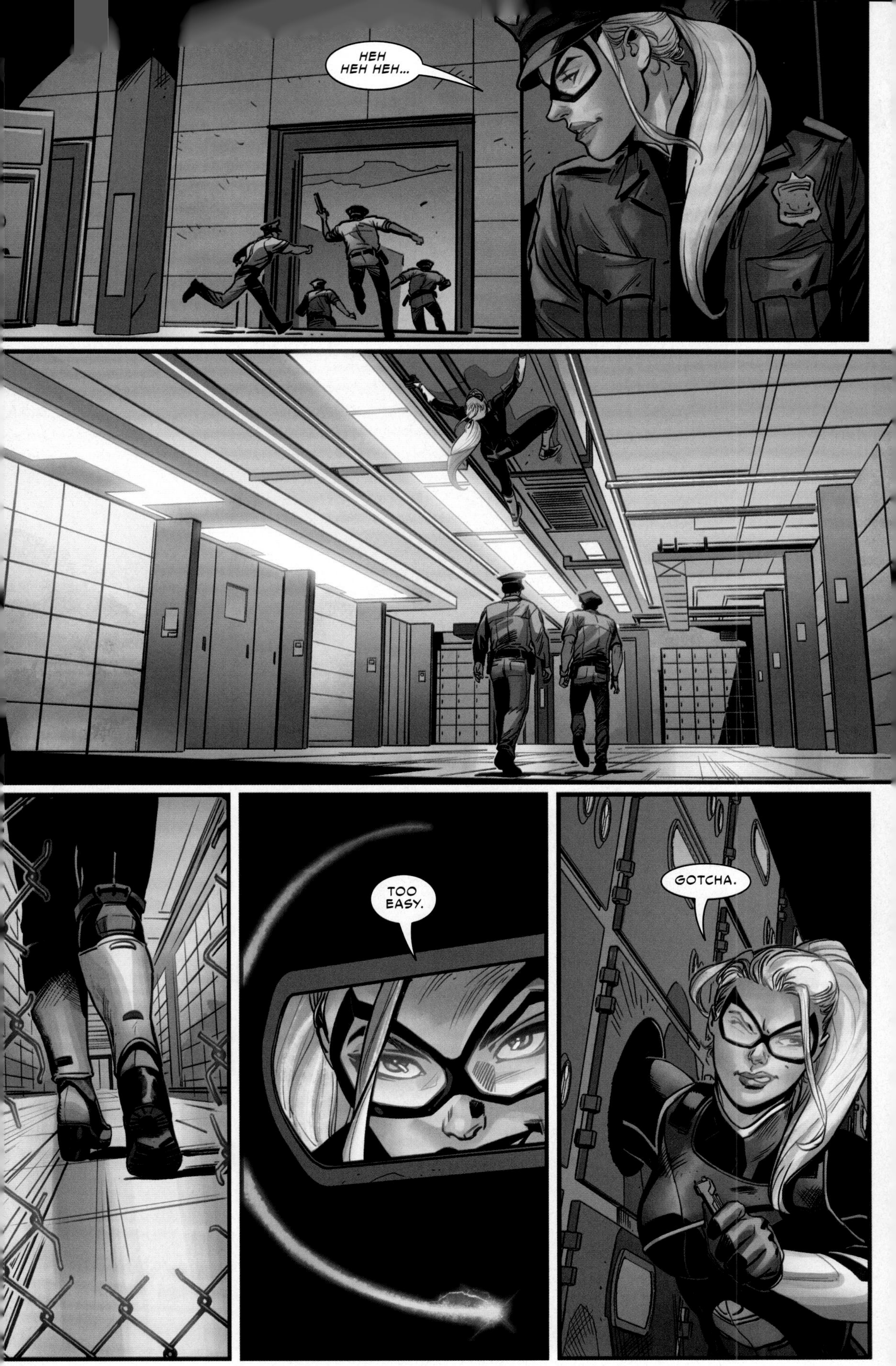
HEH HEH HEH...
TOO EASY.
GOTCHA.

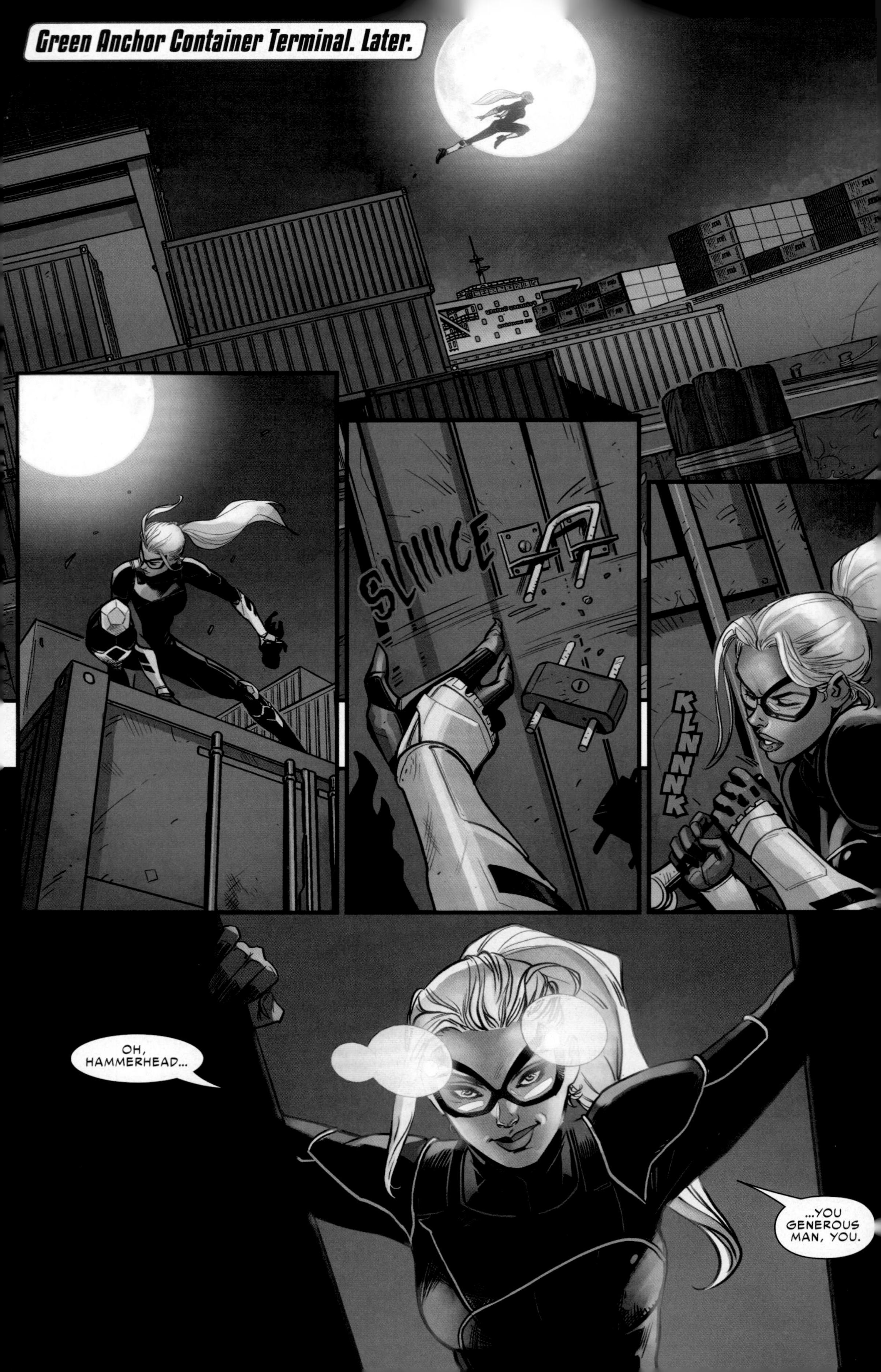
Green Anchor Container Terminal. Later.
SLIIICE
KLNNNK
OH, HAMMERHEAD...
...YOU GENEROUS MAN, YOU.

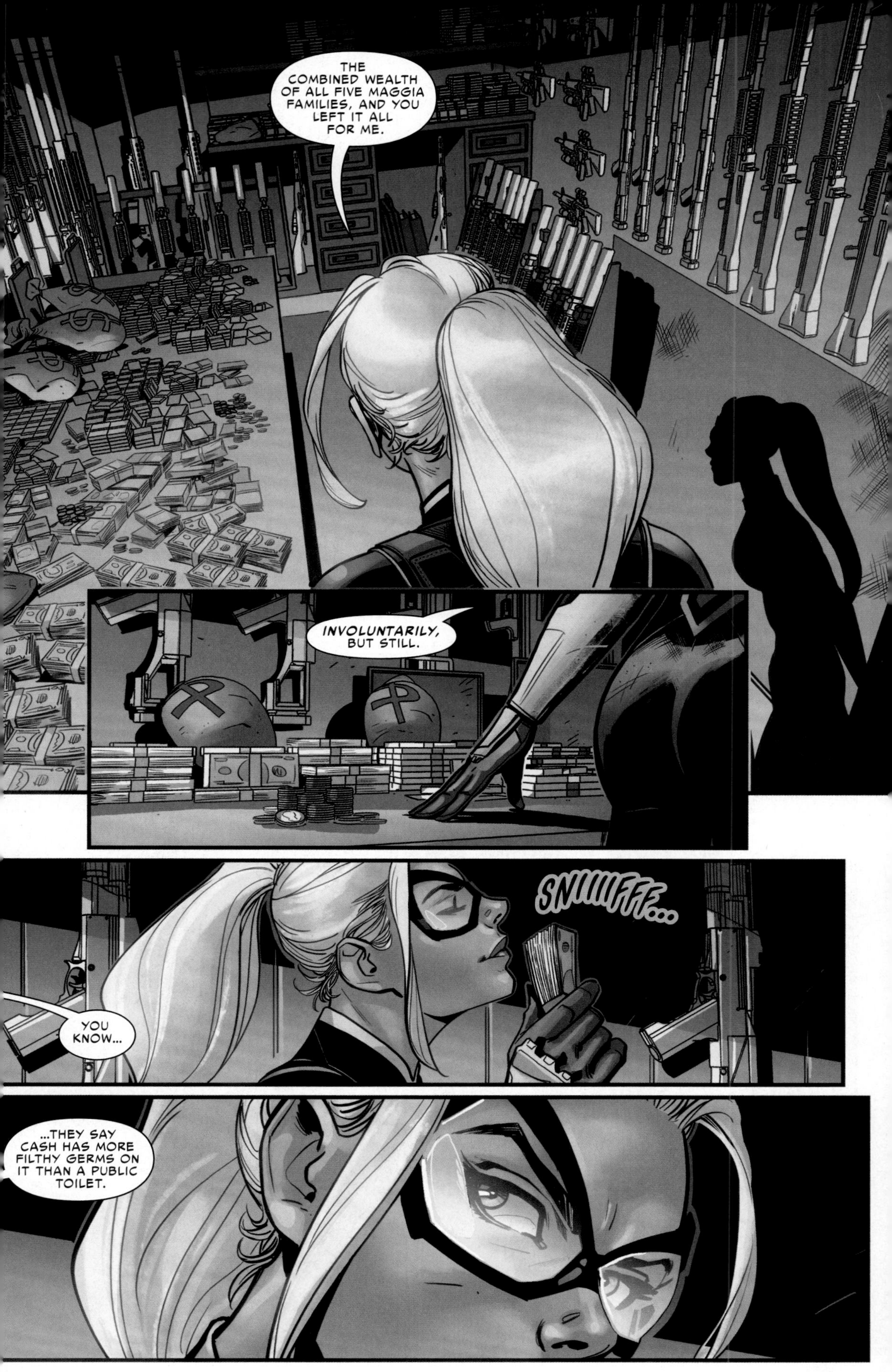
THE COMBINED WEALTH OF ALL FIVE MAGGIA FAMILIES, AND YOU LEFT IT ALL FOR ME.
INVOLUNTARILY, BUT STILL.
SNIIIIFFF...
YOU KNOW...
...THEY SAY CASH HAS MORE FILTHY GERMS ON IT THAN A PUBLIC TOILET.

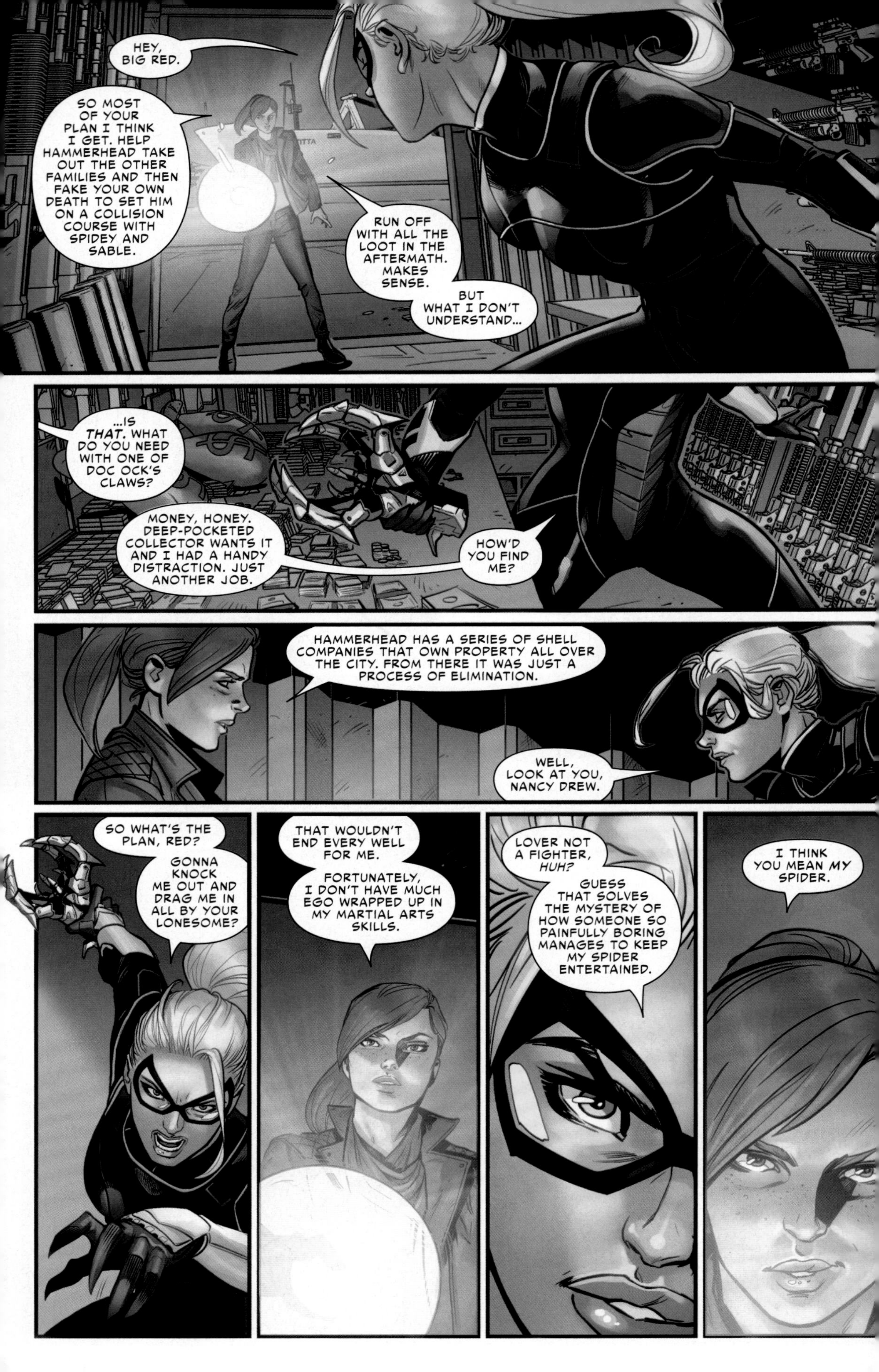
HEY, BIG RED.
SO MOST OF YOUR PLAN I THINK I GET. HELP HAMMERHEAD TAKE OUT THE OTHER FAMILIES AND THEN FAKE YOUR OWN DEATH TO SET HIM ON A COLLISION COURSE WITH SPIDEY AND SABLE.
RUN OFF WITH ALL THE LOOT IN THE AFTERMATH. MAKES SENSE.
BUT WHAT I DON'T UNDERSTAND...
...IS *THAT.* WHAT DO YOU NEED WITH ONE OF DOC OCK'S CLAWS?
MONEY, HONEY. DEEP-POCKETED COLLECTOR WANTS IT AND I HAD A HANDY DISTRACTION. JUST ANOTHER JOB.
HOW'D YOU FIND ME?
HAMMERHEAD HAS A SERIES OF SHELL COMPANIES THAT OWN PROPERTY ALL OVER THE CITY. FROM THERE IT WAS JUST A PROCESS OF ELIMINATION.
WELL, LOOK AT YOU, NANCY DREW.
SO WHAT'S THE PLAN, RED?
GONNA KNOCK ME OUT AND DRAG ME IN ALL BY YOUR LONESOME?
THAT WOULDN'T END EVERY WELL FOR ME.
FORTUNATELY, I DON'T HAVE MUCH EGO WRAPPED UP IN MY MARTIAL ARTS SKILLS.
LOVER NOT A FIGHTER, *HUH?*
GUESS THAT SOLVES THE MYSTERY OF HOW SOMEONE SO PAINFULLY BORING MANAGES TO KEEP MY SPIDER ENTERTAINED.
I THINK YOU MEAN *MY* SPIDER.

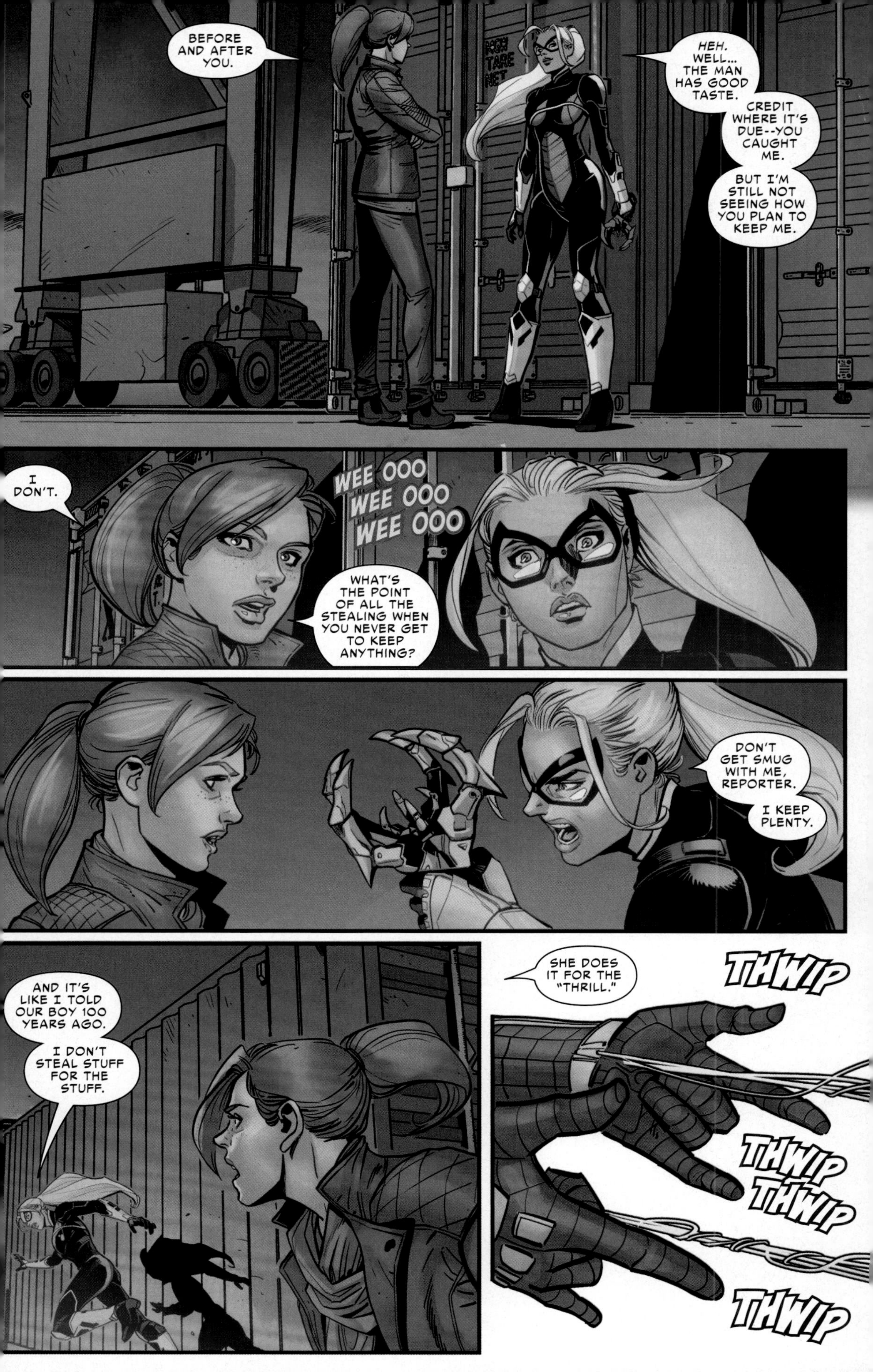
BEFORE AND AFTER YOU.
HEH. WELL... THE MAN HAS GOOD TASTE.
CREDIT WHERE IT'S DUE--YOU CAUGHT ME.
BUT I'M STILL NOT SEEING HOW YOU PLAN TO KEEP ME.
I DON'T.
WEE OOO
WEE OOO
WEE OOO
WHAT'S THE POINT OF ALL THE STEALING WHEN YOU NEVER GET TO KEEP ANYTHING?
DON'T GET SMUG WITH ME, REPORTER.
I KEEP PLENTY.
AND IT'S LIKE I TOLD OUR BOY 100 YEARS AGO.
I DON'T STEAL STUFF FOR THE STUFF.
SHE DOES IT FOR THE "THRILL."
THWIP
THWIP
THWIP
THWIP

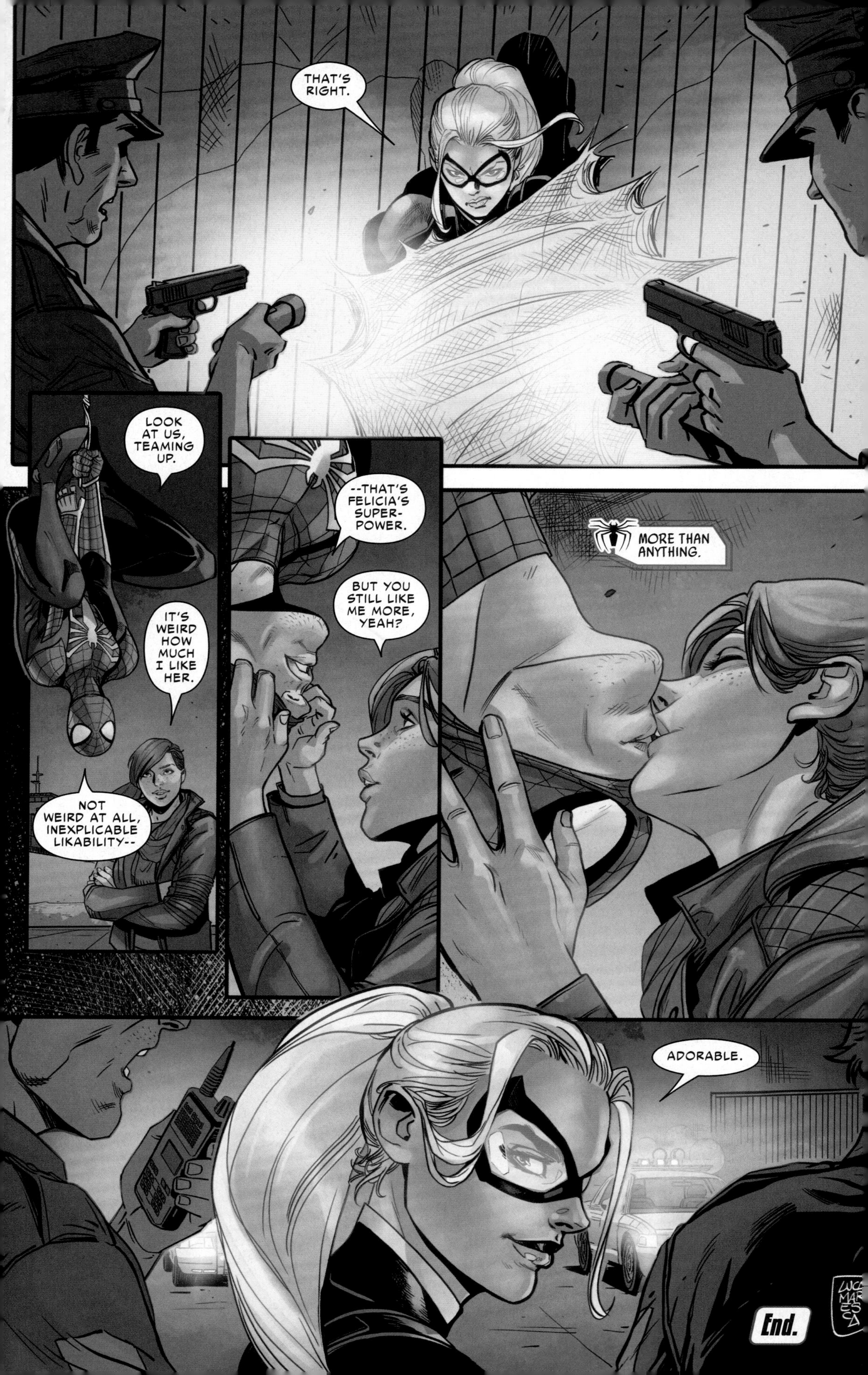
THAT'S RIGHT.
LOOK AT US, TEAMING UP.
IT'S WEIRD HOW MUCH I LIKE HER.
NOT WEIRD AT ALL, INEXPLICABLE LIKABILITY--
--THAT'S FELICIA'S SUPER-POWER.
BUT YOU STILL LIKE ME MORE, YEAH?
MORE THAN ANYTHING.
ADORABLE.
End.

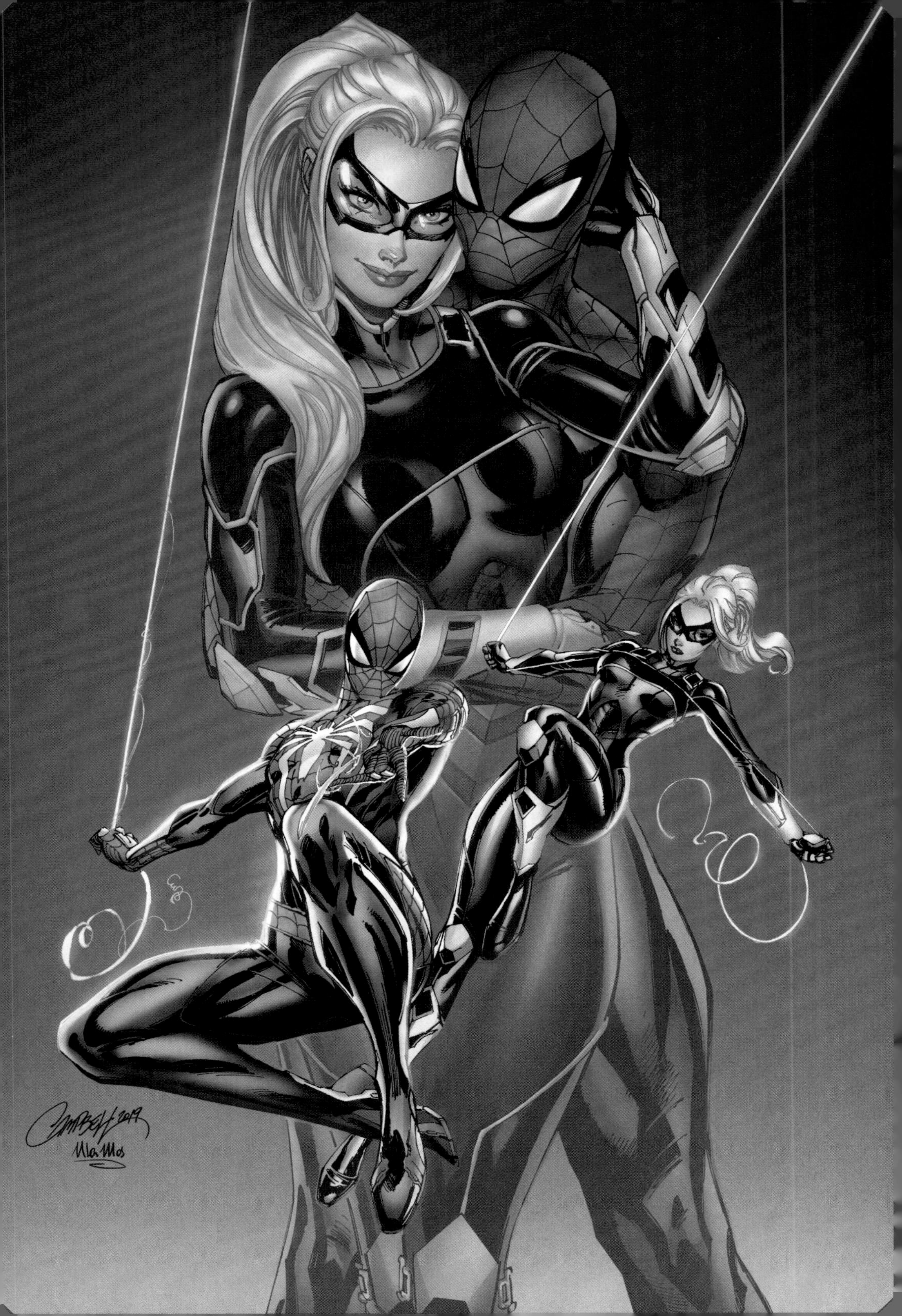

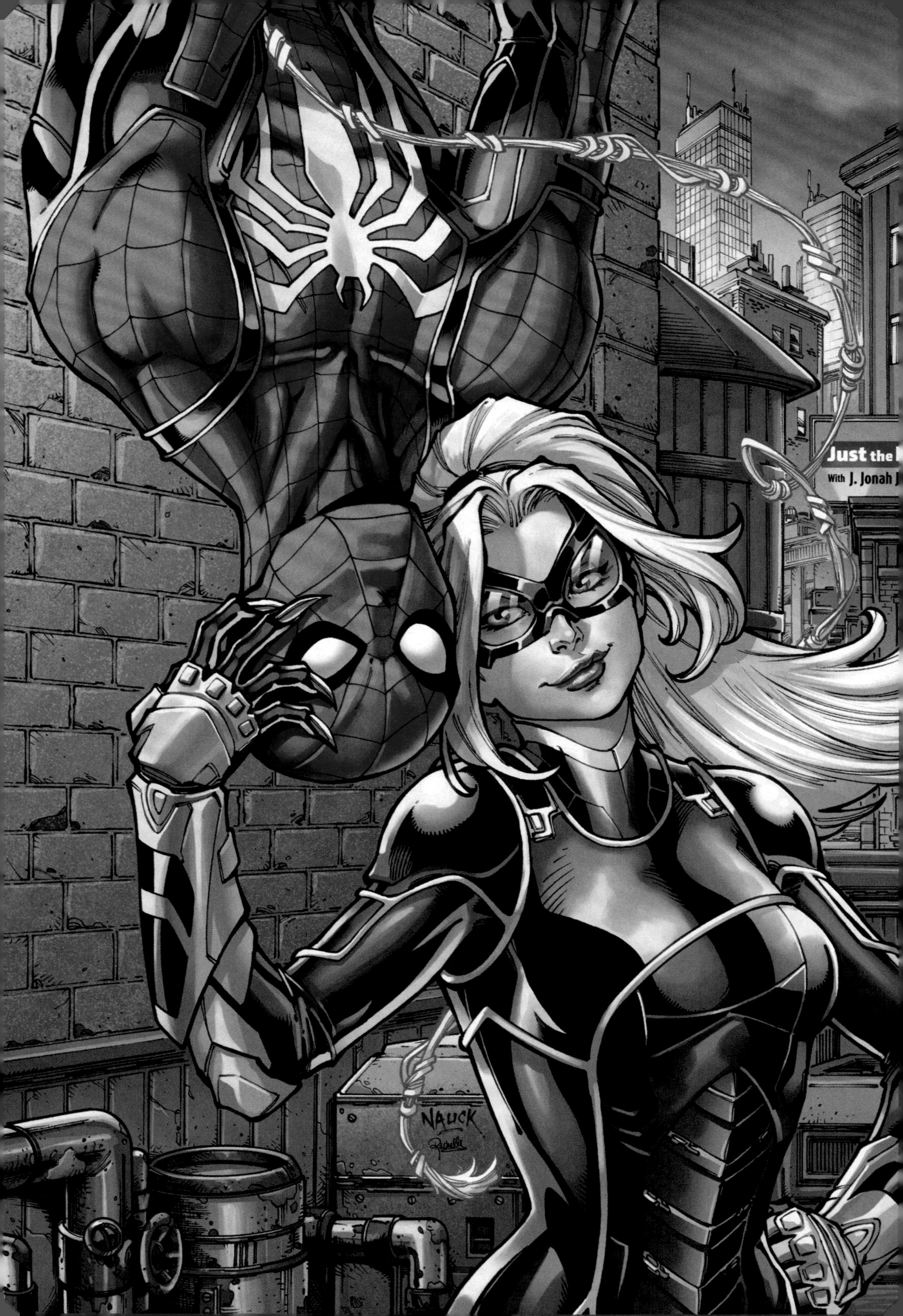
Just the
With J. Jonah
NAUCK

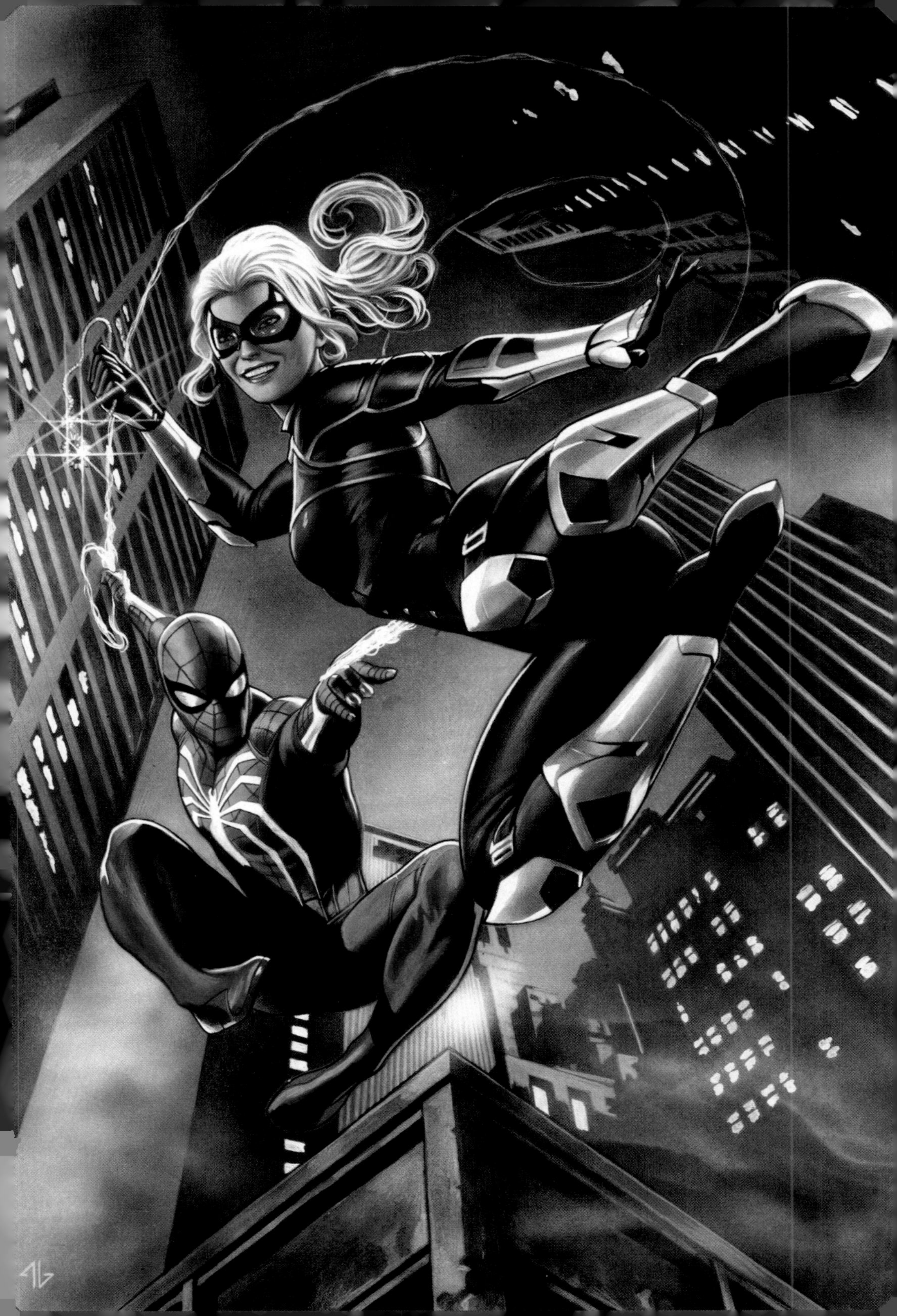

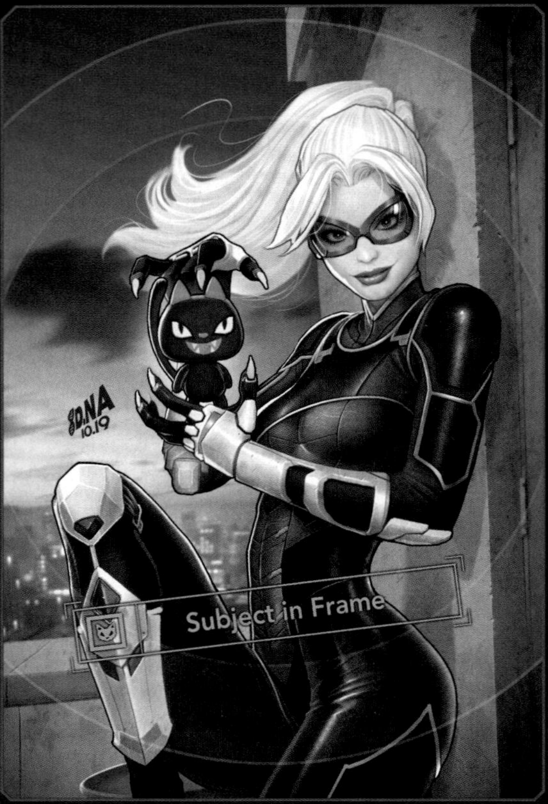
Subject in Frame

DAVID NAKAYAMA
#2 VARIANT

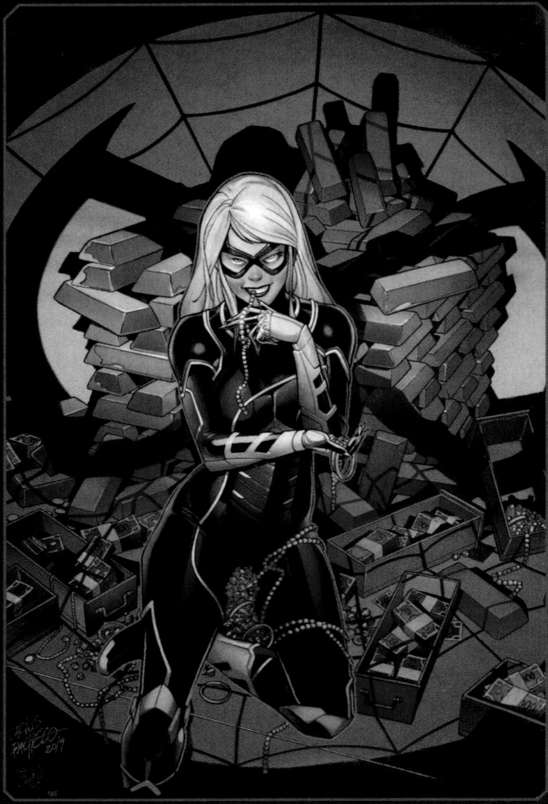

CARLOS PACHECO, RAFAEL FONTERIZ & FRANK D'ARMATA
#3 VARIANT

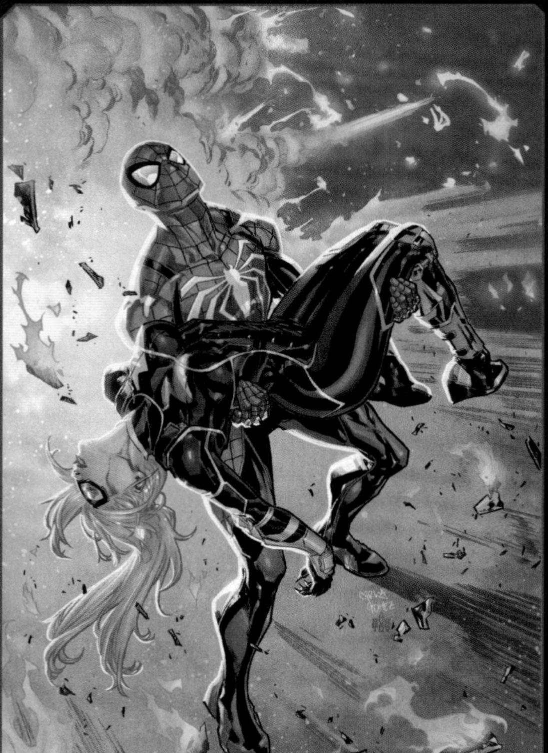

CARLOS GÓMEZ & JESUS ABURTOV
#4 VARIANT

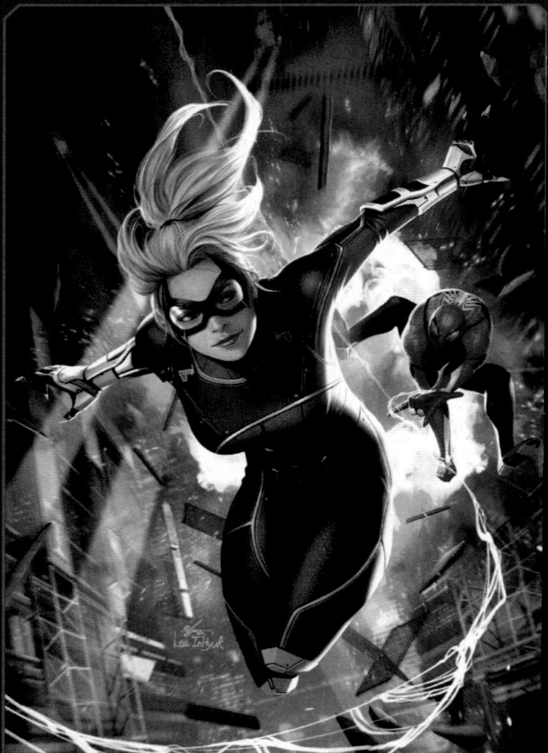

INHYUK LEE
#5 VARIANT